PRIESTLEY

JUDITH COOK

BLOOMSBURY

First published in Great Britain 1997

Bloomsbury Publishing Plc, 38 Soho Square, London W1V 5DF

Copyright © 1997 by Judith Cook

PICTURE SOURCES
Courtesy of Lady Barbara Wykeham: pages 3; 4 *bottom*
Courtesy of the University of Bradford: page 15
All other material courtesy of Tom Priestley/
the Estate of J. B. Priestley

The moral right of the author has been asserted

A CIP catalogue record for this book
is available from the British Library

ISBN 0 7475 3036 X

10 9 8 7 6 5 4 3 2 1

Typeset by Hewer Text Composition Services, Edinburgh
Printed by Clays Ltd, St Ives plc

CONTENTS

Introduction

Remember
J.B. Priestley O.M. 1894–1984
He loved the Dales and found 'Hubberholme, one of the
smallest and pleasantest places in the World.'

At Hubberholme, at the far end of Wharfedale, there is only
an ancient church with a rare rood screen (neither zealous
Reformers nor Victorian 'restorers' bothered to journey so far),
and old pub called the George and a couple of farms. The
River Wharfe runs fast under an ancient stone bridge and in
mid-June the churchyard is smothered in hawthorn blossom in
every shade of pink from the palest off-white to deep rose, while
outside the churchyard the hedgerows are thick with buttercups,
meadowsweet and clover: an idyllic spot in which to choose to
be buried.

Across the Dale lies Bolton Castle, where the young Mary
Queen of Scots was imprisoned shortly after she had fled to
England from Scotland. Her strange enigmatic motto haunts
us still: 'In my End is my Beginning'. Its sentiment might also
apply appropriately to the life of John Boynton Priestley, born
in Yorkshire who, after a journey lasting ninety years, returned
to it at the last.

Jack Priestley was immensely successful, extraordinarily pro-
lific and could switch between the disciplines of essayist, novelist
and playwright with apparent ease. His popularly remembered
persona is that of the bluff Yorkshireman puffing on a pipe,
probably imagined with a pint in his hand, giving his forthright
views on the issues of the day; a straightforward, uncomplicated
extrovert: Jolly Jack Priestley. Since his death he has also been
cast in the unlikely role of a north country Don Juan flitting

compulsively from woman to woman while his progress through life is seen as sure-footed, unshadowed, almost like a character out of his best-selling novel *The Good Companions*.

But the man underneath that public persona was a great deal more complicated, a man marked forever by his experiences during the 1914–1918 War, a man not only given to deep introspection but also to insecurity and bleak depressions. So perhaps it should be said now what he was not: he was neither uncomplicated nor a classic extrovert. A deep thinker, he was once described as 'the last of the Sages'. Nor was he in any real sense in which the words are used a Don Juan, Yorkshire or otherwise.

Least of all was he Jolly Jack Priestley.

CHAPTER 1

Beginnings and Childhood

He was born in September 1894 in the dying fall of the Victorian era and grew up in the brief interlude of the Edwardians, on which he would always look back as a golden age, forever separated by the unbridgeable chasm of the First World War. He returned to that time and the years preceding the War again and again in novels and plays as if it were Eden before the Fall, while in his autobiographical essays he recalled with nostalgia the Bradford where he had been born, the Bruddersford of *The Good Companions* and *When We Are Married*, with which Jack Priestley had a love–hate relationship throughout his long life.

The city was almost entirely a product of the Industrial Revolution when the introduction of spinning and weaving machinery, combined with a reliable supply of good water, swept handloom weavers out of their villages and into the sheds of the wool mills. In less than a hundred years, its population increased five-fold, which gave rise to the problems and politics that shaped the Priestley family.

J. B. Priestley came from local stock on both sides of his family. His paternal grandfather had been born about 1840 into a poor Bradford family and worked from his early teens in one of the town's mills. It is likely that he never went to school and remained illiterate all his life as, according to Priestley's eldest daughter, Lady Barbara Wykeham, he signed with a cross as witness to his son's wedding. He was, however, a highly skilled craftsman, and rose to the respected position of overseer or overlooker, in charge of a number of looms and those who worked them. During the 1860s he married a Scots girl, one of an influx of migrants who came south, seeking work in the mines, mills and manufactories of England.

Priestley had only shadowy memories of his grandfather, who

died while he was still a young child, but after his grandmother was widowed she came to live in the family home. Years later he wrote of his debt to her in the *New Statesman* in an essay entitled 'Growing Old':[1]

> When I was very young we had my grandmother living with us, and whenever my parents went out for the evening, my grandmother fed and entertained me. After we had eaten our rice pudding, she revealed to me the daily life, customs and folklore of the West Riding in the 1840s and 1850s. Ten university lecturers and twenty certified teachers could not have given me as much as she did: in sheer quantity yes, but not in quality. What was there, illuminating everything, was the magic that begins with personal experience and demands a certain detachment, close to wonder.

Priestley's father, Jonathan, was born in 1868, one of several children. He did so well at school that 'by some miracle of thrift', as his son later put it, money was found to send him to a teacher training college, a rare luxury for a working-class boy without any money: the usual route into the profession was through years spent as an ill-paid uncertificated pupil-teacher.

After Jonathan qualified he returned to Bradford to take up his first teaching post at Whetley Lane Primary School. He also became deeply interested in politics. He was, his son wrote years later, 'unselfish, brave and public-spirited, the kind of man socialists have in mind when they write about socialism'. Jonathan was raised on stories of the privations of the Industrial Revolution: a local Bradford journalist, the late Peter Holdsworth writes, in his memoir *The Rebel Tyke*,[2] of the town in the mid-nineteenth century as a hell-hole of dire poverty, sickness, infirmity, near starvation, drunkenness and the dread of a horrific old age. Working conditions were often appalling and ragged children, stinking cellar dwellings and brothels were commonplace. A local surveyor's report on the state of the streets, published when Jonathan was a child, describes so much filth lying around that the air was foul and doctors gave public warnings of the dangers of cholera. Not surprisingly, therefore, Bradford had a history of industrial unrest, lockouts and riots leading to injuries and even death. At twenty-three, Jonathan witnessed a violent confrontation when a bitter strike at Manningham Mill culminated in hundreds of millworkers congregating in the square outside Bradford's town hall. The police were unable to control the crowd, and a riot erupted during which many were injured.

In 1891, Jonathan married Emma Holt in St John's Baptist Chapel and the couple set up home at 34 Mannheim Road, one of a number of small but substantially built terraced houses in what was known locally as the German quarter. There was a close trading connection between Bradford and Germany; some local businesses were German-owned and a number of German and German-Jewish families had settled in that area. Mannheim Road formed part of a network of streets named after German cities, including Heidelberg and Bonn. The main road running up to the 'German' terraces was, and still is, Manningham Lane, at that time flanked by the larger houses of prominent Bradford businessmen. Its best-known pub, the Belle Vue, was the headquarters of a number of local societies including the Pickwick Club. At the time of Jonathan's marriage, Manningham was a quiet and respectable part of town.

There are only two surviving pictures of Priestley's mother, Emma, the best of which is a studio photograph of her taken with Jonathan, probably during their honeymoon in Blackpool. He wears a jacket and tie, light-coloured trousers, and a cap set at a rakish angle. Beside him, Emma is wearing a plate-like hat with a huge, striped bow, a single-breasted jacket over a long checked skirt, and is flourishing a frilly parasol. Both have the fixed expressions of a period when photographic subjects had to keep rigidly still for several minutes.

Throughout his long life Priestley claimed that he knew little of either his mother or her family, that she had died almost immediately after his birth and might have been of Irish extraction. His rare references to her were romantic. She was, he thought, a mill girl, possibly 'plucked' by Jonathan from her 'clogs and shawl, back o't'mill' background', 'a free and easy rather raffish working-class life where, in the grim little back-to-back houses, they shouted and screamed, laughed and cried, and sent out a jug for more beer'. People who not only lived 'back o't'mill but were only too happy to do so, blewing their money on beer, fish-and-chips and music halls'.[3]

He told two stories about her: that she was turned out of a straight theatrical performance for laughing too loudly and at inappropriate times, and that once, when she grew tired of a long-drawn-out meeting of educationalists taking place in the front parlour of her home, she fixed a hat on a broom handle and paraded round and round in front of the high window to persuade those men inside that it was time to finish. Of the rest of the Holt family he wrote only that Emma had a brother, Tom, who might have worked in the music halls before keeping a public house.

It might well be that Jack was told little of his mother, but it cannot be true that he knew nothing of the Holts for it has not been hard to discover a great deal more about them even at this distance in time – there are people still living in Bradford today who remember them well, especially Tom Holt, and indeed Priestley kept in touch with at least one member of the family well into his adult life. Whether or not Tom Holt did actually play the music halls at one time is not known, but he certainly went on to become one of the most popular and best-known publicans in Bradford, let alone the Manningham area, landlord of the Volunteer Hotel in Green Lane. The pub was opposite Green Lane Primary School of which Jonathan Priestley eventually became headmaster. Tom Holt was a flamboyant figure, described by those who recall him as 'a real character', so much so that the Volunteer was known throughout Bradford simply as 'Holt's'. One of my informants, Joe Mercer, told me that when he was a little boy he remembered his father having a metal matchbox on the front of which was a caricature of Tom Holt, while another, Mrs S. Blamires, sent ancient sepia photographs showing the annual 'Holt's' charabanc trip, for every year Tom Holt gave his regulars a treat in the form of a trip to the coast or the Dales. It is, therefore, impossible to believe that Priestley knew nothing of his popular uncle. As to the picturesque description of Emma as a mill girl in her clogs and shawl, that too is suspect for it is almost certain, from what can be recalled locally, that she worked for her brother as a barmaid before her marriage, either full- or part-time. Was her background and that of her publican brother considered altogether too 'raffish' for a strict Baptist family, which is why the myth of the girl at the back of the mill grew up?

Further proof that Priestley did not only know about the Holt family, but actually kept in contact with them, comes from a Mrs Marjory Wilson who still lives just outside Bradford and whose family on both sides had close connections with the Holts. As well as Tom, Emma had another brother, Joe, whose wife took in respectable lodgers on a regular footing, and at one time both her maternal aunts lodged with Joe and his wife so that they would be close to their work in the spinning sheds of Lister's Mill. When Joe's wife died, hers was one of the last Bradford funerals at which a horse-drawn hearse, complete with plumes, drew a coffin through the streets. Afterwards Joe Holt lodged at the home of another of Mrs Wilson's relatives, Bill Turton, at 7 Trees Street, Manningham. Bill was a tailor and according to Mrs Wilson 'Mr J. B. Priestley' used to send cast-off suits to Joe, who had fallen on hard times, suits which were altered to fit him by Bill Turton. A final link between the Holts and Mrs Wilson is that her own father, who was blind, used to play the piano at the Volunteer 'for singing and entertainment' and indeed did so right up until the last night it was open before its demolition, though by that time Tom Holt was no longer the landlord.

Jonathan and Emma had been married for three years before the birth of their only child on 13 September 1894. According to Peter Holdsworth, Emma suffered a protracted labour, which lasted over forty-eight hours, and the child's birth was registered forty days later at the office of Bradford's registrar, his father's occupation duly noted as 'schoolmaster', and the baby's name 'John'. The 'Boynton' appeared much later. It has no apparent family connection but was the name of a small town in Yorkshire's East Riding. Nobody knows why Priestley added it: perhaps he felt that for a would-be writer 'J.B. Priestley' sounded better than plain J. or John Priestley. Another theory is that the second name and initial were added to distinguish him from J. Priestley senior. In any event, he was throughout life known as Jack.

Emma died when her son was two of an ovarian cancer, on 15 October 1896, aged thirty-one. Hers was the first of a run of soft-tissue cancers in the Priestley family. Ovarian cancer is still hard to diagnose and it is possible that she already had the disease when she gave birth to Jack. After her death, Jonathan employed a housekeeper briefly while Jack was passed round a series of relatives.

According to Peter Holdsworth, Priestley once told him that he truly believed his father had been very much in love with Emma when they married but that he had found she approached life much more light-heartedly than he did. After her death, he was 'somewhat uneasy', looking out for any 'too-carefree' trends his son might have inherited.

Two years after Emma's death, Jonathan married again, a shopgirl called Amy Fletcher. He made an excellent choice for she was dearly loved by her stepson who wrote of her: 'I had a stepmother who defied tradition by being always kind, gentle and loving. I was happy at home. Yes, I was happy there, so wherever my desire to write came from it certainly did not come out of any frustrated or neglected childhood.'[4]

Yet in his last book, a collection of autobiographical essays, *Instead of the Trees*, published when he was in his eighties, he was still speculating on the mother he never knew, 'who must have died just after I was born', adding that 'nobody ever spoke to me about her'. He wondered if perhaps he looked more like her than he did Jonathan, who was fair to gingerish, blue-eyed, round-headed, hot-tempered and occasionally violent (he sometimes threw the odd pot!), where Jack was darker with greyish eyes and could keep a rein on his temper.

CHAPTER 2

Growing Up

Shortly before Jonathan married Amy, Jack was sent to the infants'
department of Whetley Lane School where Jonathan had taught
and where his first teacher took an immediate dislike to him.
'I can just recall that stupid woman's face, square and forever
frowning in my direction, as I remember my own terror and
despair, at an age when you don't realise that time may soon
change everything, when you feel small, helpless and apparently
doomed, arriving day after day with fear curdling your "inside".'[1]
The woman must have been stupid, he continues, 'because she
cannot have had any imagination at all and must have been
quite unfitted to be in charge of young children'. He adds that
if he had only had a mother 'she would have realised what was
happening and marched down to Whetley Lane and told that
woman what she was doing to him'.

On 15 November 1903 Amy Priestley gave birth to her daughter and only child, Winnie. Although the age gap was too great for
Jack and Winnie to be close companions when they were young,
Jack never thought of her as anything but his full sister, and his
'kind and gentle stepmother' showed equal affection to both.

Jonathan progressed up the professional ladder from Whetley
Lane to Belle Vue School and from there to Green Lane Primary
School where he was appointed headmaster. When Winnie was
one, he moved his family to what was considered in the Bradford
of the day a 'posh' address, 5 Saltburn Place off Toller Lane,
another terraced house, but a new one, close to what was then the
edge of the town, near fields with views across open countryside.
He fought hard to prevent any more houses being built nearby
and for a while the Priestleys had only two neighbours in Saltburn
Place, the Thompsons and the Wrights, both of whom owned
shops in North Parade, one of the town's best shopping streets.

The house owners in Saltburn Place had to pay for the street's upkeep and Jonathan persuaded his neighbour to agree to trees being planted along it. He would also jump up from the dinner table to rush outside and rage at lorry drivers who used it as a short cut: they had no business, he said, to use a residential street for that purpose.[2]

In his book *The Edwardians*, Jack describes his home in some detail: 'Although in the middle of a terrace, it was on a far larger scale than Mannheim Road, with more rooms, including two attics.' On the ground floor there was a kitchen with a range, where the family ate when they were by themselves, and a front-room or parlour where they dined when there was company. Beneath was a basement, also with a range, which had a sink and housed the mangle for the family laundry. Both ranges were coal-fired and had to be lit daily. The work of cleaning out and lighting the ranges every morning fell of course on Amy, along with the rest of the heavy domestic work and all the family baking, including not only scones and cakes (which the family ate with cream on Sundays as a treat) but also all the bread. 'We were always good eaters in our house,' Winnie told Jack's friend Diana Collins.

If baking day was hard work it was nothing to washday. All the water was boiled before the garments were 'dollied' in a tub, then squeezed through the heavy mangle. You could smell that Monday was washday, said Priestley in a 1943 radio programme: 'It was a day when mothers, wives and sisters were busy and short-tempered and menfolk there on sufferance. The house was full of steam and suds where menfolk crept about, carefully negotiating the lines of washing in the backyard.' In the atmosphere of rubbing and wringing out and mangling, lit with lightning flashes of irritability, 'the comfort-loving and gluttonous male had a poor day of it', not least because the house was cheerless and the meals, 'late and flung at you, both meagre and monotonous: scrag end escaping from its string, melancholy cabbage and potatoes done anyhow and bits of fruit pie with the lumpy residue of Sunday's custard'.[3]

Amy had had little formal education but she had an enormous respect for it, and considered Jack a budding genius, presumably because he was always reading and enjoyed broadcasting his knowledge from an early age. Alongside all the cooking, cleaning, washing, housework and childcare she began to educate herself, first reading the English classics, then Tolstoy and Dostoyevsky, and she saw a season of Greek drama at a Bradford theatre – she was deeply shocked by *Oedipus Rex*. As well as giving Jack affection and a secure home, in her quiet way she also gave him an inherent respect and liking for women which never left him.[4]

Jonathan's 'abiding passions' were socialism and education. A born teacher, he told his son that education was the great golden gateway to the countries of the mind. He filled the house with teaching colleagues, whose voices rose with the force of their arguments, and young Jack would linger among the pipe smoke, the smell of hot toddy ('for which we had those silver sugar crushers and, remember, whisky was three-and-six a bottle then . . .'), enjoying the visitors as comic characters. People, he notes, who cannot appreciate such characters in literature and find them overdrawn must have lost their childhood memories. 'When we are very young, it is the friends of our parents, so enormously themselves, so seemingly unchanging, like immortals, who create for us our first comic characters . . . it is useless to insist, as austere and unimaginative criticism often does, that people are not really like that, for there is a time when they are and it is a time that continues to exist out of reach of critical opinion, a time we remember when we no longer recall which critic said what.'

Jonathan was also a pillar of Westgate Baptist Chapel, seeing no conflict between his Christianity and his socialism. Florence Wood, now over ninety and still a chapel-goer, can still recall attending Sunday School as a small child 'when Mr Jonathan Priestley was our Sunday School Superintendent and headmaster of Green Lane School. He was very strict and brought his discipline into the Sunday School.' Her older brother was at school with Jack. In 1994 when she opened the chapel's Christmas Fair, she reminded the congregation of how Jack had described Westgate as a hive of activity which 'did not close its doors on Sunday evenings and open them the following Sunday . . . Whoever came to Westgate was warmly welcomed and nobody went away feeling lonely.'

Yet, his son recalled, Jonathan was never a Puritan, although he remained a 'strict and intolerant' Sabbatarian, never buying a Sunday newspaper, and denouncing 'any attempt to bring colour and gaiety into the grey weary length of a provincial

Sunday'. Apparently this was not just on religious grounds, for
he argued that even leaving aside religion, one day in the week
should be different from the rest. Perhaps inconsistently, though,
on Sunday nights after chapel he would bring home a clutch of
friends to what was always an open house and they would have a
'roaring good time shouting each other down about socialism'.
As he grew older, Jack complained that he could not see why
his father should have the kind of Sunday night *he* liked, but
prevent his son from spending his as he would have wished:
visiting concerts and the theatre or flirting with pretty girls in
cafés. Somewhat gnomically in a piece in the *Listener* in 1959 he
wrote: 'I came to know, as youths do, more about what went on
in Bradford on Sunday nights than my father did, and soon saw
that it was the ugliest, most uncivilised, most degrading evening
of the week.' At other times there was no restriction on fun and
socialising, and Christmas was one long party, with good food,
hot toddy, clouds of pipe and cigar smoke, charades and party
games. There was a piano and Jack was encouraged to learn
to play, as everyone in the family was expected to take part in
home entertainments.

Every summer, the Priestleys went on holiday, always travelling
overnight to take advantage of the cheaper fares. The family
would try to sleep while Jonathan chatted to other passengers.
Unlike their friends and neighbours the family did not go to
commonplace Blackpool or Morecambe but to exotic resorts
like Bournemouth where they would walk for miles, visiting
everything on foot.[5]

Jonathan also encouraged his son to take part in a wide range
of activities, from football and cricket to visits to the theatre and
the local Playreaders' Club: he was an accomplished amateur
actor and read every play on which he could lay his hands. He
was deeply interested in natural history and took his son for
long walks in the countryside outside Bradford. always on the
look-out for new flowers.

One of the most evocative descriptions of those early days
comes in *Outcries and Asides* (1974) when Jack recalls the place
Whitsun held in the Bradford of his youth. On Whit Sunday the
children would parade through the streets in new clothes, while
on Monday there were treats and trips out into the country, a
tradition which lasted in many northern towns and cities until
the 1950s; poor families would hock themselves for months to

provide their children with new clothes for 'the Whit Week Walks'. The children were taken off in cleaned-up coal carts and enjoyed sports, such as egg-and-spoon and three-legged races, followed by mugs of tea and buns. Growing lads 'greeted the dawn of sex' by chasing the girls round the fields, the girls giggling and screaming as they were caught, yet 'all we did when we caught them was let them go though probably all that chasing and screaming, with so many girls, often quite fleet of foot, allowing themselves to be caught by us as they shook their curls at us and cried it wasn't fair, represented an archetypal sexual game'. Priestley considered, however, that this had more to do with letting off steam, some small rebellion against the determined jollity and organisation of the superintendent and deacons. 'Even so these were good days, returning us exhausted, full of buns, and with the smell of early June grass still pleasantly haunting us.'

At the age of thirteen Jack won a scholarship to Belle Vue High School. He learned fast, and fretted when teachers made the same points over and over again, which he had grasped the first time. He thoroughly enjoyed sport, especially football, but not gymnastics which he described as 'Czech mass antics'. He loathed woodwork and metalwork, though with hindsight he felt that he might have enjoyed both had he come to them as an adult.

The shining light of his school life was Richard Pendlebury, who taught him English. A charismatic personality, he was a local boy who had been educated at Bradford Grammar School before going on to St John's teacher training college in Battersea, London. As a young man he spent his long vacations studying French at the universities of Grenoble, Nancy and Geneva and was appointed to Belle vue High School in 1898. Pendlebury was only forty-eight when he died in the inferno of the Western Front five months before the end of the First World War. He believed strongly that time is precious and must never be wasted. His qualifications, wrote Priestley many years later, were modest by today's standards, 'He did not have a Ph.D. for a thesis on the use of the semi-colon in the late works of George Eliot . . .', but he loved good writing and knew how to communicate his enthusiasm. Jack was convinced that the plays, poems and essays Pendlebury discussed with his class helped make him the writer he became, and considered that his own feeling for literature was inseparable from the admiration he had felt for his schoolmaster: 'I can see him and hear him again, quite clearly across the years that changed all human history.'

Jack's first experience of love was divided almost equally between two 'goddesses'. The first was Miss Mabel Sealby, a stage artiste. Jack fell for her when he went to a Theatre Royal pantomime in which she had appeared as Principal Girl. He saw her only once and never wrote to her, but the lively soubrette with her black curls haunted him for years for 'she was not one of your altogether-too-demure anaemic creatures'. Her name blazed out at him whenever he saw it and, when the local paper ran the story that she was probably leaving the cast after 'some saucy-curl dispute with the management', Bradford became for Jack a place of dark desolation. Mabel Sealby appeared only once at the Theatre Royal, in the 1905–6 production of *Cinderella*, when Priestley was eleven.

Jack's other love was the girl next door, and he was confined to looking longingly at her through the side window of the parlour. It should have been easy to get to know her better but contact between the two was discouraged as the families had fallen out. As this was well known locally, the two young people were never invited to the same parties or picnics. She never gave Jack a look or a smile; they never exchanged a word.

Priestley started writing in his early teens, school stories based on what he read in comics and magazines. 'They used to begin "Hurrah, Greyfriars at last," cried Dick, or something like that, but they never got beyond a page or two.' At one time he started a newspaper: the first edition included four serial stories, but he had no idea how he would either develop or end them. The first issue was laboriously handwritten to be passed around among his schoolfriends, but the venture never went beyond the second edition, which was only half the size of the first.

At fifteen he found school little more than an irritant and began to yearn for adulthood. He became angry when his teachers told him that more effort was expected of a boy whose father was a well-known and respected headmaster. Jonathan was unsympathetic, and reminded his son how fortunate he was to have the luxury of a good education when the secondary schooling of so many promising, bright children consisted at best of afternoons spent in the classroom after working in the mills from dawn until noon.

Jonathan had hoped he would go on to higher education but the idea did not appeal to Jack. He knew that to win a scholarship meant hard work, which he was not prepared to do. Nevertheless, he had boundless self-confidence: he believed that he could do whatever he set out to do and as he reached his sixteenth birthday he realised that he wanted to write.

Faced with Jack's determination to leave school, Jonathan was neither angry nor reproachful. To Jack's astonishment, his father told him that if he was to leave school he should take a job in the wool trade. 'It was as if a fanatical teetotaller had told his son to get a job as a barman. My father himself would no more have gone into the wool trade than he would have joined the Foreign Legion.' It had taken Jonathan immense effort to lever himself out of a family life that had been dependent on that industry, but if Jack was to turn his back on education, he must go where 'a lad who had anything about him . . . could learn a trade and earn his own living among the wool merchants, the combers, the spinners, the weavers, the dyers and finishers, and the exporters. That way he could acquire a nice girl, a house of his own, a bedroom suite, a piano and a pram, with whist drives and chapel high-teas-and-concerts in the winter, and the summer rising to a peak in ten days' holiday at Scarborough or Morecambe.' But Jonathan must have been disappointed, and although he sent his son into the wool trade, he never trusted those who ran it: 'To him and his friends there was a composite and symbolic "wool man" – and I can still hear them pronouncing the words with scorn – who was the enemy of teachers and the good life . . . he had, I suspect, a mental image of a "wool man" that could have been used to represent capitalism in a socialist cartoon. But into the wool trade I must go.'[6] So he went.

CHAPTER 3

The Swan Arcadian

Jack Priestley left school without any qualifications. However, he applied for a job at the firm of Helm and Company, was interviewed and, 'probably because I didn't really care what happened', taken on. The firm's offices were in the Swan Arcade, long since pulled down and 'developed'. From archive photographs it was a fine Victorian arcade, of which only a few examples now survive.

Priestley immortalises life in a north country industrial city, immediately before the First World War, in series after series of autobiographical essays. In one he introduced himself in the persona of the 'Swan Arcadian',[1] a bright and lively-minded young fellow with views that he was eager to impart, increasingly vain of his appearance, and becoming steadily aware that he wanted to write for his living.

Priestley's descriptions of Bradford's appearance are almost photographic. Much of the Victorian architecture was on a grand scale, fit for men who would 'cut up for a pretty penny'. Later in life Priestley despised those who thought the towns and cities of the West Riding ugly, and accused them of looking not with their eyes but through the prejudices of their idea of Victorian industrialism. Even as a lad, hurrying to his stool at Helm's, he was aware of 'exquisite compositions of light and shadow, of smoke and sunlight, and dark stone'. But probably the memory that still lingers with those who remember his wartime *Postscripts*, the BBC radio broadcasts of 1940, is that of the pie.

It was the centrepiece of the window of a small eating house and was of gargantuan proportions, 'a superhuman meat and potato pie with a magnificent, brown, crisp, wrinkled, succulent-looking crust'. Puffs of steam continually issued from under the crust. It was still there, puffing, when Priestley went into the shop after Bradford had been bombed. The shop owners recognised him and revealed to him the secret of how the perpetual puffs were produced – a secret Priestley took with him, as he had promised, to his grave.

The pie remained in the window until 1955 when the owner's widow retired and the shop closed.

Helm's offices were on the third floor of the arcade with imposing entrances in three different streets, the most imposing of all in Market Street nearest to the tram stop. Jack was not the office boy – there was usually one lad even lower down the ladder – but whenever the office boy left Jack had to fill the inkwells, put out clean blotting paper, uncover the typewriters, work the copying press and take huge bundles of wool samples to the post office, 'a chore I particularly detested'. While he said of his novel *Bright Day* that it was not autobiographical, the work experiences of the young Gregory Dawson mirror those of Jack Priestley. He particularly detested the sample side of the business, fearing his 'golden youth' would somehow slip away with the sheets of blue wrapping paper. But, just occasionally, incoming parcels would strike a romantic note such as the camel hair which brought with it desert dust that transported him to the golden road to Samarkand, or real oddities like the parcels of Chinese pigtails, cut off by state decree, destined to become dolls' hair.

Helm's exported 'tops', wool that had been processed and was ready to be spun into yarn. Most went to Europe, but a small proportion ended up as far afield as America. All the outgoing samples had to be listed in a 'bag book' and one of Jack's tasks was to keep it up to date – he used it as a cover to read in office hours. He also had to write to the companies that transported the wool by rail, canal or ship, which again he used to his own advantage, building up relationships with them that enabled him to travel abroad cheaply to Copenhagen and Amsterdam.

Helm and Company ran a tight ship. Staff were expected to arrive on the dot of nine o'clock and, on arrival, Jack, in common with other junior staff, had to put on a checked overall known as a 'brat'. Office conditions were Dickensian and labour-intensive. Many documents were still handwritten by the clerks who sat on tall stools at high desks, and Jack learned to use one of the two primitive office typewriters. Every letter had an upper and lower case key, and Jack blamed the fact that he never learned to touch-type on the impossibility of learning how to do so on such a battleship of a machine.

The staff had a strict hour for lunch but, unlike the time of arrival, that for going home was uncertain. At whatever time the staff were told they could leave, they still had to ask the boss if there was anything more they could do. Jack was unfortunate in that while most wool bosses had wives and children to go home to, his did not: 'I had to ask permission to leave the office from the one man whose business was most of his life, who was capable of spending Christmas Day or Good Friday brooding over samples and ledgers.'

Years later he wondered why he hadn't been sacked. He was lazy and careless and, by Bradford office standards, wore the wrong clothes, while the time he took when sent out on an errand was 'positively scandalous. True, I was paid very little, but even on that low rate I was bad value.' He could only think that in some way he represented the kind of person his elderly and austere employer might secretly like to have been, had he not repressed that side of his personality – idle, smoking, drinking, girl-chasing, verse-writing and floppy-tie-wearing. Also, unlike most men in the trade, Jack's employer was well read and would send him out to find a good new book for him, knowing that he might not see him again for an hour. Jack would take the opportunity to smoke a pipe, forbidden in the office, and observe the passers-by 'through an almost stupefying haze of Cut Black Cavendish'.

At home he had turned his one-time bedroom into a den. His father agreed to install a gas fire in it but anything else Jack wanted he had to provide himself: 'We were not poor and lived comfortably, but there was no money to spare, certainly not for any fancies of mine.' He pinned up reproductions of pictures he liked and turned orange boxes into bookcases. Two small armchairs filled the space between his bed and the gas fire.

In his den, behind the dormer window, he could indulge himself. There he became not only a writer but also a 'poet, story-teller, humorist, commentator and social philosopher'. Outside, Priestley the Dandy made his appearance. Percy Monkman, an old Bradford contemporary and friend of Priestley's youth, talking to Peter Holdsworth in 1986 at the age of ninety-three, remembered Jack in those days as an 'outlandish-dresser', who wore a Tyrolean-style hat, a vivid jacket and smoked a corncob pipe.

To those who worked in the Helm warehouse, Jack was something of a joke. When he panted in with his bundles of samples, he was greeted with shouts of 'Na, lad! Ah see tha's gotten that daft bloody coat on again.' It was a sports jacket in chrome green, considered inappropriate in the office. Jack often felt he would have probably been happier working with the men in the warehouse than in the office.

Jack's clothes and attitude were also a source of comment outside work. Winnie recalled that friends and neighbours found him baffling. He was said to hold 'hoity-toity notions' and wear unsuitable fancy clothes. One woman stopped Winnie's mother while she was shopping to warn her that her stepson was 'too full of hanky-panky', and Jonathan was constantly asked: 'Whatever are you going to do about your Jack, Mr Priestley?'

Writing in 1972, Priestley made an unequivocal statement about his sexuality. He was, he said, an elderly heterosexual male, 'lusty indeed in his day and even now no envious fossil, who has enjoyed the physical relations of sexes, and with no objection to *that*, no shrinking from *this*, and without the feeling of guilt which seems to disturb some of my distinguished colleagues'. In the early days of the twentieth century a physical relationship with a girl of his own age and class was virtually impossible, and Priestley made do with romance. Out with friends on a Saturday night, the glimpse of a face, 'unknown and fair, a flower among puddings', would cause him to push through crowds for a better look before discreetly following his quarry to another part of the town. Such a blossom might even lure him to some cold and distant chapel on a Sunday evening. It took a young man then, he said later, as long to persuade a girl to hold his hand as it does 'one of today's young bloods to get her into bed with him'.

Jack was even more tantalised on a visit to Copenhagen when, staring over the ship's side, he looked down on 'thousands of beautiful girls on bicycles, like an invasion of Rhine maidens'. Taking breakfast in a courtyard he found himself opposite a factory inside which he could see delectable girls at every window, looking out, pointing and giggling. To him Copenhagen was a magic place, where the dockers looked like businessmen, the lager was good, there were exotic lunches of open sandwiches and where in the evening he strolled in the Tivoli gardens under 'a hundred thousand soft-coloured lights'.

Enchanted by his visits to Copenhagen and Amsterdam, Priestley began to visualise himself as some Central European character in a novel and searched Bradford vainly for the equivalent of a Continental café society. He had to make do with the local Lyons in Market Street, a substantial building on two floors. On the ground floor sat solid citizens in search of a sustaining meal, while Priestley and his friends, 'we golden lads', would make straight for the upper floor where they would monopolise a couple of tables for hours at a cost of roughly sixpence a head. Also in its favour were the waitresses, sharp young women mostly from London or Ireland, who would keep tables for the young men and pass on messages for them. Once Priestley and a friend persuaded two of them out for a Sunday walk on the moors and high tea. Jack's girl, who was Irish, was pretty enough but tedious; she recited bad poetry or told him at length every detail of the melodramas she had seen in the theatre, the equivalent of today's television soap operas.

The young men held their discussions against a musical background provided by a trio made up of a flashing-eyed violinist, who looked Italian but was a local man, a fat pianist who 'appeared to take no interest either in the music or anything else and might as well have been playing in the Gobi desert', and a cellist with short hair and a clipped moustache, whose appearance suggested a cross between a croupier and the dissipated secretary of a gold-mining company.

Now that he was at work and old enough to go into pubs, he became aware of the hypocritical lives lived by many local businessmen, solemn and frock-coated on Sunday morning as they went to church with their wives and children, 'coarsely raffish' away from their families. Managers who were obdurate if the mill girls wanted another shilling a week could later be found in distant pubs turning the prettiest and weakest of them into tarts.

Priestley could not see this as right, even if the women and girls were hardly models of feminine refinement, and it was a theme that appeared later in at least one of his most popular plays. Sometimes he left the office just as the women were flooding out of one of the largest mills and 'I would find myself breasting a tide of shawls, and something about my innocent dandyism would set them screaming at me, and what I heard then, though I was never a prudish lad, made my cheeks burn.' In those days it was still the custom in the wool mills for the women to get hold of some unfortunate new male employee and 'sun' him – pull down his trousers. Priestley put this down to a rare opportunity for women, restricted by fathers or husbands at home, at the mercy of male employers and overseers at work, to get something of their own back. And the strict code of behaviour followed by the better-off did not apply so rigorously to young mill girls, who, once they were officially courting, would allow their fiancés a great deal of licence without any censure from families or neighbours, as long as a marriage took place when the girl became pregnant.

At the age of seventeen he fell 'half in love' with a girl called Ethel, an unusually independent young woman for those days as she ran her own typing agency. Her office was just across the street from his own. At least part of the attraction was that she was older than him, but she must also have reminded him of Mabel Sealby, for Ethel, too, was a 'saucy dark lass, like the woman Shakespeare seems to have loved and hated, with raven curls, bold eyes, a white skin'. After months of gazing from a distance, he asked her out and thereafter she would accompany him to the theatre where they sat in the sixpenny gallery. Coming out of the theatre one rainy night, she allowed him to kiss her under the brim of her floppy tweed hat, the hair which escaped from underneath glittering with rain drops. She often kept her office open after normal working hours, sometimes especially for him, and typed out his first pieces of writing in exchange for kisses. 'She could only have been paid in kisses, for I had no money.' He never forgot her and often wondered why she had been prepared to work overtime 'for someone as young and oafish as I was', and concluded that perhaps she was soft-hearted, as is the way of 'saucy' girls.

He had a busy social life and many friends. Among these was George, an old school friend, who had won a scholarship to Cambridge. Like Jack, George played the piano, but could not sing, while Jack fancied himself as an interpreter of comic songs. On one occasion they earned themselves a guinea at a Saturday night concert at the Mechanics Institute, where Jack was billed in the programme as 'Jack Croly, of the Leading London and Provincial Halls'. The performance was a disaster as Jack could not remember his words. George and Jack remained friends even after the former went up to Cambridge but it was never quite the same: his jokes and anecdotes about university life were alien to Jack.

Several of Priestley's contemporaries went on to the local art school and won scholarships to the Slade from where they would return in the vacations with stories that were 'epics of starvation'. Two had once decided to save money by making a stew that would last a week, a plan which came to nothing when the pan fell off the gas ring and deposited its contents all over the floor. Most daring of all was a 'Bradford-to-Slade man' who *lived* with his art-student girlfriend.

But none of the tales of student life in Cambridge or London tempted Priestley to leave Bradford. People in the city were indifferent to what went on down south, and Priestley wrote, 'Bradford seemed to offer me all I wanted from a town.'

CHAPTER 4

Into Print

Between 1910 and 1914 Jack served his 'apprenticeship' as a writer and, although he did not realise it at the time, as a dramatist.

In those immediately pre-war years the music hall was still at its height although its era was coming to an end. While 'the halls' lingered on after 1918, providing a training ground for much-loved comedians such as Arthur Askey, Jimmy Jewell and Eric Morecambe, they were supplanted first by silent films then by the 'talkies'. Priestley remained a music-hall lover all his life, paying his final homage to it in his novel *Lost Empires*.

At this time Bradford had two theatres offering music hall, the Empire and the Palace, and a third, the Alhambra, opened in the summer of 1914. According to Peter Holdsworth,[1] the Empire was 'several cuts above' the Palace in the quality of its programmes and here Jack saw among many others the young Charlie Chaplin, W. C. Fields, before his Hollywood days, top-of-the-bill star Marie Lloyd, Grock the clown, George Formby senior, father of the now better-known comic and ukelele player, and Little Tich. He was particularly fond of Little Tich, writing in an essay in *The Balconinny* that it seemed almost inconceivable that so funny a man and Death could ever meet. He mourned that the great clown's death marked the passing not only of the halls but of a whole era of quaint theatricals from touring melodramas and acrobatic dancers to the chorus boys, with their bowler hats, pearl-buttoned coats and short canes, and the girls with their flounces, feather boas and 'dashing busts'. Little Tich mimed a series of characters from aristocratic *grandes dames* to jockeys: 'You shared with him a free human intelligence and you shouted with laughter.'

Priestley also saw nearly every straight play performed at the

Theatre Royal in Manningham Lane. Britain had two touring circuits: the theatres graded number one took in the best actors and productions, number two the rest. The Theatre Royal was a number one house and many theatrical legends played there, including Sir Henry Irving, who gave his final performance there on 13 October 1905. Taken ill while appearing in *Becket* by Tennyson, he was rushed from the theatre to the Midland Hotel where he died in the foyer.

A varied bill offered Frank Benson's Shakespeare seasons and Edward Compton's productions of classic drama, including works by Sheridan and Goldsmith, Bernard Shaw, the popular comedies of J. M. Barrie and jolly musicals like *The Waltz Dream* and *The Merry Widow*. All these productions were either on the way to the West End or touring after a London season.

Jack was fascinated by the actors. Standing in the long queue for the Theatre Royal gallery, he caught glimpses of them on their way in. The men, larger than life, wore flamboyant coats and never seemed to remove all their make-up so there was always a rim of blue-black round their eyelids. They would sweep past, trilby hats perched on rakishly brilliantined curls, merely casting a few sparkling glances at the gallery queue, 'sparkling because of the blue-black', before vanishing through the stage door. And the actresses were even more unbelievable, hardly related biologically to the women and girls of Bradford.[2]

The constant visits to the theatre provided Priestley with material to write about, and during lunchtimes spent in the office he made little scribbling books of about fifty pages, which he bound in brown paper using the office's press.

Years later, he found odds and ends of his work from that time. It was a strange mixture. There was a collection of sketches, inspired by the music halls, which used the dialogue format of popular magazines of the day, such as the 'Fluffy-haired Girl and Lanky Male Companion', 'Red-faced Girl and Surly Fiancé' and many others.

He also wrote poetry, which he admitted with hindsight could only be described as versifying, for to write *poetry* 'a man must be able to go mad while still keeping himself saner than most men'. First came the epic in blank verse. He had read Malory and Tennyson's *Idylls of the King*, and embarked on a work entitled *Lancelot: After the Burial of Guenevere*, which contained such lines as:

... Arthur came
From nowhere to a throne, and no man knows
Where he has gone. The common human cries
To him were but the twittering of birds.

The older Priestley considered that for pure literary value *Lancelot* would be lucky to fetch a penny a line.

The next effort, *Evensong in Atlantis*, was little better. This had been inspired by evenings spent alone in his attic when he had become fascinated by the myth of the drowned land, fantasising on a race of black-robed priests who served only power and forbidden knowledge. But his technical ability did not match up to the grandeur of the theme. It was, he wrote, 'very bad indeed'.[3]

The third attempt at major verse, *The Song of a Mood*, was still 'not good'. Here, Priestley, at seventeen, assumes the persona of a weary writer three times his age. The first line runs 'I think the world is dying' and each stanza ends with women of all ages stitching a shroud, heroes of all ages digging graves, while poets sing requiems. As a robust young man in a no-nonsense household surrounded by lively companions, he sometimes wondered why death held such fascination for him.

He sent it, with other examples of his work, to the Irish writer A. E. Russell. It was – and is – not uncommon for would-be writers to ask established authors for their opinion, even though this carried the risk of stopping the aspirant in their tracks: the poet Robert Southey wrote to Charlotte Brontë, who had asked his advice: 'Madam, Literature cannot be the business of a woman's life, it ought not to be. The more she is engaged in her proper duties, the less leisure she will have for it, even as an accomplishment and recreation.' Russell, however, was more encouraging: he said that *Song of a Mood* was 'very beautiful and imaginative and is also better in form than the others. You have obviously imagination and feeling but you have not yet mastered the form.' He told Priestley to keep in mind the more lyrical parts of the English translation of the Bible and Walt Whitman at his best. His criticism ran to four pages, in which he paid particular attention to Priestley's technique, 'because technique is the only thing on which one writer can really advise another since it is impossible to teach imagination or creativity'.

He also wrote short stories, which 'even as teenage attempts
. . . have hardly any merit'. One, 'An Excess of Discipline', was
influenced by Priestley's reading of the popular short-story writer
W. W. Jacobs, a favourite of Jonathan Priestley. A second, 'The
Way In', features a young clerk who has dreams of becoming an
entertainer and gets his break when he is unexpectedly called
on to take the place of a popular comedian, and 'Poor Old
Dad' is about a failed artist who wants his son to follow in his
footsteps, but instead the boy goes into business and marries a
rich manufacturer's daughter. Nearly fifty years after he had
written it, he wondered why he had thought anyone would have
considered publishing it.

Lastly, there were 'articles', sent off hopefully to newspaper
editors, accompanied by stamped addressed envelopes. The style
of these was serious, suggesting that J. Boynton Priestley was
'about 150 years old' and probably a retired clergyman,[4] and
they were larded with phrases like 'to the average man one can
say nothing', hardly guaranteed to grab the imagination of a
newspaper editor even in 1913. Later Priestley conceded that
his reflections on topics such as the cinema read as if they had
come straight from the pen of the leader writer of a third-rate
provincial paper.

He had his first success with a piece called 'Secrets of a Ragtime
King', which he had sent to the popular weekly *London Opinion*.
The new craze for ragtime music had recently hit Yorkshire, and
Priestley, on a visit to the Leeds Empire, had heard it played by
three young Americans, the Hedges Brothers and Jacobsen. That
evening he found himself yanked into a new era, 'jungle-haunted,
monstrous', an era heralded by 'Alexander's Ragtime Band' and
'Waiting for the Robert E. Lee'. Fired by the experience, he
wrote an imaginary interview with a ragtime singer. Its sheer
exuberance, which caught a popular mood, appealed to *London
Opinion*'s editor, who accepted it and sent Priestley a guinea.
Even Jonathan Priestley was impressed 'by this break-through
into print and money' – although he had no interest in ragtime
and never read the magazine. Priestley was relieved, for there
had recently been a coolness between him and his father after
Jonathan had taxed him about a rumour that he had been seen
in the town 'half-carrying a young woman'. But he marked the
occasion of his son's first success by bringing out a box of cigars
– which Priestley had been rifling for years – and offering him

a Key West. 'Together we lit up and puffed away, men of the world.'

The day on which his article appeared, Priestley, travelling to work by tram, noticed that a woman sitting opposite was looking at a copy of the magazine and wondered if she would read his own contribution, although she was not the kind of reader he had in mind: he remembered her as sour, suspicious-looking and somewhere in her disappointing forties. The sight of her, leafing idly through the magazine, haunted him for years, representing the enormity of the task facing those who want to interest an unknown readership in what they have to say. He ended his journey in a confused state of 'eagerness, pride, self-love, self-doubt and shame', a 'glory and sick-flavoured brew' with which he would become familiar.

His small success inspired him, though, and he wrote until he thought he must have used up enough paper to cover the floor of Helm's warehouse. Then came a local breakthrough: in the spring of 1913 the local Labour Party weekly, *The Bradford Pioneer*, offered him a regular column. Socialism was strong in Bradford – indeed it had been the birthplace of the old Independent Labour Party – but it was a north country British socialism that owed little to classic Marxism. Priestley said of his father and the local party that they wanted radical reform but not all-out revolution. His task on the *Pioneer*, however, was not to push party politics or to comment on the state of the nation: he was to write on the theatre, books and music, and was not paid for his work – but, then, neither were the other contributors.

His column, two examples of which survive, was called 'Round the Hearth'. Evidently the editor had misgivings about what his teenage columnist might say for at the top is printed: 'It must be distinctly understood that "Round the Hearth" is pre-eminently a personal feature so that the opinions expressed therein are not necessarily those of the paper itself. Letters dealing with the subjects treated in "Round the Hearth" are invited, and should be addressed to "J.B.P.", c/o *Bradford Pioneer* – Ed.'

The 4 April issue kicks off with a paragraph headed 'It seems to me . . .' obviously written by young Jack in his persona of the 150-year-old clergyman. '"I am conscious now that behind all the beauty, satisfying though it may be, there is some spirit hidden of which the painted forms and shapes are but modes of manifestation and it is with that spirit that I desire to become in harmony." So wrote Oscar Wilde in *De Profundis*. It is an old subject, the spirit of beauty, and one that has occupied the minds of men since time immemorial . . .,' the eighteen-year-old author gravely informs his readers. There follow Jack's views on the mind-broadening effects of travel; a note that membership of the Bradford Playgoers' Society has now reached 700; a reminder of the anniversary of the death of Oliver Goldsmith; and a comment on efforts being made not to introduce conscription. There is also a review of *Gypsy Love* which was playing at the Theatre Royal that week. Priestley notes that musicals always fill the house when all too often fine productions of straight plays do not. The current show is very good, he concedes, although it is not a typical specimen of the genre (he wished it were). Viennese musicals are definitely the best, those of Britain and America being 'far inferior, in fact most of them are so extremely fatuous that I fail to see how anyone above the age of ten can find pleasure in them'.

He also recommended the performance of a young woman called La Pia, who was appearing at the Empire, to his readers. 'She is an artiste who combines graceful dancing with novel and beautiful scenic effects, the result being a most artistic performance. A new and novel use for the Cinema is shown in her dance "Spirit of the Waves".'

Under the sub-heading *It seems to me*, in the 11 April edition Jack tackles the subject of war as 'it seems to be in the air. I am being told daily that a great war is inevitable, and I always emphatically state that I don't believe in it. Nor do I!' After stating his own views ('I am not going to deal with the economic side of the question . . .') he announces that if he had his way 'war would be abolished tomorrow'. The rest of the page is made up of a dialogue 'sketch' between himself and 'Davidson, a vegetarian'; 'requests' to various theatre and music hall managers and to football enthusiasts; a note that spring must be on the way as the Pierrot shows have returned; and a review of the current music hall bill at the Bradford Empire. Of this he says: 'The Empire bill this week is headed by Jack and Evelyn, and the male partner has such an aptitude for burlesque that the turn is one of the most amusing I have seen for some time.'

At nineteen Jack Priestley was a lad of modest talent and ambition. He saw himself eventually as a full-time writer, able to earn a pound a week, renting a cottage on the moors from which, after a sharp walk, he could take a tuppenny tramride to the town centre. Perhaps he would be joined at some later date in his cottage by one of the not-unwilling apple-cheeked local girls. One such was Pat Tempest, a neighbour's daughter, who was sixteen when he first met her. He had noticed her first as she went in and out of her house carrying a violin case. He offered to accompany her on the piano and together they would try out violin and piano sonatas, which led to cuddles in the back parlour of her home. She was pretty and, like all the women to whom he would be drawn, she was also dark.[5]

In June 1914 Priestley took the ferry from Hull to Holland. He spent several days in Amsterdam 'staring at the Rembrandts and Vermeers' before setting off for Cologne on a walking tour of the Rhine. On arrival in Germany he bought a pipe a yard long – which was for 'common use not just a souvenir' – put up in tiny inns, 'buried among leaves, swimming in green air' and strummed on pianos for the local basses and tenors where, after a good sing-song, they would call for more rounds of wine and beer. He came back through Brussels, 'a small operetta king of a capital', where he stayed in a sinister, dilapidated hotel with creaking floors and a damp bed.

His account of that long-ago walking tour in Germany ends: 'When I sailed to Hull, late at night, late in June, later still in epoch, I watched the lights of Europe retreat to a glimmer, then vanish from sight forever . . . Those lights, that shore, really were gone forever. The Europe I left that night sank into history, banishing itself from immediate experience as my Atlantis had done when the sea sucked it down.'

It sucked down with it the young Jack Priestley, who yearned after the pretty girls he saw during the summer evenings spent in Bradford's Lister Park listening to the open-air concerts. His father and friends would sit in the tiers of chairs around the bandstand smoking their pipes and criticising the music between discussing the finer points of a local cricket match, while high above the band, on a promenade, the young people of the town would congregate 'looking down through the blue haze of smoke and catching what came to them of *Coppelia* or *Les Deux Pigeons,* and all the rest, past counting, on the move in a thick sluggish stream, in which, as I realised more than once, it was devilish hard to find the only face you wanted.'

The innocent parade was condemned by chapel deacons, who saw dire consequences following the display, pursuit and capture.

> No doubt the young males were often merely predatory –
> though the worst of them never paraded in the park but,
> like two older men I knew slightly, lurked elsewhere bent on
> seducing half-witted housemaids – but the girls wearing their
> best clothes, and usually in arm-linked trios and quartets, must
> have known very well, in spite of their glad-eyeing, whispering
> and giggling, that it was here, not in the mill or the office,
> not even at home or at the chapel bazaar, that they were
> engaged in the serious business of life. And the place and
> the hour were propitious for mating: a summer evening, trees
> and grass between youth and the dark narrow streets; the hills
> above the tree-tops fading into dusk; all the people, thousands
> and thousands of them, sitting, standing, or in the slow river
> of faces on the promenade; the lighted bandstand in the haze
> below, a glitter of a scarlet uniform coming through the blue
> air, and music coming too, not recognisable, not attended to,
> a long way off, but music. A good place, a good time, for the
> beginning of love.[6]

'Strange how potent cheap music is,' says one of the characters in Noël Coward's *Private Lives*. Forty years after this scene had disappeared for ever, the catchy light melody of the day, 'In the Shadows', still danced in Priestley's head, bringing him close to tears.

CHAPTER 5

Into the Inferno

They stare from the faded photographs held on file in the archive of the Imperial War Museum, those eager young men, eyes shining with enthusiasm. Processed by the Army, they all look curiously alike. The young Jack Priestley, as portrayed in a 1914 photograph which he used as a postcard to send to family and friends, is interchangeable with other young lads from working-class Bradford, George Mitchell, Vernon Rhodes, John Cocker and Arthur Pearson, whose diaries and letters are also in the museum's archive, or with the sons of the famous such as Rudyard Kipling and Stanhope Forbes. Also alike are the yellowing letters home from those raw recruits, the same phrases about 'doing one's duty', 'fighting for King and Country', 'beating the Huns' and 'the war will be over by Christmas', used again and again whether written by a lad who left school at fourteen to go straight into the mill or by a boy who had been first to public school and then to university. All the boys made their parents' hearts swell with pride as they went to do their duty.

The only concentrated piece of writing Jack Priestley produced on the First World War was not written until over forty years later and there are only fifty-three pages of it.[1] For a long time he told himself and others that the main reason he did not attempt to write about it after leaving the Army in 1919 was because he saw no point in adding to the spate of books published on the subject, many of which were very good. Later he admitted that his experiences in that war remained an open wound that never healed.

He enlisted in September 1914, and over the years gave a series of contradictory reasons as to why he had done so. In 'Carry On, Carry On' in *Margin Released* he writes: 'I was not hot with patriotic feeling; I did not believe that Britain was in any real danger. I was sorry for "gallant little Belgium" but did not feel she was waiting for me to rescue her.' Nor had he been affected by the propaganda posters exhorting the lads 'Kitchener Needs You!' or by women handing out white feathers to those who did not want to fight, as all that came later. He had felt, he wrote, simply the desire to get into the war.

The writer Vincent Brome claims that many years later, during a conversation at the Savile Club, Priestley told him he had known even at the time he joined up that the war was something concocted by politicians,[2] but this sounds more like his father's view. The young male protagonists of *Bright Day* and *Lost Empires* enlist for different reasons. In the first, the fabric of Gregory Dawson's overly romanticised vision of the Alington family is rudely torn apart by the death of one member on a Dales picnic in the summer of 1914, and in the second, Richard Herncastle has had enough of touring the music halls with his conjuror uncle, has had a disastrous affair with an older woman and is in love with a younger one. When he tells his uncle of his decision, to the former's cynical exasperation he responds much in the words of the older Jack Priestley: 'I don't want to be a soldier. I wish there wasn't a war . . . and I don't feel particularly patriotic. All this King and Country stuff and flagwaving doesn't make me want to cheer.'

When Priestley enlisted, it had been a long, hot summer and he had returned from his holiday dissatisfied with his life. Forty years on he told Diana Collins that he had felt he had something to prove: he had spent the first three years of the war trying to be a hero and the rest trying to stay alive.[3]

In *The Rebel Tyke* Peter Holdsworth gives a touching vignette of young Priestley on that August day in 1914 when the world changed. The rest of his family were on holiday at the seaside and the house was silent. Suddenly he heard the newsboys calling in the streets outside: war had been declared.

It must have been a particularly confusing situation for Bradford people, who had been dealing amicably with Germany and Germans for years in the course of their work, suddenly to be told how dastardly, evil and vicious they were. This was particularly true for Jack, who not only had had regular contact with his German importers for four years but had only recently returned from that magical walking tour.

He did not rush off, he said, with a herd of half-plastered chums and join the local battalion of the West Yorkshire Regiment (later known as the Bradford Pals); he went to Halifax and signed on with the Duke of Wellington's West Riding Regiment, known popularly as either the Havercake Lads or the Dirty Duke's.

He was not quite twenty. In *Henry IV, Part 2*, when Feeble is asked if he knows how stupid he looks for having agreed to be conscripted he says: 'By my troth, I care not; a man can die but once; we owe God a death: I'll ne'er bear a base mind.' The young Jack Priestley had no such strong religious beliefs, but he once said that in September 1914 he had received a signal from the unknown.

So it was that Jack Priestley walked into the Swan Arcade and up the stairs to Helm's office one September morning (late again) and, after shaking hands with his boss, walked out of it and his old life for ever. Then he took the tram back to Halifax and reported to the regimental depot where a sergeant, after casting a disparaging glance at his almost new sports jacket and flannels, put him to cleaning congealed fat from the insides of huge cooking pots. For that first week he was allowed home at night, as long as he reported at the barracks at eight every morning.

A week later Private J. B. Priestley of Number 8 Platoon of B Company of the 10th Duke of Wellington's 69th Brigade, 23rd Division was on his way to his first camp in Surrey. His first letter home, addressed 'Dear People' and postmarked 23 September 1914, tells how they had to get up at three a.m. to catch an enormous corridor train, filled with raw recruits bound for Aldershot, and did not arrive until two p.m. the following day. The camp, at Frensham, held ten thousand men from a variety of regiments. The rules, Priestley moaned, were very strict. They had to be up by five thirty, spent all day 'drilling', and were in bed before nine. They slept twelve to a tent and if they wrote letters it had to be done by candlelight and was 'a very difficult business'. What he did not put in the letter but said later was that he, who had always been so fastidious, found himself taking part in the evening ritual of peeing in his army boots every evening to soften them before emptying them outside the tent flap.[4]

He goes on to say that he has had to borrow the stationery on which he is writing 'as neither paper, envelopes nor stamps are obtainable' because it's all work, but he is enjoying himself, writing in the early morning before going off to wash in a lake about a quarter of a mile away. So please would they send him stationery, stamps and other things because there is only one canteen for all 10,000 and there is no money, only tickets, as up to the time of writing no pay had been given out, which he has been told could lead to 'serious trouble'. There have also been 'a number of deaths', on which he does not elaborate, but, in spite of all this, he has never felt better in his life.

At this stage in the war there were still plenty of experienced soldiers to show the recruits the ropes. Many had served in India and carried little tins of curry powder with them with which to flavour tasteless meat. They were cynics to a man, knowing every trick to avoid doing anything that was not absolutely necessary, never volunteering if they could help it. Young Jack found their attitude surprising, particularly their lack of enthusiasm for being sent to the front, for he himself was 'genuinely anxious to get into some fighting'. At Frensham he found many lads from Bradford and elsewhere in the West Riding, some of whom like himself had previously worked in mill offices, others in the mills themselves.

The early volunteers were given months of severe and intensive basic training, lasting ten hours every day; they lacked only firing practice as there were insufficient rifles to go round. There was also a shortage of khaki for uniforms, and Priestley was mortified at having to hand in the one he had been given on the day he enlisted in exchange for a 'convict-style' outfit in dark blue, from which the colour ran when it got wet. When he went home on leave that Christmas he tried to conceal it by draping himself in a long black overcoat, for which he had swapped a jacket, and wearing a huge black forage cap that gave him, he fancied, 'a half-raffish, half-sinister' look. His hopes that his brave appearance might impress the girls were dashed when they laughed heartily and asked him which service he had joined. But at least by Christmas his regiment had removed to Aldershot barracks which, by comparison with the wet tents of Frensham, seemed like the Ritz.

The only accounts of what happened to him and how he felt at the time are contained in a mere handful of letters written between September 1914 and the summer of 1916.[5] However, the archive of the Imperial War Museum contains diaries and accounts, written by other young men from Bradford, who served on the Western Front at the same time as Priestley.

In February 1915, to the sound of a military band, the young soldiers were marched out of Aldershot, to the cheering of the crowds lining the streets, on a roundabout route to Folkestone where they were personally inspected and harangued by Kitchener before leaving for France. Priestley wrote, from a 'dilapidated barn somewhere in France', in a letter dated 'Saturday': 'The cheering crowds as we left England, the marches on fearful roads with ton-weights on our backs; the long rides in cattle trucks – it's all like a dream. There are no YMCAs or canteens or anything else round here. Will you please send me some tobacco (duty free) and matches or anything else. My address is: L/Corporal Priestley No. 12398 [he had had his first promotion], 10th S.B. West Riding Regt., British Expeditionary Force. Cheer up: Jacky, with love to all at home.'

In the next letter he gives a chilling account of life on the Western Front. It is dated 14 March 1915:

Dear People – We are 'soldiering' (as the Tommies phrase it) in earnest now. We have just been in the ghastliest part of the whole Western Front. There is nothing like it. We relieved the French there and they look relieved too. You must have heard of the famous 'Labyrinth'; well, that's it. Great hills, half blown away with enormous shells; villages absolutely raised [*sic*] to the ground; old trenches full of heads, legs and arms, bloodstained clothing and old equipment. Talk about 'souvenirs'! The place is one vast morgue, it has been taken and retaken so many times. The front line trench is a ditch about three feet deep; there are no communication trenches, you simply crawl up in the dark and lie in the trench until relieved, which is often 24 hours. The German trenches are very close, in some places only twenty yards away, and there is great execution with bombs and aerial torpedoes. Luckily my company went into the reserves, for those who went into the front line lost very heavily.

And there was snow, sleet, blizzards and about a slice of bread a day to eat. We've marched and marched, slept in cellars (a few inches under water) while all around the great shells were roaring and blasting.

There are a number of huge, military burial places, both French and German, round about and when the big shells ploughed their way into these, the result was gruesome in the extreme. There is nothing in the British line to equal this little lot. However, we are now back some way from the line, billeted in a town.

He then grumbles that the French troops are better fed and treated than they are 'and the British public can put that in their pipes and smoke it!'

It is unusual for such a vivid description to have got through the censor and he must have known he was taking a chance, for he exhorts his family not to send his letter to the local paper as so many proud parents were doing, since there were plenty of military people back home to give another side to it all. Lastly, we have what must be the final appearance of Jack the Swan Arcadian and centenarian commentator on matters artistic. Confirming that he had received a parcel from 'Miss Southwark', he says she had told him that she has 'offered her play to Miss Herriman, who refused it on account of the long speeches. Miss S', he pontificates, 'uses literature as the handmaiden of politics and sociology – a great mistake. The point of view is always too obvious, this spoils her work which is otherwise very good, being sensitive, sympathetic and possessed of much kindly mature humour – the last a rare thing nowadays.' He was still only twenty and he was writing this after days spent among the rotting remains of human beings.

Also serving on the same sector of the front, Bois Grenier-Laventie-Fleurbaix, was another Bradford lad, George Mitchell, who had enlisted in the West Yorkshire Regiment in August 1914. There is a gap in the Priestley correspondence after that last letter until August 1915, but Mitchell described some of the actions in the small diary he carried with him.[6] On Wednesday, 28 April 1915 he wrote:

'Rumour was we were "going in" too and we marched off at 6 p.m. through [Laventie] which has been thoroughly shelled. Practically everything in ruins. Terrible desolation . . . Curious feeling of elation as was my first time under fire. Marched on to ruined village at Fauquissant, past "Dead Men's Corner". Bullets occasionally whistled down street. Trenches are not like the last lot, not trenches at all but merely a sandbag parapet 6 to 7 feet high and 3 to 5 feet thick. All open at the back.'

There is a similar description of that part of the front in *Margin Released* where Priestley remembers there were no 'real trenches at all', only breastworks of sandbags which contained, unbelievably, catapults, 'big ones, the kind the Romans used'.

Diaries kept by the Bradford boys during that period of the war all recount the same things, the endless bombardments, the shortage of rations, the feeling of always being 'fagged out', how a close mate 'got his', news of the failure of the latest attack and, overall, the terrible, sickening stench of death. George Mitchell, marooned in a listening post, 'simply prayed for the day to come up' and scribbled a few lines of a verse popular with the lads:

> I want to go home, I want to go home.
> Shrapnel and whizzbangs around me do roar.
> I don't want to go to the trenches no more.
> Take me over the sea where the Germans can't get me.
> Oh my, I don't want to die, I want to go home.

In *Margin Released* Priestley remembered his time in a listening post on that same sector of the front and how he found himself staring so hard at black nothingness that 'it stopped being black or nothing but began to crawl with greyish shapes. I would then shut my eyes for a few moments and when I opened them again the shapes had vanished.'

And all around was the everlasting noise. 'Youth, hard training, a genuine desire to get into the war at some point, had turned me into a brave soldier but I was less and less brave, in that sense, the more I saw of the war.' Terror, he wrote, came first through the ear. The First World War with its massed artillery was the most deafening of all time. 'The sound hit you harder and harder as the months passed, as time went on, the vast cannonading, drumming hell into your ears, no matter whether it was their guns or yours, began to wear you down, making you feel that flesh and blood had no place in this factory of destruction.'

George Mitchell's orders for those in the trenches when not in action shows that there was little rest even then, with sentry duty, cleaning and servicing weapons, repair work, cooking and eating, latrine duty, night patrols and night working parties. 'No trench will ever be vacated when attacked,' the official orders conclude, 'the enemy to be met if necessary at the point of a bayonet.'

The trenches on that sector were filthy, wet and most of the men were infested with lice. Years later, watching a performance of R.C. Sherriff's *Journey's End*, Priestley wrote that the dugout in the trenches as portrayed by the set designer 'looked to me like a suite at the Ritz' compared with the reality.

Priestley's next letter home is dated 8 September 1915 and is from 'somewhere in . . .' near Neuve Chapelle. For a few days, he wrote, they had been camped in a deserted, partly ruined farmhouse, all huddled together on the stone floor. He thanked his family for the welcome parcel, which he was sharing with everyone as they were soon to move on yet again. 'You have doubtless heard a lot about YMCAs, canteens and concerts for the troops, but I have never seen anything of them yet. I have never had my trousers off yet since I left England . . . The fellows across the way are in pigsties.' If anyone wanted to send anything he would be grateful for tobacco, chocolate, a tin of vermin-killer, a pocket-sized writing pad, shaving powder and a good razor but they had better not send them just yet. He enclosed a pound towards the cost.

Ten days later he wrote to thank his father for a parcel and its contents, though he longed for some fruit. During the last week they had marched

> till we dropped, slept in fields, marched again and so forth. This is our third day in the Fire-trench or First Line Trench. My home at the moment is just off Watson Avenue, which branches off Shaftesbury Avenue. I've seen a few Germans but only through the periscope. Every now and then bullets and shells come whizzing over our heads. At night it is very weird; we are all on the alert and star shells – like rockets – are sent up now and again – making the place look bright as day. The nights seem to stretch out to eternity. Rats and mice, wasps and gigantic bluebottles abound in the dugouts.

But he was in good spirits, if filthy.

On 26 September he found himself in the front line immediately before what became known as the battle of Loos, he and his fellows in full kit and so weighed down with extra cartridges and bombs they could hardly move as they waited to climb the scaling ladders all along the fire-trench. During the usual bombardment before the industry advanced over their heads, 'invisible express trains seemed to be passing both ways'. He felt that once he had climbed up the ladder in front of him his expectation of life was such that even a cat wouldn't last five minutes. But 'I had a lucky war.' Because the attack on the right had not gained sufficient ground, it was decided not to send in his company.

On 8 October he wrote home again thanking his family for a parcel, but grumbling that it had taken a long time to come and asking why they did not send smaller ones through the *Telegraph* 'as these only cost fourpence whereas this parcel cost 1s. 4d. and the contents are not worth much more . . .' He also complained that he received fewer letters than anyone else in the platoon. It was bitterly cold and monotonous in the trenches: he spent the nights on sentry duty and listening and, as he found it difficult to sleep during the day, they passed like a lifetime. He was disgusted with the officers, who continually badgered and hampered the men with 'silly little rules and regulations other regiments don't have to submit to', and finally he became so angry with having to bully men to obey 'this and that little order that I've been thinking of reverting to the ranks, so don't be surprised if you have to address me as "private". The "rest" we are supposed to get when relieved from the trenches is a GHASTLY FRAUD.' He and his men were no better than 'supernavvies'. Could they send him 'some substantial food – such as a stand-pie or tinned pudding – and yes, by all means the *Times French Literature* sheets'.

They had rushed to enlist, in that hot August and September of 1914, for the war that was going to be over before Christmas. Now it was by no means sure it would even be over by Christmas 1915. But at least it couldn't get any worse. Could it?

CHAPTER 6

Flowers From Dead Men

During the autumn of 1915 and the following winter the weather was appalling, first heavy rain, then sleet and snow. It was so bad that there were few mass attacks; instead raids took place into enemy territory; during one Priestley found himself trapped in no man's land, unable to get through the barbed wire entanglements that the artillery was supposed to have cut. The men were exposed in the flashes of star shells and pistol lights, 'asking to be machine-gunned out of this world'. On one occasion Priestley and another soldier crawled back, illuminated in bright light, half carrying and half dragging between them a third, badly wounded, man.

The trenches, by now steadily filling with mud and water, were regularly bombarded by the Germans with enormous shells known as Jack Johnsons, and for days on end, wearing six pairs of socks, high boots and a sheepskin jacket, Priestley had to slither along the communication trenches with messages. He was covered with lice and never saw a hot meal. Some of the worst nights were spent carrying huge coils of barbed wire along the flooded trenches under shellfire: 'I saw men, no weaklings but powerful fellows, break down and weep. It was not the danger, which might have been even worse – though I lost every close friend I had in the company that winter – but the conditions in which the lower ranks of the infantry were condemned to exist, month after month, worse conditions than the Germans and French ever knew except briefly in battle . . .'[1]

In his letters he kept the worst from his family, either for fear of worrying them or because of the censor, but sometimes what he was experiencing broke through. He wrote to Jonathan of the difficulty of getting up and down the trenches through the mud and water, and 'the most appalling thing is to see the stretcher bearers trying to get the wounded men up to the Field Dressing Station'. He described the bombardment one Saturday morning as 'fearful' and he and his mates crouched in their dugouts expecting to die. One shell burst in Priestley's trench, 'miraculously' wounding only four men – including himself on the thumb. 'But poor Murphy – your Murphy, you know – got a shrapnel wound in the head – a horrible great hole – and the other two were the same. They were removed soon after and I don't know how they are going on. I've seen some terrible sights and endured some hardships, but believe me, I never lost my nerve and strange to say, I felt a strange exultation of the soul at the expense of the body. *Do not be afraid for me; – I am not afraid.*' The letter ends, significantly: 'I suppose I am a man now, and am certainly going through an ordeal. Perhaps it would be as well if everybody went through some test of manhood.'

The end of November brought a brief respite when he was sent back behind the lines to the Third Corps Headquarters to act as a clerk. Here, at least, he had a bed, food and a chance to wash even though the hours were very long, the only recreation being walks in the bitter cold in the grounds of an old château. But he hated his clerking job and longed to get back to the trenches.

It is hard to believe that this was really how he felt at the time, but if it was, his wish was soon granted and he went back up the line to discover that in his absence his closest friend, Irvine Ellis, had been killed. A shell had hit the trench, killing two and wounding fifteen others. 'Ellis was not killed on the spot,' he wrote to his father on 3 December 1915, 'but died a few hours later. Poor Irvine! – he enlisted at the same time that I did and we were together all the time; his cheery companionship helped to lighten many a dark hour.' Shortly afterwards he received a pathetic letter from Irvine's sister on behalf of their mother, asking for news. They had heard rumours of her brother's death but had had no confirmation and she had found it hard to believe. He replied to her, and passed on her address to Jonathan in case he would like to write too.

On 12 December he wrote to Winnie: he had heard that she had wanted a letter 'from the trenches' and told her that he would be spending Christmas in one. 'I thought Bradford was a bad place for rain, but it is the Sahara Desert compared with this miserable country. There is little fighting now because both sides are suffering from awful conditions.' But they had been under bombardment only the day before and did not look, he told her,

remotely like the soldiers she would see at home. He thanked
the family for his Christmas parcel and hoped she was getting on
all right at school. A letter to his stepmother on Christmas Eve
enclosed a pretty handkerchief for Winnie, bought in a half-ruined
village three miles behind the lines. He had not had time to go
any further to where he might have bought nice, if expensive,
'souvenirs'. What, he enquired, was the white powder in a tin?
Vermin powder? Tooth powder? Baking soda? The contents of
the parcels sent to the troops from Bradford, he told her, were
laughable – 'the whole contents aren't worth sixpence' – but
those from Halifax were splendid, containing candles, toffee,
a cake, plum-pudding, tobacco, cigarettes, matches and a large
tablet of soap but still 'the rain it raineth every day'.

He spent New Year's Eve in the trenches too, writing his letter
by the light of a guttering candle in a dugout only two feet high.
It had been 'a nightmare'. The troops in front had made a bomb
attack on the German lines and they had been ordered to support
them. 'It was literally hell on earth.' He had spent most of the
time crouched in the mud beside a machine-gun, stunned by
the noise, sickened by the smell of cordite. The artillery from
both sides lit up the sky, revealing the red streaks of shells going
both ways. This was followed by an incessant stream of bullets
also from both sides, along with bombs and trench mortars so
that the sky blazed with a mad medley of shells, searchlights,
star lights and green and red rockets. 'That was our introduction
to the year 1916. This morning I learned we lost 80 men and
several officers, so that it cost us pretty dearly . . . This is the
morning of January 2nd. We go back into the firing line this
afternoon for four days.' On a lighter note he says he has heard
of something called Mackintosh's Chocolate Toffee de Luxe. 'It
sounds so weird I'd like some, if you can procure any please.'

A few days later he was sent with a party to dig new trenches
less than fifty yards from the German lines where, of course, they
were spotted and shot at, two men killed outright. Yet such a task
wasn't remotely considered 'VC business, just a working party'. His
battalion, he wrote, was now getting something of a name: at one
time there had been three hundred men in it, but new reserves had
continually to be brought in to bring it up to strength owing to the
heavy casualties they had suffered. His chances of coming home
on leave were pretty remote, 'unless I happen to get a Blighty'.

The letter proved prophetic, for a few days later he was wounded in the hand by a rifle grenade that dropped right into the bay of the trench, killing one and wounding four. 'I've had some narrow escapes this last day or two and since I got wounded they've made me very nervy . . . the part of the line we hold now is absolute "Hell"; the French said it was the worst part of their line, not counting Verdun.' But it was not a sufficiently serious Blighty to allow him home and, after a brief stay in a convalescent camp on the coast, he was soon back at the front. He was under pressure to take a commission but refused it; he wanted to remain in the ranks with the men, many of whom had become close friends and had gone through so much with him; within a few months nearly all of them were dead.

The beginning of February found the battalion camped in trenches running through the middle of a large French cemetery, surrounded by ornate tombs interspersed with simple white wooden crosses of the British dead, 'the most pathetic graves in the world'. In his letter of 2 February he grumbles at Jonathan for sending him 'Navy CUT tobacco, insead of Navy MIXTURE or Smith's Glasgow FULL STRENGTH (medium won't do at all).'

In March the division moved to the Carency–Souchez front to relieve the French, a journey that would now take about forty minutes in a car but then took several days. The sector into which they crept, through the snow, was sinister, with names that became notorious: Notre Dame de Lorette, Souchez, Vimy Ridge . . . Gone were the trenches with their jokey British street names. In *Margin Released* Priestley wrote that it was madness to launch attacks from such a position as the Germans were not only well dug in and better equipped, but also entrenched on higher ground only twenty yards away. But the decision was taken to 'keep the men on their toes' and 'we went through the mincer. It was not long before our own B company, with a nominal fighting strength of 270, had been reduced to a grim and weary seventy. Two hundred men had gone somehow and somewhere with nothing to show for it.'

Spring came, and behind the areas of desolation were scenes 'good enough for Pissarro and Sisley', as Priestley put it in *Margin Released*. Pulled back for a few days' rest, he and his men were billeted in a mining village with a huge slag-heap that reminded him of the towns and villages of the Yorkshire coalfield. But even the village was within range of one of the Germans' huge naval guns, which fired shells of 'monstrous' calibre. One minute they would be relaxing in the sunshine, the next they would join the villagers behind the slag-heap waiting for the 'Shirr-brirr-bump!' of the shell; then the smoke would clear and another six houses would have been destroyed.

At the beginning of June they were again sent up the line.

Curious you should mention the loss of trenches at—— as that is the terrible place we took over from the French three months ago and we are only just on the left of it now. The company strength is now seventy when it should be at least 260 and there are others decimated even more. None of the ranks have had any break back in England for at least ten months, while some of the officers have been home three times . . . They sent every kind of shell over, gas shells (it was quaint to see the French children with gas helmets on), tear gas shells (everybody's eyes were watering and sore), incendiary shells, shrapnel and last, but not least, the enormous Johnsons. I tried to imagine Saltburn Place being shelled in a similar manner, but it was too horrible to think about. They crash through houses, roads and steel girders, like going through paper. And the concussion!

Our heavy batteries just near thunder in response, and our stretcher bearers had to keep dashing down to the dugouts to bring out the wounded, poor maimed creatures – burnt, twisted, torn and many of them dazed beyond immediate recovery with the sheer noise.

Gas was being used by both sides, and there is a graphic description of its use by the British. Private George Mitchell was detailed into the Gas Corps along with Will Griffiths of the Bradford PALS; the two had known each other before the war.[1] They were sent to a mining village, inappropriately called Philosophe, for what was euphemistically described as 'cylinder work'. 'What a hole – though there are still a few frowsty-looking inhabitants knocking about.' They were then moved on to Vermelles, half a mile away, where special emplacements had been dug for the 'cylinders', disguised as fire steps. A gas attack was ordered in drizzling rain for five fifty a.m. and they loaded the 'cylinders' to let them off.

Got a big mouthful from the first cylinder and then *of course* pulled my helmet down. We had only 2 pipes for 12 cylinders and had to change over when one was empty. God, what a game! The rotten apparatus they had given us was leaking all over the place. We were working in a cloud of gas. We sweated ourselves to death and only got 8 off. All gas had to be turned off by 6.30 a.m. At 6.30 the infantry had to go over the parapet.

Soon the wounded were being brought back:

We saw some horrible wounds and bandaged up a good number. All at once a number of men (unwounded) came back with a tale that they hadn't been able to get through the barbed wire . . .[2]

One beautiful June morning, when the platoon rations had arrived, Priestley sent Private O'Neill down the communication trench to bring up some water – 'and sixteen years went by before we saw each other again'. He had just helped a young soldier who had recently joined the platoon to carry the morning's rations up to a dugout to be divided among the men, and was putting the bread, meat, tea, sugar and tinned milk into neat heaps: 'There I was then, deciding on each section's share, when I heard a rushing sound and knew what it meant and knew, though everything had gone into slow motion, I had no hope of getting away before the thing arrived.' The Minenwerfer shell landed slap in the trench only two or three yards from him. The explosion caused the trench to cave in.

Priestley was one of the lucky ones: his companions were able to dig him out but they, along with two hundred 'Volunteers' from the Bradford PALS, had to go 'over the top' on 29 June to check if the heavy shelling had cleared the barbed wire. 'It hadn't,' wrote Private Gilbert Isles, 'and only forty men returned.' The remnants of other regiments, he said, were then hurriedly put together and in the next action he was the only one left alive out of two Lewis gun teams. After days when all around him were wounded or killed ('I saw the Colonel, doctor and RSM shot down trying to get away'), he was severely wounded and sent home with gas gangrene.

In Yorkshire crowds gathered daily outside the offices of the *Sheffield Telegraph*, *Bradford Telegraph* and *Huddersfield Examiner* waiting for the long lists of dead and wounded to be printed and posted up. Jack Priestley had spent nearly eighteen months on the front line and almost all those who had volunteered with him were dead. The Western Front, Priestley said, had become an abattoir in which thousands of young men were blown to pieces. Another aspect of the carnage was revealed in little-known correspondence from the archive of the artist Stanhope Forbes, whose only son was killed eighteen days after he went to the front. His father received a letter from a Catholic priest who had buried him, who said, in answer to why the boy's personal possessions had not been returned to his family, that the dead, as they lay unburied in the sun, were robbed by soldiers on their own side, many of whom had served beside them for weeks or months. 'I don't want this to be published', he wrote, 'for it will only add to the pain and sufferings of the relatives.' He asked Forbes not to judge the thieves too harshly, for ordinary men had been turned into brutal and callous beasts by the hell they had undergone.[3]

Priestley's last letter home ends: 'Enclosed are flowers plucked from the parapet, probably growing out of dead men; there are plenty in these parapets. It's no uncommon sight to see a hand or foot sticking out.'

Priestley had no memory of being brought out of the front line, first to a casualty station, then to a field hospital in Souchez and finally to a military hospital at North Evington, near Leicester: for most of the time he was unconscious. 'All I knew at the time was that the world blew up!' He was considered lucky to be carted away in one piece, but he was now partly deaf and running a high temperature, which kept him in bed for weeks. His first recollections, through a haze of delirium, were of seeing his father and stepmother staring mistily at each other across his bed.[4] The casualties were also visited by local performers who entertained them with the songs they least wanted to hear, such as 'We don't want to lose you, but we think you ought to go . . .'

Once Priestley was convalescent, he was sent to another hospital, this time in a country house in Rutland and which 'belonged to light comedy'. After what he had been through, the scene that greeted him there was one of pure farce. People were frantically rushing around, 'beautiful VADs could be seen in tears and everyone was talking of "Arthur" '. Arthur, it transpired, was butler to the family who owned and still lived in the house, a portly young man who had somehow evaded conscription. Charged with getting a housemaid in the family way, he had admitted the offence, broken down full of remorse and had threatened to end it all: 'A full chorus of panic-stricken females, consisting of the family, housekeeper, cook, assorted maids, nurse, the starched and red-crossed debs, had implored him to forgive them their cruel reproaches by abandoning his plan to commit suicide, and, almost as a favour, he had agreed.'

There were ten wounded men in the house, visited daily by a doctor who looked and behaved as if he were eighty, and of whom it was said that he had treated a village girl for dropsy until the birth of a child had proved his diagnosis wrong. Priestley was a definite hit with the VADs, one of whom suggested that he took up polo when he recovered. When it was discovered he could play the piano he was recruited to accompany a daughter of the family who played the violin. He felt he was living in an absurd, dreamlike world, blown out of the bitter chalk of Artois 'into some tale of roses, mown grass and dawns without gunfire'.

When it was considered that he was sufficiently recovered, he was sent first to a camp in Ripon, 'a place apparently run by sadists', to undergo tough training to restore his physical fitness, then to Alnwick in Northumberland, which seemed like Siberia but where the men were well treated. He drifted through the first six months of 1917 in a daze, often drinking too much, and when a local well-to-do woman offered a £20 prize for an essay by a soldier he wrote one, 'though my heart was not in it, because my heart was not in anything'. He won, and spent the money on more beer. It was then that he decided to take a commission and was temporarily attached to the Third Battalion on Tyneside to await officer training. This was another piece of good fortune, for otherwise 'I might have been at Passchendaele, where Haig, who ought to have gone up there himself, was slicing my whole generation into sausage meat held above a swill bucket.'

Sent for training in North Wales, he was finally jerked out of his apathy and played football for the first time for three years, earning a place in the company team; he also wrote 'satirical odds and ends' for both print and performance. He made no close friends – 'there was no time' – but found his colleagues friendly and pleasant. He dined in the officers' mess 'to prove we didn't eat peas off a knife', sat the necessary examinations, passed, and was given an allowance to buy a new uniform, including a warm greatcoat and a Sam Browne belt. 'We were officers, free forever from cookhouse fatigues and carrying coils of barbed wire.'

He was commissioned into the Devon Regiment and spent further months either in barracks at Devonport or on training

courses in Cornwall, his evenings spent strolling along Plymouth
Hoe 'eyeing the bright-eyed girls', already spoken for by sailors,
or going to the cinema to see early Charlie Chaplin films – until
he was sent back to France on a troopship full of Americans.

When they arrived Priestley was one of a party of six sent out
to the front. He never knew what happened to his travelling
companions, only that two, those who had been particular friends
in Devonport, were killed within days. The battalion he joined
was far below strength and encamped in a railway cutting into
which the Germans dropped gas shells. While running up and
down ensuring that the men were wearing their masks, some gas
seeped in through his and he spent most of the battle unable to
see or breathe properly. Eventually he saw a dim figure coming
towards him through the gas. Realising that it was a German, he
pulled out his revolver and pointed it at him for 'after all, he was
not to know that I had been on two revolver courses and never
could hit anything'. The lad was about sixteen and gibbering
with fright. Priestley pushed his prisoner off in the direction of
the British lines, then collapsed in a shell hole, unable to breathe.
Here he was found by stretcher bearers who removed him from
the field – and also from the war, for the Army Medical Board
decided that he was now unfit for active service.

Priestley spent the final months of the war in the Labour Corps
Department, near Rouen, auditioning artists for concert parties,
then in a prisoner-of-war camp for Germans near Calais. Almost
his last posting, immediately after the Armistice, was to take
charge of a company sent up to the Lille–Roubaix–Tourcoing
area to do salvage work. It consisted of seventy or eighty British
soldiers, all unfit for active service, and some seven hundred
prisoners. Although the war was over, conditions were still
appalling. After they arrived in early December Priestley was
given a map reference for a proposed camp site. When he
went to the place to check it out he found it consisted only of
waterlogged shell holes and presumed there must have been a
mistake. No, he was told, there was no mistake and no further
delay would be tolerated. He must make camp straightaway. He
wrote back to his HQ saying the site was unsuitable even for 750
fit men, let alone a company of sick ones.

The next day a carload of 'red tabs and brass hats arrived,
important chaps with staring eyes and those voices that are the
equivalent of hard stares . . .' Priestley stood his ground: he told

the newcomers to look at the place themselves, that he would not move his men there and, as the war was now over, if they wanted to court-martial him they could get on with it. He won his case and his men were put instead into an old German hut encampment.

One morning in the early spring of 1919 'in some town, strangely chosen in the Midlands – and I have forgotten both date and place – I came blinking out at last into civilian daylight'.[5]

Priestley never recovered from his war experiences. In *Margin Released* he writes: 'I felt, as indeed I still feel today and must go on feeling until I die, the open wound, never to be healed, of my generation's fate, the best sorted out and then slaughtered, not by hard necessity but mainly by huge, murderous, public folly.' Mrs Rosalie Batten, his last secretary, recalls that in his mid-eighties he would suddenly stop what he was doing and stare into space. 'Then he would say, "It was terrible, terrible . . ." and I knew he was thinking about the First War.'

Not only was he unable to write about it for the best part of half a century, he could not talk about it either, least of all to those nearest and dearest to him. He wrote of how, when his parents visited him in hospital, he had found himself unable to communicate with them. He said too little,

> 'never really tried to grasp their hands. *Speak now and I will answer* . . . But too often we don't speak in this sense, certainly not in my family. We are affectionate and have plenty to say on general topics, but never have we spoken heart to heart, not I to my father, not my children to me, and so far, perhaps, not their children to them. With us, the Lord our God is an inhibited God, visiting the awkward silences and unspoken endearments of the fathers upon the children unto the third and fourth generation.'

In the light of all that had happened to him, it is certain that the young ex-soldier who walked out of the Army into the spring sunshine of an unremembered Midlands town bore scarcely any resemblance to the amusing lad who had enlisted five years earlier. His friend and fellow-Bradfordian the late John Braine said of him: 'I think the real Jack Priestley died in August 1914 somewhere on the Western Front. He came out of it apparently without any neurosis but I think he actually did die. But a writer was born and what all those millions and millions of words were really written for was so that he wouldn't remember the 1914–1918 War.'[6]

CHAPTER 7

Brief Diversions

It was not only Jack Priestley who had changed at the end of the war: so had Bradford. His and its 'time of innocence [had] long gone', as Peter Holdsworth puts it.[1] Holdsworth was theatre and film critic for the *Bradford Telegraph and Argus* for over thirty years, twice winning the regional Drama Critic of the Year award. On retiring he was invited to become Vice-President of the Bradford Playhouse and Film Theatre, of which Priestley was President for twenty-five years. He met Priestley through his work and came to know him well. Over 2000 of Bradford's young men had been killed and only 223 came home. And that was just the Bradford PALS. As we know from Priestley's letters, the losses in the Duke of Wellington's West Yorkshire Regiment had also been very heavy and the Bradford to which he returned was a bleak place, devastated by loss, haunted by memories of those who had gone. Almost all the friends of Jack's boyhood had vanished as if they had never existed.

While he was considering what to do next, Priestley approached the *Yorkshire Observer*, a daily newspaper, and offered to write a series of articles on walking in the Dales. They agreed to pay him a guinea for each piece published, and during the summer of 1919 he set off into the country, taking with him, as he writes in his book of short essays *Delight*, published in 1949, 'an enchanted passport', a commission from an editor for which he would be paid. It was his first and nothing that came after meant 'half as much'. It was therapeutic, too. He walked his favourite paths in a landscape of great beauty and deep peace. He could set his own pace, choose his itinerary, please himself, and it had the added advantage that when he turned in for the night at some isolated country pub he was tired enough to sleep. The articles were published under the pseudonym 'Peter of Pomfret'. No one knows why he chose this name, but Winnie said, 'I've a hunch he took it from something he had read.'[2]

By the time he returned from his walking tour he had made up his mind what he would do. The Forces Rehabilitation Service were offering small grants to ex-officers who wanted to go to university and Priestley, to the pleasure and relief of his father, decided that he would, after all, go up to Trinity Hall, Cambridge. His first choice was to read English and history, but he later switched to history and political science. The grant was small and throughout his time there he had to supplement it by writing and giving lectures and talks. Dorothy Fieldsend, who had taught him as a boy, told Peter Holdsworth: 'The war was at last mercifully over with its million dead, though "JB" survived its horrors and was now studying at Cambridge. During the long vacation he came to our school to lecture to our senior girls on the Shakespearean Theatre. He brought with him a delightful, meticulously made model of the Globe Theatre, complete in every detail, down to tiny metal balls to be rolled across the floor of the loft to imitate the sound of thunder. I remember being fascinated by this, as I have been so many times since by his extraordinary capacity for communicating to others his own enormous interest and detailed knowledge of people and places.'[3]

From his return to Bradford and throughout his time at Trinity Hall he continued 'keeping company' with Pat Tempest, who was working in Bradford Central Library, but he never wrote about his relationship with her during that time.

He was not very happy at Cambridge. Once when he was discussing university, he said: 'I'll tell you this, if you're a real writer then you don't need ever to have been to university; if you're not one, and you can't write, then going to every university under the sun won't make you one.'[4] He rarely spoke of his own experience at Cambridge. Like many of the undergraduates who went up after serving in the war, especially those from backgrounds where there was little money, he thought the new intake of well-heeled, upper-class young men shallow and immature. He had found himself surrounded by eighteen-year-olds who could have stepped out of the pages of Evelyn Waugh's *Brideshead Revisited*. Caught between those elegant young men with their college blazers and ties, and the dons and lecturers who had returned from the war determined that every old tradition should be meticulously maintained, Priestley felt out of place. His experiences had matured him in

a way he felt unfitted him for Cambridge life and he was also convinced that behind his back his peers mocked his Yorkshire accent:
'Cambridge regarded me as a north-country lout of uncertain
temper.' Another great divide was lack of money: his grant of £120 a
year, plus his infrequent earnings, forced him to live frugally. By the
time he entered his second year and moved into digs he was living
on bread, cheese and eggs: 'I ate so many boiled eggs – very cheap,
that year – that I have never properly enjoyed them since'.[5]

In those far-off days the university provided tea, 'crammed with
muffins and crumpets and fancy cakes, and I remember how it
irritated me to see men I knew, around four o'clock, carrying
fat bags of confectionery. And I never provided anybody with
those Cambridge breakfasts of buttered eggs from the kitchen.
I lived a spare, inhospitable existence, totally unsuited to my
temperament.' The weather was either too hot or too cold. He
had gone up during a miners' strike and had to study in a room like
a refrigerator, huddled in an overcoat, while the summers proved
almost too hot to bear for he took his first tripos examination
in a May heatwave, his dripping hands sticking to the paper
and his writing – 'never a good feature' – more illegible than
ever. He found the countryside dull after the dramatic Yorkshire
landscape, all fens and depressing fields, although he spent his
leisure time going for long solitary walks. Within a comparatively
short time he was wishing he had chosen Oxford instead. 'You
went to Cambridge to acquire knowledge and to cope with the
enormous teas and bad dinners. You could go to Oxford for any
ten of fifty good reasons. Beyond it were Bath and Wells and the
Cotswolds. Beyond Cambridge were Diss and Siberia.'[6]

A 1977 television programme about the university showed a
picture of Cambridge life that, for Priestley, was as far removed
from what he had seen in 1919 as life in Tahiti, particularly where
sexual relationships were concerned. In his day, he grumbled, the
undergraduates had had to live like monks, because few girls were
available and even fewer who would offer sex without marriage:
in 1977 there was 'none of that old stuff – arguing late over beer
and pipes about idealism and materialism, the individual against
the State, but instant skirt-dropping and bed work'.

He was twenty-five when he returned from the war and it seems
likely that he was still sexually inexperienced. Since he had a strong
sex drive it is hardly surprising that he admits to having suffered
intense frustration. Vincent Brome quotes him as saying once

that the sight of any woman was nothing less than 'magical', that the itch to communicate physically was almost overpowering and that there were times when 'you had to carefully restrain straying hands'. He recalled standing outside the old Empire in Bradford one day shortly after he had been discharged as a slim young girl in a yellow frock passed by, a floating vision of beauty, and how his hands trembled as he watched her and 'I was overtaken by sheer lust.'[7]

According to her daughters, Pat Tempest visited Priestley in Cambridge, but they did not know what had passed between him and their mother. It is unlikely that a well-brought-up young woman would have risked ruining her reputation. However, on 29 June 1921, eight days after acquiring his BA, Priestley married her 'with as little fuss as was reasonably possible', he wrote later.

It was, though, a wedding of some note, not least because of Jonathan's standing in the Bradford community. It was celebrated in the Westgate Baptist Chapel in modest style, as is confirmed by Mrs Florence Wood who still remembers it although she was a small child at the time.

Pat Tempest is a shadowy figure, of whose family little is known. Priestley once said they had Spanish origins but he never disclosed what they were. A photograph taken in 1924 shows the couple together, Pat posed under a parasol. She is attractive, but the most striking thing about her is her physical likeness to Priestley's second and third wives, Jane Wyndham Lewis and Jacquetta Hawkes: all three were dark with strong features.

Pat was the obvious choice. As her eldest daughter, Barbara Wykeham, puts it, 'she was very pretty, really delightful looking and smiled a lot; she had also written to him all through the war, visited him when he was in a convalescent home and all that kind of thing. Daddy said that after the war, when he was still at Cambridge and had enough money from his grant and his tutorials, he could afford – just – to have a wife and also (and I can't quite say how he put it) it was sort of expected of him as she had stood by him right through the war.' Pat's younger daughter Sylvia considers that that had been important to him: 'I think she was the stability that helped get him through and he thought, Here's my sweetheart at home, she hasn't got married, she's waited for me and I shall marry her.'[8] In 1918 Priestley paid for the publication of a collection of poems he had written just before the war. *The Chapman of Rhymes* is dedicated to Pat. He had been determined to put the work in print in case he never returned from the war, so that at least something of him would remain. When he grew older he thought the standard of work appalling and destroyed every copy he could lay his hands on. In the 1970s it did not please him to discover it in a bookseller's catalogue of rare editions at £250.

Priestley remained at Cambridge for a year after his marriage, engaged in 'postgraduate research on how to make ends meet . . .', and began to contribute to the *Cambridge Review*. Not only was this a prestigious outlet for his work, it introduced him to his lifelong friend Edward Davison. Davison had been born in Glasgow four years after Priestley and in the space on his birth certificate for the father's name there is only a blank. His mother had left Glasgow in the 1890s to become a governess to a family called Shields who lived in a large house in the countryside outside Leeds, after which the story reads rather like a Catherine Cookson novel: she was seduced by the master of the house and fell deeply in love with him, bearing him two children, Edward in 1898 and a daughter in 1902. Finally, after his wife died some fifteen years later – and, according to Edward Davison's son Peter, with great reluctance – he married his faithful mistress.[9]

Edward's early life had been miserable. Some excuse was found for his mother to return to Glasgow before her pregnancy became impossible to conceal, which is why he was born in her home city. When she returned to Yorkshire her baby was put out to nurse with a family on Tyneside where she visited him infrequently. He left school at the age of twelve, to work in factories, offices and in a music hall because his father either could not or would not support the children of a second household. In 1914, aged sixteen, he lied his way into the Royal Navy, went through the war and then, like Priestley, went up to Cambridge on an ex-serviceman's grant. Unlike Priestley, though, he loved it. These were, he told his own son, his golden years. He was a brilliant student, taking a first-class honours degree in English and history under the tutorship of Sir Arthur Quiller-Couch and the historian G. C. Coulton. His was a high Cambridge profile and he was regarded as the most likely young poet to inherit the mantle of Rupert Brooke. He edited the *Review*, played leading roles in Marlowe Society productions, directed by George Rylands, and entertained visiting celebrities to the university such as Walter de la Mare, Siegfried Sassoon, Hilaire Belloc, Sydney Webb and Arnold Bennett. His first volume of poetry was published in 1920, when he was twenty-two, to great acclaim. His poems were also published in the *London Mercury*, whose editor, Sir John (J. C.) Squire, was so impressed that he offered to supplement Davison's grant out of his own pocket. His only setback appears to have been an unhappy love affair that ended in a broken engagement.

The friendship between Priestley and Davison never faltered even though the latter spent most of his life in America. The two wrote hundreds, if not thousands, of letters to each other right up until Davison's death in 1970.

It was quite likely to have been Davison who prompted Priestley to find a publisher for a collection of pieces that had appeared in the *Review*, which he supplemented with others. It was not unusual at that time for local bookshops to publish young authors and this was what happened in Priestley's case: both *Brief Diversions* and *Papers from Lilliput* were brought out in 1922 by Bowes and Bowes Ltd.

Brief Diversions is a curious mixture of epigrams, anecdotes, stories between 250 and 400 words, and poems which are a pastiche of popular poets such as:

> I never see her walk into a room
> But what I think: Ah, now the fiddling's done,
> The world's brave footlights leap to stab the gloom,
> The curtain lifts and see the play's begun . . .

Many of the short stories would seem to have been influenced by ancient legends in which Death is portrayed as a person (a classic example is the Arabian tale known as 'Appointment at Samara'[10]), which was the nearest Priestley came to admitting a preoccupation with mortality. In 'The Uninvited Guest', a fancy-dress party is given by a rich man who has invented a new way of adulterating milk for babies. As in Edgar Allan Poe's *The Masque of the Red Death*, a guest appears strikingly costumed as Death, but in Priestley's story he wins a prize only to reveal himself as the real thing. *Brief Diversions* is a slight work but received surprisingly good reviews – the critic Edmund Gosse was especially enthusiastic. Priestley was carried away: 'One tiny quick shot – and *bang* – the bullseye! Like a man playing a fruit machine, I cupped my hands for the clanging spill of the jackpot. And nothing happened.'

Papers from Lilliput is a series of essays, whose titles all begin 'On', a popular convention of the period. One of Priestley's favourites was 'On a Certain Provincial Player', which featured Bridge Frodsham, an eighteenth-century Yorkshire actor. Frodsham rarely left Yorkshire and spent almost his entire career playing at his local theatre in York, but he once made a ten-day visit to London when he called on David Garrick, then at the height of his fame, whom he treated, much to Garrick's fury, as his equal. This book was also well received, but no publishers clamoured at Priestley's door to sign up an amazing new talent, no editors sent letters beseeching him to contribute to their newspapers and periodicals.

So what next? After being awarded his MA the obvious course was the one he had spent his youth trying to avoid: teaching. However, now that he was under mounting pressure to earn a living, for Pat had recently become pregnant, he began to study the appointments columns of educational journals and *The Times.* In a contribution made to a book edited by John Lehmann in 1957, *Coming to London,* he writes that the only posts carrying any kind of prestige appeared to be in universities of which no one had ever heard, situated in the far outposts of the British Empire, and where the salaries offered were quoted in the local currency so that he had no idea what in real terms they were worth. In desperation he applied for what was known as Extension Lecturing, and had to give a sample lecture in a village deep in the fens 'to a large, yawning dean and six gloomy workers'. Much to his surprise, as he knew his lecture had been poor and that the dean disliked him, he was accepted and was told that he could begin his Extension work – which sounds similar to today's Access courses – in North Devon at the beginning of the next autumn term.

As the summer ended, with the prospect of teaching in North Devon growing inexorably nearer, Priestley made the decision that changed his life for ever – a decision that was received with bitter incredulity at home in Saltburn Place and with amazement by his tutors at Cambridge, apart from Sir Arthur Quiller-Couch. Quiller-Couch admitted to having reservations as to the wisdom of the course Priestley was about to take but encouraged him nevertheless. 'Q', as he was known, was generous in his encouragement of new talent, although he could hardly have guessed that Jack Priestley would become one of the two best-selling British authors of the 1930s and that another of his protégées would be the other. She was Daphne du Maurier.[11]

Priestley decided to take a gamble. He wanted to be a professional writer and he was convinced that he had the ability to do so. This was all very well but his entire capital at that time consisted of fifty pounds, the baby was due the following March, and he knew no one of influence in the London literary scene; he had no entrée into the magic circle of those who had been together to public school, then Oxbridge, had entered the world of letters, belonged to the same clubs and employed each other's sons.

However, it was easier to freelance in the 1920s and 1930s than it would ever be again. When he discussed the tribulations of the writer's lot with the in the early 1970s, he said that he did not envy today's hopefuls for in the 1920s, when there was no competition from radio or television and people read for information as well as entertainment, far more publications had been looking for freelance contributors.

In September 1922 he was twenty-eight and he felt he had wasted enough time. He was haunted by an advertisement which appeared in the popular press and showed a series of male faces getting older and more anxious as the years passed. The caption asked if your present post offered you a pension, which Priestley thought a soul-destroying ambition.

There is no way of knowing what Pat thought about it, but early in the autumn they went to London to search for a flat and found one in Walham Green, then considered a somewhat seedy neighbourhood, on the ground floor of a block of apartments called King Edward's Mansions. It was spacious, had seven rooms and the rent was seventy-five pounds a year. It would have stretched the Priestleys' budget to breaking point had they taken it on their own, but as Edward Davison had just been appointed editor of a London magazine, the *Challenge*, the obvious thing was for him to join them and share the expenses.

Over the next few weeks they decorated it and went shopping for second-hand furniture in the Fulham and North End Roads. Priestley, carried away at having so much space, bought a Broadwood grand piano on hire purchase.

He then set out to conquer London.

CHAPTER 8

Dark Hours

The first few months in London were good ones, the three young people full of optimism, and the Priestleys enjoyed setting up home, even though breaking into the magic circle and earning a living was not easy. The rent and housekeeping bills had to be paid and looming up ahead was the expense of Pat's confinement: even though in 1923 little care was available during pregnancy, the doctor had to be paid for every consultation, as would everyone involved in the delivery of the baby, whether it was born at home or in a private nursing home.

But Priestley applied himself with a will to finding work. Edward Davison gave him space in the *Challenger*, and J. C. Squire, whom Priestley admits he had felt compelled to contradict within 'ninety seconds' of meeting him, commissioned some work from him for the *London Mercury*. Squire also mentioned Priestley to a number of other literary editors and publishers, including Robert Lynd of the *Daily News*, who gave him regular reviewing, and John Lane of the Bodley Head, who took him on as a reader. The help was invaluable.

However, writing of Squire in the 1960s, Priestley admitted that the relationship had always been embarrassing, for although they recognised each other's talent and admired each other's work, 'we didn't enjoy each other's company. I can imagine many reasons why he could not enjoy mine. I thought his talk contained too many large statements impossible to believe. He began as a Socialist rebel and ended a High Tory . . .'[1]

Priestley spent one morning a week at the offices of the Bodley Head, deciding what was worth reading and reporting on ('throwing out the 1000-page history of Jerusalem in blank verse or the reminiscences of a busy life in Stockport'), then taking the manuscripts home to read after he had done 'other work'. For this the Bodley Head paid him six pounds a week, a not inconsiderable sum in 1923 when, as he recalled, you could buy a seven-course dinner in Soho for half a crown. Among the writers he recommended for publication were Graham Greene and C. S. Forester.

The 'other work' began to grow and he added the *Bookman*, the *Spectator*, the *Saturday Review*, the *Daily Chronicle* and *The Times Literary Supplement* to the titles for which he wrote essays and reviews. Of all the commissioning editors with whom he came into contact, the one he admired most was Robert Lynd, Literary Editor of the *Daily News*, whom he described as 'an enchanting character', as well as a fine critic and essayist, in whose company for more than twenty-five years he 'fleeted the time carelessly as they did in the golden world'. 'Of all the scores and scores of writers I have known, I think Lynd and Walter de la Mare were the most delightful characters and companions.' Walter de la Mare invited Priestley to his home at Anerley in south London to play charades, which Priestley adored. The life of the writer is lonely, he said, compared to that even of painters and sculptors, let alone actors. 'Authorship is a demanding and unhealthy occupation. You sit alone for long hours spinning the stuff out like a spider. Creation may be all very fine but getting it down on paper is a hard task.' Charades were a blessed relief from his work – and they also allowed him to indulge himself as a performer.

He was fortunate that the essay was still a popular form of writing and, although Priestley can be criticised both in early and later essays for self-indulgence and, sometimes, repetition, it was a form in which he proved masterly. John Atkins in his book on Priestley's philosophy and literary work, *The Last of the Sages* (1981), denigrates the essay because the 'essayist always wears the same mask' and concludes that it had disappeared, victim of its own frivolity. Priestley himself recognised that the old-fashioned essay had vanished with the passing of the great literary magazines but, as he proved himself, it did not disappear altogether even if it was now called an 'opinion' or 'think' piece.

On 4 March 1923, Pat gave birth to their first child, Barbara, and it is interesting that Priestley describes himself on the birth certificate neither as a writer nor as an author, which even his daughter thought he would have done until she looked it up, but as a journalist. Pat had had a sickly pregnancy and the birth was not easy, but the plethora of family snapshots show that the Priestleys were delighted with their baby daughter. The pictures include two showing a young, fairly slim Jack Priestley holding the new baby as if he thought she might break, and Barbara suspects that she was the only baby he handled at such an early age: although Priestley loved small children, babies rather frightened him.[2]

Pat's health did not pick up once the baby had arrived and she seemed stricken with an unexplained malaise. Nor were her problems confined to her health. When she had married Priestley and joined him in Cambridge, Pat had happily shared his life and interests for she was a lively and intelligent young woman and she adored him. Indeed, she had continued to accompany him to social and literary events for some time after the move to London, until the later stages of her pregnancy.

Barbara's birth made it hard to continue to share Priestley's social life, but her presence was still only part of a problem that had already began to develop. As a writer, critic and reviewer, Priestley was expected to attend many of the frequent and specifically literary parties, and while he wrote later that he had felt ambivalent about them it is evident that he had enjoyed them; he was after all, highly regarded by such luminaries as John Lane, J. C. Squire and Robert Lynd, and was, too, an amusing and witty talker.

But in those hotbeds of malicious gossip, bright talk and professional oneupmanship, Pat found herself increasingly out of her depth, not least because of the attitude of the southern literati towards someone they considered a rather unworldly young woman from the north. Pat, like her husband, had a pronounced Yorkshire accent, which she had seen no reason to alter, but while in his case it was tolerated, even considered amusing, in hers it was not, however bright she might be. As Barbara said, 'Daddy would overcome it by being frightfully funny and everybody would think it was all a great joke', but Pat's accent was considered 'quite ghastly' and she was seen as just another provincial wife. But even Priestley did not escape censure and Barbara quoted Virginia Woolf's description of him as a ' "tradesman writer" – a *real* snob there! Anyway, for whatever reason, she [Pat] soon just couldn't cope, whereas Daddy actually sparkled. Literary parties were absolutely his idea of heaven and he was fine as by that time he was already writing books.'[3] Pat's social role, therefore, became that of the wife who stayed at home, looked after the baby, welcomed the friends her husband brought back, cooked for them and listened while they talked the night away.

John Lane, of the Bodley Head, published a collection of Priestley essays, *I For One*, and then commissioned a book, *Figures in Modern Literature*, after having Priestley recommended to him by J. C. Squire, to whose *London Mercury* Priestley had been contributing for some time. In those days the commissioning of even a modest book merited a splendid lunch for the hopeful author and Lane's favourite venue was the Café Royal. After a lavish meal ending with cigars and liqueur brandy, he would produce a contract 'designed to keep poets in garrets, in which thirteen copies sold would count as twelve, 10 per cent to 12½ per cent royalties after 10,000 copies had been sold, first refusal of the next four books, all for an advance of fifty or twenty-five pounds. But he was a good host and had many fascinating anecdotes: it was like lunching with literary history', according to Priestley in his contribution to John Lehmann's book *Coming to London*, published in 1957.

During the summer after Barbara's birth, Priestley pounded his typewriter at home during the day, finished *Figures in Modern Literature* and then embarked almost at once on a second Bodley Head commission, *English Comic Characters*, of which he remained proud for the rest of his life: both Charles Laughton and Ralph Richardson told him how much they had enjoyed it and how useful it had been to them. The book is worth reading for the chapter 'The Illyrians' alone, a perceptive and delightful examination of the characters in Shakespeare's *Twelfth Night*. Priestley ends it by imagining Sir Andrew Aguecheek leaving Illyria and arriving in that Shakespearean paradise – to which Priestley returned again and again throughout his writing life – Justice Shallow's Gloucestershire orchard in *Henry IV, Part 2*:

> ... for there he would find company after his own heart, the great Shallow himself and Silence and Slender, and take his place among such boon companions, seat himself at the pippins and the cheese and try to disengage from his tangled mind such confused memories as remained there of Illyria and the roystering Illyrians, his foolish face aglow beneath the unfading apple-blossom.

His work was going well, but his personal life was another matter. In an essay, 'Dark Hours', in a collection entitled *Apes and Angels*, he wrote, in 1927, of the night horrors that afflict the sleepless:

> In these dark hours there is no escape, not even by any dizzy ladder of thought, and your mind goes round and round, drearily pacing its cage . . . This self consciousness of the dark hours, unable to fasten on anything outside itself, forever denied communication, its thoughts wearily jangling around the old circus ring of the mind, is a glimpse of Hell. These are the terrors with which the preachers should threaten us. The old-fashioned place, we know, would soon become companionable. I have no doubt that it would not take us long to develop a taste for molten metal and brimstone, and that the fiends themselves would soon become companionable. But these dark hours of the night and the spinning mind, if prolonged, would only gain in terror and despair. They are the true nightmare.

It came from the heart, for the years from 1924 to 1926 were, after the First World War, the worst of his life.

Within six months of Barbara's birth Pat was pregnant again and far from well: she had the sickness of the first pregnancy but strange stomach pains too. It gradually became clear that something was very wrong with her. Throughout February and March 1924 the stomach pains worsened and by mid-April she was in such agony that on the advice of a young doctor, Peggy Scott Brown, who was a personal friend, she was admitted to Guy's Hospital.

In his biography of his father,[4] Peter Davison mentions several emotional involvements Edward had before he fell in love with the woman who became his first wife, but says nothing of Peggy Scott Brown. She and Edward had met when he was at Cambridge and she had been a medical student. According to Pat's daughters, Peggy was the love of Edward's life but the relationship came to nothing. After qualifying as a doctor she married someone else, but always remained a friend of the Priestleys and was Barbara's godmother.

Towards the end of April it was decided that Pat could not continue with the pregnancy and, although she was then only seven months pregnant and the survival rate for premature babies in the early 1920s was poor, she gave birth by Caesarian section, during which her doctors investigated what was causing her so much pain.

Sylvia Priestley was born on 30 April 1924 and was described at the time as the 'miracle baby' for she was the smallest and most premature baby ever to have survived in Guy's maternity wing. She was wrapped in cotton wool and placed in an incubator, which was little more than a warm box packed with hot-water bottles. The good news was that the baby had survived delivery and was putting up a real fight for life. But the investigation had revealed that Pat was suffering from advanced cancer of the bladder.

Faced with a future that seemed unutterably bleak, Priestley decided to move his family into the country in the hope that rural living and country air might help his wife recover, at least for a while. He rented a house at Chinnor Hill in Buckinghamshire, found for him by friends from his Cambridge days, Gerald and Rosemary Bullett, who were next-door neighbours. Another friend, the poet Frank Kendon, also lived close by.

Although at first Pat improved a little, she was unable to cope with the house and two babies, which meant that Priestley had to employ a cook-housekeeper. Remarkably, Sylvia flourished and there was soon nothing to show that her survival had ever been considered miraculous.

Then fate struck Priestley another blow. He learned that his father, who had not been well for several months, was seriously ill. Jonathan, the dedicated teacher and socialist, the pillar of the chapel, the keen cricketer, the lively amateur actor and doughty fell walker, had suddenly become, at only fifty-six, a frail old man hardly able to walk unaided and whose memory was fading.

On one of the last occasions the two met, they called in at a pub and drank their final pint together. 'He was easy in his mind about me at last, indeed pleased and proud,' Priestley told Peter Holdsworth. 'He did not know, because I never told him, that my wife, only in her twenties, was already going in and out of hospital with the cancer from which she was to die the following year and that in London, where he thought I was doing so well, I was half out of my mind with overwork and worry.' Years later, Winnie told Holdsworth: 'I'm still sorry Father didn't live long enough to see how revered a writer Jack became. He would have been *so* proud!'[5]

Jonathan Priestley died in June 1924 of stomach cancer. He never knew what he was suffering from and it is not clear whether his family did or not. But the manner of his death raises a number of questions. Jonathan and Emma had both died of soft-tissue cancers, Jonathan of the stomach and Emma of the ovaries. Pat died of cancer of the bladder, which spread to the pelvic floor, and Amy Priestley of cancer of the uterus. Perhaps it was coincident, but Barbara Wykeham thinks there might be another explanation. It is now known that chemicals used in the dyeing process can cause cancer, particularly of the bladder. Emma, Jonathan, Pat and Amy had all grown up and lived in an area dominated by a great chimney, known as the 'Lister chimney' after the company owning the dyeworks of which it formed part, and Lister's were specialists in dyeing velvet, for which certain types of chemicals were used.

The options for treating cancer were limited, but both Priestleys felt that anything was worth a try; so she underwent crude, primitive and gruelling radiation therapy, which resulted in her feeling even more ill without any improvement.

It was at some time during those terrible weeks between Pat's first admission to hospital in April and Jonathan's death in June that Priestley first encountered Jane Wyndham Lewis.

CHAPTER 9

Jane

They met at yet another literary party. Jane and her journalist husband, Bevan Wyndham Lewis, were great party-givers but this one had been organised by Jane alone as Bevan was on a walking tour of the Pyrenees with a party of friends. Jane's family, the Hollands, were originally from Devon but her father, who was a marine surveyor, had been settled for a long time in Wales and it was here that she was born and brought up. She was one of a large family of siblings and had always been known at home as 'Winifred'. At this time it seems to have been popular to use a name other than one's own: the marriage certificate of Jack and Pat Priestley gives his name as John, without the Boynton, and Pat's as Emily.

Jane's family lived in a grand house in Cathedral Road in Cardiff and there had been nursemaids, cooks and other general servants. At some stage, though, her father's business failed and the family were forced to sell up. They crammed themselves in with their nearby cousins. Epsi Hutchings recalls the house as being full of lively girls and she adored Jane/Winifred, who was considerably older than she was. She also remembers that there was great friendship between their families and that of the neighbours the Novellos – the girls used to play with young Ivor, who preferred acting out plays with their dolls than involving himself in boys' games.[1]

Jane was clever and went to Bedford College, part of London University. She had a particular bent for languages, easily becoming fluent in French and Italian and eventually in Russian and Portuguese. She had met Wyndham Lewis after she had come down from university but the marriage was not a success. Although they had a daughter, Barbara, later known as Angela, by the time she and Priestley met, Bevan was involved in a very public affair with a married woman, Marjorie Cole.

It has been said that Jane determined to marry Priestley as soon as she set eyes on him. The reality, though, was different. In a letter written to her sister Ena some time in the late spring or early summer of 1924 she described, as she wrestled for the first time with a typewriter, how Teddy Davison had rung her the previous Friday to say he was coming to her party and asked if he could bring his friend, 'the famous Priestley'. Jane was not impressed:

> They came and "D" brought lots of songs which he sang and Priestley accompanied – extremely badly, his head swaying in ecstasy, his tongue well out. All quite unnecessary because he hadn't even the most primitive idea of time. We also talked. It was rather difficult because "P" usurped my usual role and I sat and listened. He is typical literary Cambridge . . . rather boorish but extremely clever, I imagine.

She went on to say that Ena had made a big impression on Davison, who had evidently told Priestley about her forthcoming book.

> Priestley asked a lot about your book. His advice to you is to go on with it at all costs. Apparently he is a reader for John Lane and he asked me if I would ask you if he might see the book when it is ready. He says even if he couldn't advise Lane to take it, he could probably give you sound technical advice. I thanked him very much. He may be very useful, don't you think?[2]

It is possible Priestley was attracted to Jane from the start: she was his physical type, dark, strong-featured and lively: indeed as a young woman she was beautiful, and she remained handsome into old age. Priestley, as he constantly reiterated, was strongly sexed and in a desperate emotional state. She was locked in an unhappy marriage and felt publicly spurned by a husband who made no secret that he found another woman more attractive. Pat was either in hospital or at home in the country, which left Priestley alone for weeks at a time. By June 1924 they had become lovers. It is quite likely that initially neither thought of it as anything more than a passing affair, but by the end of

June, at about the time Jonathan died, Jane discovered she was pregnant.

There is no clear account of what happened next because Priestley never discussed with his children the circumstances leading to his second marriage, and if he wrote to anyone about it, the letters no longer exist. However, shortly after her pregnancy was confirmed Jane left Bevan, lived for a short time somewhere in the country, then took a flat in London in Boundary Road, near Lord's Cricket Ground, where on 4 March 1925 she gave birth to a daughter, Mary. A footnote to Mary's birth and her registration under the name of 'Wyndham Lewis' came in 1930 when Priestley formally adopted her, but he did not adopt Jane's elder daughter Angela. This meant that Mary became a beneficiary of the later Good Companions' Trust, whereas Angela did not. Bevan wanted to remarry and agreed that Jane might petition against him for divorce, which became absolute on 2 November 1925.

Priestley was now without the constant support and friendship of Edward Davison: in the summer of 1924 Davison had met his future wife at a London party. Natalie, pretty, red-headed and clever, came from a New York Jewish family and was about to return to the States. Edward, who was immediately smitten, walked her back to her lodgings and the two agreed to correspond. Early in 1925 he went over to America to pursue the courtship and the two were married in 1926. He never returned to England, pursuing an academic career in the States to the end of his life, but he knew about Priestley's liaison with Jane from letters to him in the autumn of 1925.[3]

Pat spent much of 1924 and the early part of 1925 in Chinnor with spells at Guy's Hospital, and Pat's widowed mother looked after Barbara and Sylvia. She is remembered still with love and affection. 'Wonderful, wonderful Granny Tempest,' was how Sylvia described her grandmother. 'She looked after us in the Chilterns and later in London. She planned these excursions and holidays for us.' 'We went everywhere by train,' Barbara recalled, 'days out at the seaside, holidays with relations in Penarth.'

According to Barbara, '[Granny Tempest] had a most relaxed attitude to children. We were never *made* to eat things – there was always plenty of bread-and-butter and if you didn't like what there was you could always fill up on that. You could also get down from the table if you wanted and didn't have to sit around bored while the adults talked, though sometimes I'd sit under the table and listen to the conversation.'

By August 1925 Pat was having more useless, expensive treatment in Guy's and Jane was still living in Boundary Road with Barbara/Angela and Mary. Priestley was also providing for his stepmother, who was in dire straits as Jonathan had died before pensionable age, and she and her daughter Winnie were struggling to manage on Winnie's small teaching salary.

There was a brief gap of a little over a year between Priestley's *English Comic Characters* and the appearance of his next book, a biography of George Meredith commissioned by Macmillan as part of a series, *English Men of Letters*, edited by J. C. Squire. When Priestley realised that he had to get down to the book, which might prove a turning point for him as a professional writer, he had been to London to see Pat in Guy's. She was in great pain, and Priestley returned to Chinnor Hill

> so deep in despair I did not know what to do with myself. I was nearly out of my mind with misery. Finally, just to pass the time while I was at the bottom of this pit, I decided to write something – anything – a few pages to be torn up after I felt less wretched. On my desk was a rough list of chapters for the Meredith book. I chose one of the chapters, not the first, and slowly, painfully, set to work on it. In an hour I was writing freely and well. It is in fact one of the best chapters in the book. And I wrote myself out of my misery and followed a trail of thought and words into the daylight.[4]

Priestley felt that the ability to get on with the job and write whatever the circumstances was what separated the truly professional writer from the amateur. Writing the Meredith biography, he said, did not lighten his woes or remove the anguish, but a kind of release was born and good work done out of the necessary concentration, the act of writing. To any aspirant writer he would say that it is better not to attempt to be one but that

> if you *must* be one – then, I say, *write.* If you are a great genius you will make your own rules; but if you are not – and the odds are heavily against it – go to your desk, no matter how high or low your mood, face the icy challenge of the paper – *write.* Sooner or

later the goddess will recognise in this a devotional act, worthy of benison and grace. But if what I am saying seems nonsense, do not attempt to write for a living. Try elsewhere, making sure the position carries a pension.[5]

George Meredith is a perceptive, sympathetic and critical appraisal of a now somewhat neglected writer. For Priestley Meredith was more than just a poet of nature – the popular view – but a man, in the words of Priestley's friend Diana Collins,

> untouched by the Victorian controversies between religion and science, creation and evolution, that induced a sense of strain in so many Victorian writers. [Priestley] viewed Meredith as a true pagan who rejected the "old war between the spirit and the flesh ... He sees that animal life is not something to be gradually eliminated but the broad foundation of our spiritual life, the body must be disciplined but not subdued, for brain and soul its leaders and not its enemies will have need of its vital energies.

He found in Meredith a splendid buoyancy and completeness, not simply *a* poet of nature but *the* poet of nature, more truly than Wordsworth, 'who was always wanting nature to be leading to something more, some kind of mystical and spiritual vision ... If everything is God, then nothing is God,' Jack concluded. 'Pantheism is neither a religion nor a philosophy, but a certain poetical state of mind.' He had reservations over Meredith's attitude to death, feeling that he deliberately shut his imagination to it, but paid homage to Meredith's comic talents and fiction, comparing him to 'a man who cannot pass the salt without spilling it and yet is able to juggle with six plates and a whole cruet'. The book was published in 1926 and, in spite of the difficulties Priestley experienced when he was writing it, was well received by the critics.

Much later it became clear that Pat had known of Priestley's emotional turmoil, but she was also fully aware of his struggle to make ends meet, the heavy demands her illness made on him and the problem he had in fulfilling the literary obligations that provided their only means of income. Only two of her letters survive,[6] the first undated and written from Chinnor Hill probably in the mid-summer of 1925, and the second from the Bright Annexe of Guy's Hospital. Both are to her mother-in-law, Amy Priestley, and both show nothing but concern for the enormous problems facing her husband.

> Many thanks for your letter. I am a wretched correspondent these days as my energy, physical and mental, doesn't amount to much and there isn't even much news. When I'm not in Guy's, I am in a hammock in the garden, and that's all there is to it.
>
> We are trying to find a house in town as we have given our landlady notice. Jack has made up his mind that we ought to get back to town as I have to go into Guy's every few weeks now and the problem of getting up increases. It will be a ghastly job moving. I daren't think about it. I'd love to come up in August but I doubt whether I could stand the journey. We've had to get a cook-housekeeper, she's a very nice woman, a widow and very obliging.
>
> The babies are very well and Sylvia can walk now by herself and is a much finer kid physically than Barbara, which is rather a mystery to me.

She moves on to the vexed subject of the car or, rather, Priestley as a driver.

> The car is smashed up again. Every time we go out in it something goes wrong, so Jack is going to sell it. The people at the garage say we shall get practically nothing for it but it's better to give it away than for Jack to work himself to a shadow to pay for its repairs. Our expenses are going to be very heavy and we shall need every penny, so we think it best not to fritter away any more money on the car. . . Jack is up to the eyes and is trying to finish another book by next week. Love to all – Pat.

The second letter is dated 25 August. Amy had suggested she come and help but Priestley had rejected her offer.

> Please don't go on worrying about me because I am well looked after here.
>
> I hope Jack didn't hurt your feelings by asking you to postpone your visit. (He's having a devilish time at present.) If he says so, do please respect his wishes. I know you want to help, of course,

but everything is *very complicated,* he's every bit of time taken up with planning things out. I think we have got a house but a lot of details have to be fixed up.

I'm sorry you haven't been able to see the kiddies. I've seen precious little of them myself. But please have a bit more patience. It is desperate that we should be settled in a house and very soon. I don't want Jack to have to worry more than is necessary. It isn't as if I'm on my deathbed or anything – as a matter of fact, it is not as easy to die as one might think . . . Hope you both had a good time in Scotland and so cheer yourself up, Mum – With love, Pat.

The house that Priestley 'fixed up' was in Scarsdale Villas, Kensington, and the following September he moved the family in. On 1 October 1925 he wrote to Davison telling him that he had just spent a week in the Lake District where he had met the novelist Hugh Walpole, 'whom I liked immensely, by the way'. Walpole had given him what he considered useful and sensible advice on the subject of lecturing, of which 'he has done an enormous amount in America and is one of their very favourite people'.

Then he gets down to more important matters. They are in the new house but far from settled.

Pat is back and seemed very well for a day or two, but has just had a bad relapse. I had to get a doctor at four this morning. It's an awful business when she's so bad, particularly as I shall have to earn a lot of money, as these last few months have been all expenditure and no income. I like the house immensely, and have taken very kindly to my new study. There's plenty of work to be done when only I can get at it.

Here it becomes obvious that Davison knew about Priestley's relationship with Jane.

Jane has just moved to Church Hanborough, Oxfordshire (College House). Bevan has been telling her that you and I (me this time as well) have been slandering him all over Fleet Street. The idea is perfectly preposterous, seeing that everyone I know in Fleet Street knows far more about him than I do. Obviously I can't make a fuss, but I shall do what I can to put a stop to this nonsense . . . I haven't seen Jane since she left town, though we've written regularly. We shall have to see one another soon, but things being so bad here, we are trying to put it off for as long as possible. It won't be easy to find a meeting place, either.

A fortnight later he wrote again to Davison, explaining that things were now very bad indeed. After a brief respite, Pat had collapsed and 'doctors and nurses' had had to be called in at all times of the day and night. 'Finally, a week ago, she was in such agony that the doctor said she would have to return to hospital quick.' This time, though, Pat could not face a return to Guy's and more pointless treatment. Priestley had contacted Peggy Scott Brown, whose tutor had a position at the Royal Free Hospital, then in Gray's Inn Road, and asked for help. Pat was admitted to a side ward of her own where for days she lingered between life and death. Then, to everyone's surprise, she rallied and was more comfortable than she had been for months, due to heavy doses of morphine. The drawback was that it made her forgetful and rather childish. 'But she can't help wishing that for all our sakes it was done with. Pat is worn out and longs for complete rest. Fate has played with her like a cat with a mouse. Her mother too is almost worn out with the business. And as for me, I too feel pretty far gone.'

Finally, on 25 November 1925, Pat's long torment ended. Her death certificate records the cause as (1) Sarcoma of the pelvic floor and (2) Exhaustion. She was barely twenty-nine. To Barbara and Sylvia, aged respectively thirty-two months and nineteen months when their mother died, Pat is now only a blurred, shadowy figure. Members of the Priestley family seemed to remember little of her. Diana Collins[7] was told that Winnie and Amy had not much liked Pat: they had thought her scatterbrained and that she would not be able to run a house properly or keep up with Priestley – she had not been, in fact, 'good enough for "our Jack"'. Barbara once asked Winnie why she hadn't liked Pat. 'She was then a very old lady and I asked, "What was it you had against her?" and she replied, "Well, she went upstairs and cracked the basin!" You mean, something fell off and cracked the basin?" I asked, "I don't know," said Winnie, "she never said a word about it." That was Winnie, you see. Poor Pat, poor thing. Goes into her boyfriend's house and a glass falls off a shelf . . .' And is remembered seventy years later.

Neither of her daughters feel that if Pat had lived the marriage would have lasted, mainly because of Priestley's literary career. If Pat found the social side of his work hard at the start of his career, it is unlikely she would have enjoyed it any more when he hit the big time as a bestselling author and fêted celebrity.

Jack Priestley was eighty when at last he tried to talk to Barbara and Sylvia about their mother. He invited himself to stay with Barbara and asked for Sylvia to be there too so that he could talk to them both. Yet, when it came to it, he had little to say. He told them how their mother's family had been neighbours of the Priestleys, that she had worked in the library and that they had played duets for piano and violin together: that she had waited for him and written to him all through the war and that he thought he had, in his fashion, loved her at the time they married, but that in the long term it probably would not have worked.[8]

When Pat died Jack Priestley was thirty-one. Within seven or eight years he had lost his friends in the war, his much-loved father and, finally, his young wife. In burying her, he finally buried his youth.

CHAPTER 10

Picking Up the Pieces

'You will have heard my bad news,' Priestley wrote to Edward Davison on 3 December in his first letter to his friend following Pat's death. 'Pat's end, which took place in her sleep after she had been having prodigious quantities of morphia, was a good one and a great release for her and all of us, but nevertheless, when these things come, they are a terrible shock. One sees the whole pitiful thing in high relief. She was unbelievably brave and unselfish right up until the end . . .' He would be keeping on Scarsdale Villas, he said, and Mrs Tempest would continue to keep house for him and look after the little girls 'and of course in about a year's time I will marry Jane'. He was about to embark on a five-week cruise of the West Indies, able to do so because he had been commissioned to write a weekly essay for the *Saturday Review,* for six guineas a week, and he also had 'plenty of other work on hand'.

For the time being life continued without disruption for the two small Priestley girls with their beloved granny. Nobody spoke of Pat, and the sisters now recall having been told only that Mummy was 'dead': 'If people disappear, somebody's got to explain to the children what's happened, but what do the children really think? Well, you think the lady who's stepped into her shoes probably murdered her! You know what children are like, we all read about such things in stories by Grimm and Andersen. The only certain fact was that she was "dead", but nobody explained to us what "dead" meant. When I was about six, we had a holiday at Marazion in Cornwall in a rented house and somewhere along the coast we came upon a dead seal washed up on the beach. I remember it coming as a terrible, terrible shock for there was that awful thing decomposing on the beach and it absolutely threw me. Had that happened to Mummy? Is that what she was now like? If only people had talked to children then in a sensible way.'[1]

Priestley's output between early 1926 and 1929, a period that ended with the publication of *The Good Companions*, was immense and covered almost every field. There were collections of essays, *Essays of Today and Yesterday, Open House, Apes and Angels, The Balconinny, These Diversions* (a collection which he edited and to which he contributed one essay himself; it was while preparing this book that he met Hugh Walpole), another biography, of Thomas Love Peacock, two books of literary criticism, *The English Novel* and *English Humour*, and his first attempts at fiction with *Adam in Moonshine, Benighted* and *Farthing Hall* – the last he co-wrote with Hugh Walpole. He also took his first tentative steps into drama with an adaptation of Peacock's *Nightmare Abbey*, which came to nothing, and several other draft scripts.

The flood of work was due in part to his extraordinary creative energy, but also because he was driven by the necessity of catching up with the debts caused by Pat's medical bills and having to support two households. It is also likely that he was sending money to Bradford for Amy and Winnie.

In his letters to Davison during that period a number of general themes and regular grumbles crop up. A. D. Peters and Priestley first met when both were at Cambridge, and not only did they become great friends, but Peters was also Priestley's major business partner and his agent. No agent could have been more devoted to promoting an author – it is clear that Peters worked hard for Priestley, especially in the home market – but in his letters to Davison Priestley constantly aired his low opinion of America and its publishers. He devoted no small space to this and to describing the deals to which he had had to agree, and the apparent refusal of publishers on both sides of the Atlantic properly to promote his work – the everlasting cry of the author who is not a bestseller and therefore not considered a 'property'. Both he and Davison tried to sell each other's books to publishers in their respective countries, usually without success. Priestley was also contemptuous of J. C. Squire and the *Mercury* – to which, however, he continued to contribute:

Two parts of 'Talking' have been turned down by Squire here, one of them the last part which I really think a good piece of

writing. The other two parts are appearing in *Blackwoods.* I'm
not angry about Squire, but just a wee bit sore, particularly
when I think of the way I've been pestered for the last nine
months to write something, anything, for the *Mercury*, and also
because of the rot Squire does print . . . his remark about it being
below my average is bilge. He doesn't know my average to begin
with . . .[2]

Priestley's first letter to Davison after his return from the West
Indies shows him painfully picking up the pieces of both his
professional and personal lives.[3] He was at last embarking on a
novel (*Adam in Moonshine*), not least because he hoped it would
make him some money after the expense of the last two years but
also because it was an exciting new challenge. Jane was somewhat
depressed over a quarrel she'd had with 'most of her family'. He
did not say that this was because of their relationship, but it is
implicit for, while they were making plans to marry as soon as
was decently possible, they were at present keeping this decision
to themselves, though 'I make no secret of the fact that we are
very good friends.'

On 16 February he wrote to Davison and Natalie, congratulating
them on the announcement of their forthcoming marriage. He
and Jane expected to marry early in September and her family had
finally accepted this. He had also told Mrs Tempest, who indicated
that Pat had known of his relationship with Jane, possibly even of
the existence of Mary, for 'Mrs Tempest . . . knew Pat's feelings
about it and knows how much I need a wife and the children
a mother'. She is, he says, 'quite glad': she and Jane had met
briefly and got on well with each other, which seemed to bode
well for the future, and the family spent jolly weekends at 'Jane's
place', which is how he referred to College House.

By the end of March he had written 20,000 words of *Adam in
Moonshine*, which he confidently expected would be published
in the autumn both at home and in the States. Both Jane and
Gerald Bullett, to whom he had shown it chapter by chapter,
were enthusiastic, and he was finding it fun to write.

Adam in Moonshine and *Benighted*, which followed close on its
heels, are apprentice works. Priestley would say of writing fiction
that he would find beginning a novel a slow business but that he
gathered confidence and speed as he went on, ending with a fine
flourish. But John Atkins in *Last of the Sages* says of Priestley's minor

works that they give the impression of the exact opposite: they get off to a flying start, then develop engine trouble midway round the course. *Adam in Moonshine,* the story of a young man who is caught up in a kind of fairy story but then finds himself involved with a bunch of anarchists, is an attempt to marry two genres, the Jeffery Farnol romance with the modern thriller, and falls between two stools. When it was published the following year the reviews were mixed, and Priestley grumbled to Davison about the critics' inability to see what he had been trying to do or to appreciate the novel's 'underlying irony', insisting instead on regarding it only as a fairy-tale romance.

In *Margin Released,* he admitted its failures: he had intended it to be all fine writing and nonsense, 'a little coloured trial balloon. But the story does not move effortlessly like a balloon: it moves stiffly, creaking with self-consciousness.' He recalled how critics had called it an 'essayist's novel' and that Arnold Bennett had complained that it had no substance, but then Priestley had never intended it should have. When it was published in America 'it was an immediate and complete failure', but from time to time he still came across readers who had enjoyed it. 'What was truest in the tale,' he wrote, 'was my feeling for its background, the Yorkshire Dales country, for which I had – and still have – a deep affection. It was the moors and the trout streams below them, the grey stone bridges and the white-washed farmhouses, not the ravishing girls I tried to create, that had the magic.' He had, he felt, probably wasted too much time 'bathing Adam in moonshine . . .'

In *Benighted* he turned to the Gothic novel, but he also used a device that reappeared later in at least two of his plays: an apparently ill-assorted group of people who find themselves cut off in some way from the outside world. In *Benighted* the travellers find themselves arriving at a house in the Welsh mountains, where they are marooned by a storm of epic proportions followed by a landslip. They are welcomed by a bizarre couple, the Femms, and their manservant. Saul. Mr Femm is a strange invalid who lives at the top of the house, Mrs Femm would be a soulmate for Daphne du Maurier's Mrs Danvers and Saul is reminiscent of Frankenstein's monster. Two of the travellers are a married couple, the Wavertons, suffering matrimonial difficulties, and the third is a young man, Roger Penderel, who becomes involved with the wife. Penderel is still suffering from shell-shock after the war and has been unable to come to terms with civilian life. The book ends with a life-and-death struggle between him and Saul, which neither survives, but which enables Penderel to redeem himself; after which the road is cleared and the Wavertons continue on their journey, their own problems resolved.

It had been an attempt, he said, familiar enough by the 1960s but unusual in the 1920s, to transmute the thriller into symbolic fiction 'with some psychological depth but I don't think I succeeded in this', he wrote, 'although the tale itself was readable and sufficiently engrossing'. In Britain it is remembered by some as a novel of ideas when such fiction was thin on the ground. However, it did best in the USA, where it sold 20,000 copies under the title *The Old Dark House* and where there was little interest in either symbolic literature or psychological depth. It was seen and marketed as a creepy thriller in the Gothic tradition and later made into a film, one of the earliest 'talkies'.

Both novels were written against the background of the General Strike when Priestley was drowning in a sea of financial worries. He had also started the Peacock biography, not, as he told Davison, because he wanted to write it but solely because he desperately needed money.

He had tried to sell the lease on Scarsdale Villas, as it was now impossible to keep up both it and College House; but he had been unable to find a buyer and was forced to let it, which added to his worries. Although he and Jane were soon to be married, he felt he had to preserve the proprieties, so instead of moving in with her he rented a small cottage close by which belonged to the Asquith family. Moving from Scarsdale Villas meant he had to part with cherished possessions: 'I advertised the lovely Broadwood grand in *The Times*', he wrote to Davison, 'and got one solitary reply. I had it valued (£80) but I could not get more than £50 for it.'

By the early summer of 1926, with their wedding fixed for September, Priestley and Jane decided to combine their families. It must have been daunting for Jane to be faced with four young children, two of whom had spent almost all their early lives with their grandmother. She must also have been aware of Priestley's high expectations of her, based on his own loving recollections of Amy, the perfect stepmother. Both she and Priestley embarked on the venture with high hopes, both wrote enthusiastically of how well and easily the children were settling down together. But many years later those involved see it rather differently.

Barbara and Sylvia experienced the worst shock: two days after

Granny Tempest had delivered them to College House she was sent away and they never saw her again. They were stranded in a house they had rarely visited with a woman they hardly knew and who, they were told, they were to call 'Mummy'. Both women remember those early years as bleak and themselves as unhappy. Why had their grandmother been banished? 'I think it was difficult for Mummy,' recalls Sylvia. 'I suppose it was brave of her to say to herself this is the man who is just the right person for us and I must make it work and, of course, in a way he was.' According to Barbara, 'I think she felt the only way she could cope was to put the past behind her, draw a line under it and start again. As for Jack, he didn't, or couldn't, stand up to her about it – but then he never was able to stand up to strong-minded women!'[4]

Jane was not happy with the free-and-easy way the two girls had been brought up or with the Yorkshire accent they had inherited from their parents and grandmother, and made every effort to rid them of it. A nursemaid was employed and meals with their parents were formal affairs. The children had to eat everything that was put in front of them, acquire 'proper' table manners and were expected to sit quietly after they had finished eating until told they could leave the table. As they grew older and Jane was able to employ more staff, Sunday lunch was the only meal the children took with their parents. Upper-middle-class households of the late twenties and early thirties seen to have been the last bastions of Edwardian manners and the Edwardian age.[5]

Then there was Jane's own child. The first Angela knew of what was in store for her was when her mother informed her, after she had returned from a holiday spent with her grandparents in Cardiff, that some new sisters were coming. 'So not only had I been sent away, when I got back I was greeted with the fact that there were going to be some threatening new sisters and, worse still, one of them was called Barbara so I couldn't be Barbara any more. I had to be Angela.'[6] Mary, of course, was too young to realise what was happening but considers that in some ways she suffered most of all. There is disagreement as to how old she was when she discovered that Priestley was her father, although she had wondered why Bevan Wyndham Lewis treated Angela and her quite differently. The effect of the discovery was disastrous and she is still convinced that it was the cause of her later breakdown.[6]

All four women, however, stress that Jane tried to treat them all

equally. Priestley left their upbringing to her, retreating thankfully
into his study and his writing when things were difficult. But for
his daughters he was 'a very fair man', according to Sylvia, 'a
wonderful father who devised the most marvellous games for us.
He was a great one for clowning. Christmas was always splendid,
based on his own recollections of his Bradford days when it was
always "a big do". And he would do quite unexpected things. I
remember him once bringing home lots of little aeroplanes, the
kind you wound up to make them go, and we all went up to the
attics and let them off out of the window. Then we had to go
out and find them and it took ages, thus allowing him to work
in peace!' He could, they say, be moody, even rude – but never
to the children.

In June 1926 Jane wrote to Edward Davison: the children
were settling in 'well' and she was fortunate to have found
an excellent nursemaid 'who manages them all very well and
easily'. They were considering moving from Church House and
she and Jack had been to see two old houses in Pangbourne,
both with gardens and within easy reach of Reading station.
Jack, she wrote, had sold most of his own furniture and she
was busy furnishing College House with 'lovely old Welsh oak',
which she had discovered during a trip to Cardiganshire the
previous month. Once she and Jack were married she intended
to have two or three people down 'every weekend' and she was
also planning that they should give a party every month in 'the
Cavendish Road studio'. 'I am very anxious to keep in touch
with people, to meet as many as possible, to entertain as much
as possible as it needs rather a special effort when one's base is
in the country.' Jack had finished *Adam in Moonshine* ('which is
amazingly good, quite the best thing he's done') and it had been
a source of great pleasure to him as he had been getting bored
with writing essays. In a little word picture she describes him
'sitting in the window, pipe in his mouth, tortoise-shell glasses
on, rumpled hair, generally rather tousled, typing his *Saturday
Review* essay' while she lounged by the fire writing her letter.
' "Fire" sounds absurd, doesn't it, in July but it is a cold wet day
and the rain outside is steadily streaming down the windows.'

Davison had been urging Priestley to visit the USA, promising
to organise a lecture tour for him, but while he was attracted by
the idea of seeing America for himself, he was less enthusiastic at
the prospect of having to lecture. Even if he did, he told Davison

in a letter sent with Jane's, he would not want it to be the main
reason for the visit (although he realised it would be the lecturing
that would pay for the trip) as he would prefer to write about
'picturesque America rather in the spirit in which Americans
write about Europe'. He wanted to travel widely from the Rockies
to New Orleans although this would be expensive, which meant
that the lecturing could not be cut out. He would agree to do it
if it could be confined to large towns. He estimated it would take
him about four months to gather sufficient material for his book,
and thought that it would sell well as it would not be the kind of
sociological stuff several English authors had churned out 'but a
real literary travel book'. Such a trip would also enable him to
meet his American publishers face to face. *Adam* and *Benighted*,
he told Davison, had given him a real taste for writing fiction
and he now had an idea for another novel, one in which he was
'trying to get the subjective interest with the objective narrative,
working through a kind of symbolism'. He must have realised
the obscurity of this because he added: 'Think of Don Quixote
and you'll see what I mean. Instead of appealing on one definite
level, as most modern novelists do, I want to appeal on several at
once, so that if you want only an idle tale, it's there for you.'

In a letter to Hugh Walpole dated 1 June Priestley coyly
admitted that he was about to marry for the second time.

> I can't imagine how you contrived to hear I was marrying again.
> It's true and no secret, but I've only just begun to tell people. It
> was one of the things I was going to tell you, as a matter of fact.
> The lady is Mrs Wyndham Lewis, an old friend of mine and of
> the little set I used to see here, who divorced her husband, the
> humorous journalist of the 'Daily Mail' about a year or so ago.
> Like me, she has two little girls [he could not admit that one of
> hers was also his]. We are very, very fond of one another, have
> both had some hard knocks in our time, and I believe are capable
> of making something really fine out of our life together, though
> we both pretend to be sceptical about marriage. You ought to
> applaud the step when I tell you that she is the only person who
> can make a civilised human being out of me, rub off some of
> those gritty Yorkshire edges.

On 9 September Priestley and Jane were married ('with as much
discretion as I could muster') and, leaving their children with the

nursemaid, embarked on a motoring tour of Wales. Priestley told his daughters that he married Jane because he needed a mother for his children, he felt obligated to her because she had had a child by him, and he was lonely.

What is clear, though, from his letters about her to other people and those he wrote to her when they were apart, especially in the early days, is that he felt a deep affection for her that suggests far more than a marriage of convenience. He gave her financial security, eventually great wealth, and an introduction into a world she found fascinating, but he made no secret of how much he respected her opinion on what he wrote. She gave him affection, and organised his life in such a way that he could write unhindered by practical obstacles. Jane had a natural flair for finance where Priestley was hopelessly inept, so she took on the ordering and organisation of all his affairs, lifting an enormous burden from him.

But she suffered from continual health problems and it seems that at least some were psychosomatic; her way of coping when things were going wrong emotionally was to take to her bed. Priestley was never an easy partner, and for years Jane ruefully accepted, with one major exception, his infidelities, but there is little doubt that they caused tension.

One of her most attractive traits was the strong sense of humour she shared with him. 'That was the really endearing face of Jane,' said Barbara. 'Daddy could always get her to giggle. I remember some formal lunch one Sunday with some Americans which was really heavy going. Suddenly Daddy began playing with the orange peel on his plate, then he cut it into a set of huge teeth which he put in his mouth, then turned round and gave Jane a ghastly grin. She started to giggle, then couldn't stop laughing – we were all finished by that!'

CHAPTER 11

Mr Walpole and Dear Old Jack

The Priestleys and their combined family settled in at College House and he took over what Barbara describes as 'a nice room over the gardener's shed and what was once a coach house – the kind of place where they used to keep hay above the horses. He made himself a quiet little writing place there and he'd disappear into it every day and work and work.'[1]

Priestley and Hugh Walpole had become close friends. In 1925 the publishers Jarrold had invited Priestley to edit a series called *These Diversions* and he had approached Walpole, one of the most popular novelists of his day with twenty books behind him, to contribute to it. Walpole, the son of a bishop, was ten years older than Priestley. He had been born in New Zealand but had come to England as a child and was educated at King's School, Canterbury, and Emmanuel College, Cambridge. His first success was with a novel, *Mr Perrin and Mr Trail*, based on his brief teaching experience, and another, *Dark Forest*, on his work with the Russian Red Cross in the First World War. His real popularity, though, had grown out of the series of *Jeremy* books. When Priestley contacted him he was working on an idea for a series of novels, set in Cumberland, which became known as the *Herries Chronicles*.

Walpole responded at once and with enthusiasm to Priestley's proposal and told him how much he had enjoyed *Comic Characters*.[2] It was the beginning of a remarkable friendship that lasted until Walpole's death in 1941. Throughout Edward Davison's life Priestley's letters never ceased, but in the main they detail progress on the latest book, news of the family and gossip about old friends: there were few truly intimate letters. When Jack was suffering emotional turmoil in the early 1930s we know he wrote to Davison about it, but none of this correspondence has survived. In the correspondence with Walpole, however, Priestley reveals his innermost thoughts, feelings and self-doubts in a way he does nowhere else.

Walpole was the closest male friend Priestley ever had. He was almost certainly homosexual, but his name was never linked with anyone in such a relationship and the most constant love of his life was literature. But, having said that, he truly loved Jack Priestley, and Priestley reciprocated with the kind of affection one might feel for a loved and respected elder brother.

Writing in *Margin Released* forty years on, Priestley says theirs was an attraction of opposites: 'He was always wildly anxious to please, whereas I have a talent, almost a genius, for displeasing all but those near to me. He was fond of making lists, of favourite people, books, experiences and so on, something I never did even as a school boy.' In his book on Priestley, Vincent Brome uses this to infer that he neither admired nor cared much for Walpole, but their correspondence disproves this, as does the fact that the two men met whenever they could until Walpole's death.

The early letters are addressed with great formality, 'Dear Mr Walpole', 'Dear Mr Priestley', then progress to the form of the times, 'Dear Walpole' and 'Dear Priestley', finally becoming 'My Dear Hugh' and 'Dear Old Jack', while 'Yours sincerely' changes to 'Yours ever' and, from Walpole, simply 'Love'.

Priestley wasted no time in replying to Walpole's acceptance of his commission and said how gratified he was at Walpole's praise of *Comic Characters*, which was not selling well, in spite of its being supposedly a popular subject and having had plenty of publicity. Nor, apart from those in the *Daily Telegraph* and *The Times Literary Supplement*, had the reviews been good. 'It is odd,' he grumbles, 'but we now have a body of critics who *like* bad writing . . .' Somewhat surprisingly he went on to tell Walpole that he was having a bad time, that not only had his father died the previous year but his wife was now dying of cancer, he had two young children, he was working himself to death and his books 'just don't sell well'. It was the sheer necessity of keeping everything going that made him do 'the thousand things you speak of'. The explosion of feeling is all the more remarkable for the fact that it appears to be quite unique. He ends on a moving note with a reference to Pat: 'My wife asks me to express her gratitude for *The Old Ladies*, one of the few recent books which have enthralled her in her constant pain.'[3]

Walpole, ever the professional, produced his copy in six days flat, and the two continued to correspond throughout the summer of 1925. At the beginning of September, Walpole invited Priestley to visit him at his home, Brackenburn, in the Lake District, near Keswick.

His initial reaction to Priestley is well known from his diaries:

> Sept 24. Arrived Priestley – a North Country, no-nonsense-about-me, I-know-my-mind kind of little man. [Walpole was *very* tall.] But I think I shall like and respect him. Sept. 25. I find Priestley very agreeable. He is cocksure and determined but has a great sense of humour about himself and his views on literature most strangely coincide with mine. Sept. 30. Priestley is certainly a very clever man . . . he will go far.

A later entry reads:

> I certainly find Priestley an enchanting companion. I've never had a writing man for a friend before who has been so close a companion. Henry James was too old, Conrad too mysterious, Swinnerton too untrustworthy, Bennett too egoist – all *good* friends, but none of them with the sweetness and humour Priestley has.

A photograph shows them standing together in Walpole's garden in front of an enormous rose bush, staring into the middle distance and each clutching a pipe. Walpole looks considerably more than ten years older than Priestley, possibly because he was diabetic and his health never good.

On hearing of Pat's death, Walpole wrote a kind and sympathetic letter of condolence, expressing how he had felt the previous spring when his mother had died, that nothing seemed to matter except that she should be out of pain. He was, he says, especially glad that Jack had spent the week with him the month before.

> 'It was, I suppose, a risk to take but you don't know what pleasure you gave me.' He had found it comforting that someone of Priestley's talent and knowledge 'was finding that middle path between the Cranks and the Idiots that I, in my own way, had been looking for. To tell you the truth, your being here rather

spoiled my days in London. There was no one to throw his head back and laugh at the thought of my slipping down the quarry railway . . . well, come soon again.' He ends by offering his help in any way he can.[4]

Early in 1927 the idea for a completely different kind of book began to obsess Priestley. 'I knew what kind of a long novel I wanted to write,' he wrote in *Margin Released*.

> I had always been fascinated by what we, not the Spaniards, call the picaresque; ample tales in which the characters go wandering – *Don Quixote* (that supreme masterpiece), *Gil Blas*, *Tom Jones*, *Pickwick*. I saw no reason why the picaresque novel should vanish with the stagecoach. Why not one about my own England of the Twenties? No attempt to create a sort of Christmas-card past – that would have been a fake – but using as a background the England I knew and presenting it quite realistically. This idea of a contemporary, picaresque long novel haunted me, refusing to go when other people argued against it, even when they were people who knew, they said, what the reading public wanted and what it didn't want.

Tentative feelers put out to publishing houses 'aroused about as much enthusiasm as a stuffed walrus at an exhibition of watercolours. The long novel was out of fashion, expensive to print, hard to sell.'

But one person had faith in his idea. In May 1927 Priestley went up to Brackenburn again, full of his proposed novel and simmering with discontent: he could not see how he would even be able to start it as he had so much other work ahead of him. Such a major undertaking needed a long run at it and that was impossible with weekly and monthly columns, reviews, pot-boilers and series to write. Walpole gave the matter some thought and came up with the idea of a joint book, an epistolary novel to be called *Farthing Hall*. The story would be told in a series of letters between a middle-aged academic and a younger man. As Priestley lived in Oxfordshire and Walpole divided his time between London and the Lake District, they would pass the plot between them without needing to meet. Mischievously they decided to reverse roles: Walpole would play that of the eager young man, Priestley the academic: 'Though I was neither middle-aged nor a scholar, this was the role I preferred, leaving eager youth and romance to Walpole.' Walpole found it all highly amusing, hence 'Dear Old Jack'.

Fired with enthusiasm, Priestley returned home to College House, Walpole having volunteered to approach his own publishers, Macmillan, with a proposal for the novel. He did not anticipate any problems as his relationship with them was excellent: he had a long and successful track record and was one of their star authors. It was a generous gesture on his part for he had started on the *Herries* series, and in the earliest letters between him and Priestley there is discussion of 'the red-haired man', Rogue Herries. There was one other important factor: Walpole could command substantial advances and royalties where Priestley could not. With no domestic ties Walpole was comfortably off, and Priestley ruefully compared their different work styles: Walpole in his fine study, expensive pen in hand, and himself in the room over the stable banging away at a battered portable typewriter, driven not so much by a burning desire to create as the need to pay the bills.

It is clear that Walpole had told Priestley only part of what he intended, for on 4 July 1927 Priestley wrote to him in astonished gratitude:

> You're not acting as my 'father in God' but as the Fairy Queen. You've given me the best piece of news I have had for a long, long time, and if you only knew how worried and disappointed I've been all this year (and since I saw you I've heard (a) that ADAM has done nothing in America (b) dropped to about five a week here! (c) that OPEN HOUSE [one of his most delightful books of essays] is doing badly so far), you'd walk about feeling you were tighted and spangled and wanded, in short, a very large good fairy. It's going to make all the difference to me these next twelve months because now I can sit down and spend the whole time writing two good books, the one with you and my own big comic one, instead of grinding away at all manner of rot.

Walpole had arranged that the entire advance and most of the royalties would go to Priestley. He had then spoken of the proposed book to A. D. Peters, who immediately saw its potential for serialisation and thought, bearing in mind Walpole's undoubted prestige, that there would be no problem selling the book on either side of the Atlantic. Walpole set out a detailed work scheme: at the beginning of September, they would devise the plot line and the mechanics of how it would work. Thereafter they would write an agreed amount of words each week in the form of letters and meet up again when the time came to finish it. Priestley suggested it might be easier if he came to Brackenburn in September, not least because 'we never had a proper walk this last time and I never got up Great Gable again. It seems to me better that we should work out the scheme just before we're ready to begin, though meanwhile we can be filling out our respective characters in our minds.' If Walpole could get him a decent advance, he would also make a start on his new large novel. He thought he would offer it to Macmillan. A. D. Peters had put his idea for the book to Heinemann but his editor there, C. S. Evans, was

> very depressed; he says books aren't selling, etc, etc, and he succeeded in depressing me the other day. He thinks BENIGHTED good but not a seller (though rather 'too gloomy and symbolical'), therefore *not* a seller. I never knew such a fellow for blowing hot and cold. He's rapidly combining the manners of big business with the manners of the King's Road, Chelsea.

Walpole's letters became increasingly affectionate: he thought often of Priestley and longed to see him again, which evoked rare admissions from his friend:[5]

> You do my 'proud spirit' (as you call it) good. The fact is, I need more humility and more sense of humour about myself, and your attitude and chaff and so forth knock the silliness out of me. I've always been a wee bit soured I suspect (it began at Cambridge) and there's a little, morbidish Malvolio streak in me, which comes out in my thoughts about myself and my work but not when I'm thinking generally and dealing with other men's work . . . but you've had enough of this stuff to last you all your life, and I won't inflict any more on you. Yours ever, Jack.

A few days later Priestley had developed cold feet, due to the amount of work he had taken on, coupled with the fact that he had had a 'stinking' review of his Peacock biography in *The Times*. Walpole reassured him that there was nothing to worry about, least of all a bad notice by someone who had been prejudiced against everything Priestley had ever written but was always given his books to review. Priestley replied that Jane agreed with Walpole that he was worrying unnecessarily, but could he let him know as soon as he heard when he might get the advance for *Farthing Hall*: 'You see all my plans for the next twelve months hang on this: I hope to do nothing but my big comic book, THE GOOD COMPANIONS, and our joint lark.' But he had also, he admitted, taken on yet another book, this time on

> the English Novel, for Benn's sixpenny library . . . although Peters is still trying to get me an ascending scale of royalties in place of the usual flat. The terms are bad . . . but there's a chance it might have a colossal sale, for I understand the first ones have touched the 100,000 mark and of course I like the idea of talking about the novel to a possible quarter of a million readers here and in America.

The books in the series were only about 20,000 words long and the format he proposed was a short chapter about 'what we get out of a novel, and then taking a gallop right through from Defoe to our friends, cutting out the usual historical bunkum . . .' He had not been well, 'nerves twitching and not sleeping'.

In September, and to their mutual enjoyment, he and Walpole settled down to *Farthing Hall*. Walpole wrote in his diary, 'It is delightful to have Jack here – a friendship that does me all the good in the world because I respect so immensely his intelligence.' The next day, 22 September, he added: 'The book with Priestley moves. I have as expected a burning desire to get on with it.' Five days later they were 'moving at breakneck speed': both men could write fast. Then they parted company, exchanging their respective chapters throughout the autumn. On 22 October Priestley wrote to Walpole, enclosing his latest chapter, 'a tentative letter' saying that if he didn't like it he should throw it on the fire:

> I can't exploit the Where-is-Marjorie situation any more and on the other hand it would be absurd to write a long letter about other matters. Jane says that if she read this in the middle of a novel, it would only irritate her. What do you think? I leave it to you. Don't forget to give me the situation exactly with your next letters so that I know when to send Robert careering North.

At some stage Walpole must have asked Priestley why he did not consider moving near to him in Hampstead, for he replied that he and Jane had been discussing the need for a move for some time. The house was lovely, but there was no school in the village and it was too far to send the children into Oxford, 'and no company here at all; and I can't afford at present to be so out of touch with things as I am'. They had worked out that their preferred areas, St John's Wood or Hampstead, would cost him a further £400 a year, but he thought he could make up the difference 'doing little jobs I can't do here'. He and Jane had already discussed selling their house with a local agent and were going to look at some houses in London, though 'we may find difficulty getting what we want with ourselves, four children' and, revealingly, in view of how often he complains of being hard up, 'a nurse, a cook and a housemaid and a decent study for me and some sort of garden, particularly as I can't plonk money down for premiums or start buying leases, but we're going to see what is possible for the kind of rent we can afford'. He hoped one day to have two homes, like Walpole, but he would want the second to be in the north, not the south. 'This sort of stuff here is pretty but it is too relaxing and dull for me and I never bother going out to look at it.'

Again financial worries surface: if neither *Farthing Hall* nor *Good Companions* does well, he will have to look around for a regular job to provide the main part of his income.

Jane sent her love. She was busy reading Trollope again, the only novelist of his time 'she says, who gives you good sprightly heroines (barring Jane Austen of course) or women generally. It's true too, isn't it? Even Thackeray couldn't make a woman sprightly and virtuous at the same time.'

By mid-November *Farthing Hall* was far enough on for Priestley and Walpole to agree to slow down, number the chapter-letters, and decide what else needed to be in them. Walpole thought some of Priestley's letters too discursive and not sufficiently dramatic. Somewhat hurt, Priestley insisted that he had been 'more dramatic than you imagine, for even my reflective passages are really dramatic, that is they come naturally out of the situation . . . and you have been more discursive than you seem to imagine, read back and see. I want your opinion on all manner of things, not merely as "Robert", but as J. B. Priestley.' He followed this up with details of where he thought the plot might be improved, but

Jonathan and Emma Priestley in Blackpool, probably taken
during their honeymoon in August 1891.

A 'Holt's' charabanc trip. Priestley's uncle Tom, landlord of The Volunteer pub, would organise a trip every year for his regulars, either to the Dales or the Yorkshire coast.

Jack Priestley in the autumn of 1914, newly recruited to the army.

The only picture in existence of Jack and Pat Priestley together.

Teddy Davidson, Jack Priestley and Gerald Bullett in 1922.

Pat Priestley with Barbara, 1923.

Granny Tempest with Barbara, 1924.

Jonathan Priestley towards the end of his life.

Jack with Hugh Walpole while they were working together on *Farthing Hill* in 1927.

Jack in his study at Well Walk, Hampstead, at the time of
publication of *The Good Companions*.

Hugh Walpole and Rose Macaulay as godparents at
Rachel Priestley's christening, 1930.

Coleridge's house, 3 The Grove, Highgate, to which Jack and his family moved in 1931.

At 3 The Grove.

Jack at Billingham Manor, Isle of Wight, in the 1930s.

when I think of the snags, I consider we are doing wonderfully well. But if we ever do another book of this kind – and I hope we do – we really must go away together, perhaps to some little Mediterranean place in the winter, and make it half a holiday and half an orgy of high-spirited composition . . . Again, we might do a little book of letters that has no story at all but is frankly an exchange of opinions between ourselves, about Shakespeare and music . . .

'Do you know', he wrote later, 'I've brought out *five* books this year: two novels, an English Man of Letters; a book of essays; and my little history of the novel. I can't decide whether that's glorious or downright wicked; but anyhow it's an accident, and next year I shall be out of the publishers' lists.'

In the winter of 1927–8 Walpole visited the Priestleys in Oxfordshire, found the house rather bleak and cold ('like Conrad's but much happier'), but felt happy and at home with them, talking 'a million to the clock'. At the end of January Priestley went to the Lake District to finish *Farthing Hall*. When he and Walpole decided that they had the manuscript as they wanted it, Priestley set off for home with a sort of relief. Now he could turn all his attention to *The Good Companions*.

Walpole's feelings for Priestley are perhaps best expressed in a letter dated 1 April, which must have been written in 1928:

I ought to be settling down to Herries but I must write to you first. Odd your letter coming because I missed you amazingly last night. I sat in a chair and thought of you for about an hour while the American Professor chattered on (he's a good sort really and excellent company when you learn not to trust a word he says). It's funny you and I should be friends, I so demonstrative and you the opposite, but our basic feelings for one another are the same, I think, and I feel that Jane has become a kind of deeper bond between us . . .

In his reply, Priestley tries to explain that his lack of demonstrative affection did not mean that he did not care deeply for his friend:

I think you were lucky in never having – what I've always had and had badly – a social inferiority complex. From what you have told me, you assumed from the start that people would like you as you liked them; and though you got a bad knock or two when you were young, that feeling persisted. Now I think I'm a hell of a fellow in some ways – but I can never understand that anybody should find pleasure in my company, and when they do I always think there's a catch in it. That explains a lot, I think. If I was ever overbearing, rough, dogmatic with people; it was always because I felt that if I didn't assert myself, I should simply fade to nothing, just be so much ugly lumber in the room. A silly point of view and I'm getting out of it. You'd better see what your professor says about it, because I fancy nearly all Americans have got it, that's why they can't be quiet.

In no other surviving letter to anyone is he so self-revelatory.[6]
Towards the end of his life Walpole wrote of his Dear Old Jack:

Strange man – so sensitive and vain, so sure of his uniqueness, his power, his wisdom, yet with a marvellous control of his real nature (he is peevish and complaining, but I have never known him once in all these years lose his temper), so pessimistic, but with such a gorgeous sense of humour – so penurious about little things, yet so generous-minded. He is so gruff, ill-mannered, and yet how sweet he was to Mrs Brown on Sunday. He can be an admirable critic. But, through all and everything, there is a deep sweetness that pervades his whole nature, which is why I love him.

But Hugh Walpole had given Priestley something else: an inestimable Cove, 'greater than gold or diamonds; the joint book and Walpole's generosity in handing the substantial advance to his friend enabled Priestley to write *The Good Companions*, which brought with it the fame and fortune from which he never looked back.

CHAPTER 12

Fame

Even today those who know almost nothing else about J. B. Priestley can tell you that he wrote *The Good Companions*. Others have seen a television showing of the 1930s' film, with John Gielgud and Jessie Matthews. Theatre buffs may remember a stage version in 1931 and thousands saw the 1974 musical, which starred Judi Dench as Miss Trant, with music by André Previn.

By the end of February 1928 Priestley told Davison that he had written 30,000 words of *The Good Companions* and was enthusiastic about it, which was more than could be said for the publishing fraternity. He had already been told that there was no market for long, picaresque novels, but he felt his next move made matters even worse: 'For I decided that my story should be about a concert party or pierrot troupe. I knew nothing about concert parties and had to mug them up a bit.' He made a brisk tour of several cities, including Bradford, staying overnight in theatrical digs to try to pick up some colour – but his book's subject matter, he was told, was fatal: 'The monster I was planning would now be "a back-stage novel" which readers, it appeared, had always disliked.' Nor was that all. 'I had found a title that was no good. "No, old boy: think again." I did, once I had finished the book, so that my desk was littered with sheets on which I had scribbled possible alternatives. But it was no use, the white elephant would have to be called *The Good Companions*.'[1]

As yet he had no publisher for it and continually pressed A. D. Peters to find one in Britain and the USA. Priestley's letters to Davison refer frequently to the problem and, increasingly bitterly, to American publishers. Davison was finally provoked into an exasperated defence of his adopted country. It was, he wrote, quite unfair to damn a whole nation largely because of the attitude of its publishing companies.

At the end of March 1928 Priestley wrote to Hugh Walpole, 'trying to cheer myself up as Jane's been away this week looking for a furnished house at the seaside'.[2] It was raining, he had had no post to speak of, not a scrap of news from anyone and had done nothing but work all day and read George Moore's *Hail and Farewell* in the evening. 'I liked it before and think I like it even more now – some fatuities apart (there is one remark about his taste in women's breasts that is easily the most fatuous in all literature).' He had been asked to broadcast a 'little talk recalling Easter Customs of other years', his first, and he wondered if he would be taken for the Yorkshire comedian John Henry.

However, he was enjoying writing the novel:

> At the moment my little working man is helping a fellow to sell rubber dolls at a fair . . . In fact my idea of this monumental yarn is simply to amuse myself first of all. Jane says that provincial life – working and lower middle class stuff, industrial not rural – is my métier obviously and she's probably right. I really do know about these people because I've spent a lot of my time in pubs and low music halls and at football matches – especially the early impressionable years – and then again I had the first two years of the war in the ranks, living with all sorts of queer fellows. And one of the weaknesses of fiction today is that most of the novelists who can write have not an extensive acquaintance with the people and life of this country . . . I feel better after that bit of bragging. God Speed the Rogue Herries!

He ends with a note about his youngest daughter: 'If Mary dislikes anything now, she says, "There's snakes in it!" – and that's what I call literature!' The period when he was writing *The Good Companions* was a magic time. As he said later: 'I gave myself a holiday from anxiety, strain and tragic circumstance, shaping and colouring a long, happy daydream.'

Priestley coined a choice metaphor at around this time to describe how a writer feels at the start of each day: 'Every morning, you have to go in there and lift the elephant off the typewriter.' The elephant appears in a number of letters and essays and also in *Margin Released* when he writes of *The Good Companions*, harking back to his need to write a daydream. 'And because a lot of other people then must have felt in need of such a holiday, so long a daydream, the elephant suddenly turned into a balloon.'

The creative flow was disrupted in May 1928 when Priestley and his family moved from Oxfordshire, not to London, which was their final destination, but to a rented, furnished house in Deal, Kent. 'There is a little balcony,' he wrote to Davison, 'the house is bang on the sea – and we can watch ships in the Downs. My novel rolls on – now over 90,000 words – with dozens and dozens of characters in it, like a Dickens novel. I hope it will make you laugh, it amuses me enormously.'

Jane left him to it, and spent much of her time in London trying to find them a suitable base. Meanwhile A. D. Peters was still negotiating with publishers, but by July it had been decided that it would be best for Priestley to remain with Heinemann, as C. S. Evans had read the first volume of the novel and was full of praise:

> ... the only thing I can say is, bless you! In a desert of aridity which I have been traversing in the last six months, your book stands out as a green and pleasant oasis. There is not a line in it that I would wish away, and I am certain that if you go on as you have begun, we are going to produce a book that the world has got to reckon with. Appreciation so enthusiastic as this may seem a bit strange to you after my luke-warm reception of your other two books; but this is much bigger than either. It has the true creative spirit in it. It has humour, humanity and exuberance, three of the very rarest qualities of our time.

He added a warning: 'Do not let facility take the place of creation. You are a very facile writer, my dear Priestley, and you can do standing on your head what other writers can only achieve with blood and tears.'[3] The first volume had also been shown to Eugene Saxton of Harper's, in New York, which had been followed up with a meeting. Priestley had found him more sympathetic than he had expected.

Priestley's enthusiastic letters to his friends about how well the book was coming along prompted Walpole to assume, by the beginning of August, that it must be almost finished. Priestley responded:

> What on earth makes you think I've nearly done my book? Give me a chance! I've done close on 150,000 words now and expect to be working at it until the end of the year and probably later.

Heinemann would like a June publication if possible, and I
agree. I'm still enjoying it immensely and my only difficulty is
going to be in getting it even into 250,000! The people are all
real to me now and they all come clamouring for space. The
best character of all is the little working man from Bradford.
Everything about him is absolutely real and I defy anyone to
say he isn't alive and very lovable. So there! I find that a big
canvas suits me far better than a little one, and the point about
it, Hugh, is this, that the big canvas knocks out the people who
are not really novelists with full minds . . .

He would, he said, allow Walpole to read it when it had been
finished and 'sanded'. Only Jane was allowed to read the work
in progress and she was pleased, which contented him.

In September they found a house in London they thought
would be suitable: 27 Well Walk, Hampstead. Now that there
was a definite publisher for *The Good Companions* they felt secure
enough to buy rather than rent. The house was on the edge of
Hampstead Heath, and Priestley wrote to Davison: 'Keats lived in
Well Walk for a time; and so did Constable; though our house is
actually neither old nor handsome it is roomy, cheerful, amusing
and full of conveniences.'

'Have I told you about the Hampstead house?' he asked
Walpole. 'It's something between a turkish bath, a ship and a
nonconformist chapel.' He had bought it from a doctor with
a number of children so it was an ideal family home and very
handy, being close to the tube station. They would be moving
in mid-October, although this would mean more disruption.

There were also problems with *Farthing Hall.* Priestley had
corrected his part of the manuscript and suggested that he and
Walpole might have to devise a sub-title or dedicatory letter to
suggest that the book was simply a lark and not to be taken
seriously by intelligent people: 'I think we made a mistake not
hammering out a better story or alternatively not making a sheer
farce out of it. It's wildly improbable and Jane doesn't like it (she
has been re-reading it) on that ground but I disagree with her,
thinking that in spite of that fact, it is quite bright reading.'[4]

Shortly before the move he paid a brief visit to Bradford.
The previous year he had given a highly successful lecture
to the Bradford English Society on 'English Humour', which
resulted in his being elected its president. His inaugural address

is remembered because he read Chapter One of *The Good Companions.*

The move to Well Walk held him up for a few weeks but the novel was eventually finished in January 1929. It could hardly have been a worse time in which to bring out this or any other novel: it was the year of the Wall Street crash, the ripples of which spread worldwide, triggering off what became known as the Great Depression. It was also the year in which the ill-prepared and ill-starred Labour government of Ramsay MacDonald took office. These two major events led to numerous arguments between Priestley and Walpole in the early thirties, as Walpole was a High Tory.

The story of *The Good Companions* is straightforward. In the opening section we follow the fortunes of three of its protagonists. Jess Oakroyd, the little working man from Bradford, called Bruddersford in the book, has a shrewish wife, a wastrel son and as unsympathetic employer; one day he tears up his insurance card and walks out into the world. Miss Elizabeth Trant lives in the Cotswolds, has spent most of her adult life looking after ageing parents and now, a spinster nearing middle-age, is determined to strike out and change her life; she buys a car and sets off into the unknown. Inigo Jollifant is a schoolmaster at a private school; he is sacked after falling foul of the headmaster's wife and looking for something to turn up when his path crosses those of Jess, Miss Trant and a stranded, depressed concert party, the Dinky-Doos. The three play a crucial role in turning the failed Dinky-Doos into the successful Good Companions. Miss Trant puts some of her inheritance into the concert party's kitty, Jess becomes the company's carpenter and handyman, while Jollifant emerges as a brilliant composer of popular songs and falls in love with the engaging young artist Susie Dean. We follow the Good Companions around the country sharing their joys, triumphs and near disasters, including the evil machinations of the wicked West End impresario Monte Mortimer. It all ends more or less happily. Jess Oakroyd returns to Bruddersford where his termagant wife is dying and, after her death, sails for Canada to live with his beloved daughter. Miss Trant, who believed that love had passed her by, meets an old flame and marries him. Inigo's best number, 'Slipping Round the Corner', written for the concert party's Jerry Jerningham, makes him a

household name, and he, Jerry and Susie set off for the West
End and fame – but no, he doesn't get the girl at the end.

The Good Companions was published at the end of July; August is
notorious as the worst book-buying month in the year. Although
leading bookshops had been sent proofs to read, the total
advance sales were for well below 2000 copies. The book cost
10s.6d (55p), which was a high price for a hard-back novel in
the 1920s, and frightening in 1929. Nevertheless Heinemann
printed 10,000 copies, hoping that if the reviews were favourable
they might sell 7000 or 8000.

The book appeared. Nothing happened. Then, quite suddenly, as Priestley wrote in *Margin Released*, 'The balloon went
up.' Orders poured in to such an extent that other printers had
to be found to cope with the demand, copies were bound 'all
over the place' and fleets of vans were hired to get them into
the bookshops. By Christmas these had to be supplemented by
taxis, for the novel was still selling at the rate of 1000 a week.

It was all the more surprising as the reviews, apart from the
Sunday Times, had been only moderately favourable. Indeed V. S.
Pritchett said he had had to abandon the book half-way through.
The Times Literary Supplement described it a massive novel of 600
pages, 'a trifle heavy to hold but the not too sophisticated reader
will find no difficulty and a good deal of pleasure in reading it
through from cover to cover . . . Criticism is hardly called upon
to lift her head in such an expansive atmosphere.'

'What I suffered from,' Priestley wrote in *Margin Released*, 'was
the fixed idea, itself an indictment of our whole culture, that
anything widely popular must necessarily be bad. Criticism,
the worst not the best, borrowed "best-seller" from the book
trade, where it means what it says and nothing more, and
made it pejorative.' He suffered in the same way as Daphne
du Maurier, a decade later, with *Rebecca.* But in the event it
did not matter: readers of both simply did not care what the
professional reviewers had to say. Priestley wrote to Davison on
28 December 1929,

'The Good Companions' has been breaking all Heinemann's
records for daily sales, and the rush before Christmas was so
great that it cleaned them out entirely. It has sold over 50,000
over here, which is marvellous for England and at 10s.6d. too.
Evans hopes to clear 100,000 for this edition and then go on

to other editions, illustrated, thin paper, etc. In America it is now selling 2000 a week, good enough, of course, but not comparable with sales here. Harpers have done better lately, but I'm afraid their initial bad handling missed the bus for me. But of course I don't expect to be popular with the idiotic American intelligentsia, who seem to me, at this distance, the very silliest people the world has ever seen, entirely without sense or roots.

As the sales shot ever higher a kind of *Good Companions* industry grew up around it. Sentimental pictures of pairs of puppies or kittens, or children holding hands or friends of any kind, were captioned 'The Good Companions'.

According to Peter Holdsworth,[5] within three years of its publication Priestley had had enough, thundering:

On and after this date, if at any public dinner or meeting at which I am present I am referred to as 'a good companion', I shall forthwith leave the building. There is a limit and it has long ago been passed. For over two years I have suffered. I can recognise now with sinking heart, a foolish gleam in the eyes of my fellow speakers, and I know it means that they are about to call me 'a good companion'. And they all say it as if it had never been said before, as if it was a sudden bold inspiration. Never was a man so pestered and haunted by the title of a book as I am. It begins to look as if I shall go down to the grave (and that at no far distant date) as a confounded good companion.

By this time the book had sold over a quarter of a million copies and was still selling.

But nevertheless I wish I'd called it something else. And let us get this straight, once and for all: The novel is not about some people who were good companions, but about some people who organised a concert party called The Good Companions. The people in question were not idyllically good-natured and self-sacrificing (except by comparison with some of the monsters that pass as characters now in fiction). They were an ordinary set of fairly decent mummers. Sometimes they were jealous of one another, let one down, bickered and quarrelled and got drunk, were silly and stupid. There was nothing astonishingly noble about them. But in an expansive moment – after supper – these people agreed to call their concert party The Good Companions. Hence the title of the book. Hence my misery. It would be just as sensible to keep referring to me as 'an angel' because a later (and in my opinion, better) novel of mine is called *Angel Pavement*.

Thus was the myth of Jolly Jack Priestley born. Yet he was not, he emphasised, one of those jovial men who are always to be found at the centre of a jolly group. 'I walk in and out of my club so gloomily that even now the servants are suspicious of my standing. I do not slap people on the back, and people do not slap me on the back – at least not more than once.' But that was later. When he wrote so gleefully to Davison that Christmas, he simply could not believe his luck. He was fêted: no literary party or gathering was complete without him and so much money was coming in that Jane took advice on how best to deal with such unexpected wealth, which resulted in the setting up of a trust fund for the children. She was pregnant again, and this time she and Priestley could look forward to the birth of their child in comfort and security beyond their wildest dreams.

It might be thought that Priestley, having achieved such success, would give himself a long break, but after only a short holiday in Devon he began another, very different book.

If *The Good Companions* was an escape from the times, then the new novel, *Angel Pavement*, was a reflection on them. In the opinion of many literary critics, it is Priestley's finest novel. The plot is based around the mysterious Mr Golspie who, with his beautiful daughter, Lena, arrives in London one day from an unnamed Baltic port and makes his way to the offices of Messrs Twigg and Dersingham, 8 Angel Pavement, in the City of London. Twigg and Dersingham import veneers and inlays from abroad and sell them on to cabinet makers and furniture manufacturers. Like every other small firm in these hard times they are having difficulty in keeping afloat. Golspie makes a deal with Mr Dersingham, the firm's owner, which he says will rescue the business for him. He will become the firm's salesman as he has a connection with a timber firm in a Baltic state that will undercut any of Dersingham's suppliers. More than that, he will guarantee to increase the firm's sales fivefold. He makes only one stipulation: his commission must be paid before the buyers settle. The gullible Dersingham agrees. Mesmerised by Golspie and his confidence, he is carried away on a tide of euphoria; but Golspie is a trickster and when he disappears, leaving the firm in ruins, he has almost destroyed the lives of all of its employees.

Those who bought the book in eager anticipation of its being another *Good Companions* must have been surprised by what they found: a book which, although shot through with humour, is full of the gritty reality of the times. *Angel Pavement* is, most of all, a compelling story of betrayal – financial, sexual and personal – at the end of which only the women look to the future with a glimmer of hope. Discussing it with Diana Collins years later, Priestley told her that there was one other character in the novel: 'society itself'. Once again the reviews were mixed. J. M. Barrie found it even better than *The Good Companions* 'and I had not thought to find a better in my time'. Virginia Woolf commented in her diary: 'I have invented this phrase for Bennett and Priestley, "the tradesmen of letters".'

The book, which was nearly as long as *The Good Companions*, was rushed into print within months of delivery and sold by the hundred thousand. Priestley's fourth daughter, Rachel, was born safely on 16 August 1930 and her parents began to consider another move. The property on which they had their eye was 3 The Grove, Highgate, a four-storey house which had once been lived in by Coleridge.

Throughout all this period and well beyond, the river of ideas never dried up. Notebooks that surfaced only after the death of Jacquetta Hawkes, Priestley's third wife, are crammed with them: 'Play based on people's ridiculous estimates of themselves? Novel – The Hottest Summer that ever was. Play/novel? The Day of Judgement for a couple. Play – The Labyrinth – from outside, going into it, the middle. Novel – secrets, espionage. Adaptation *Tristram Shandy*. Play in which all are actors – Ouspensky's spiral – Pontius Pilate?' Dozens and dozens of ideas including one presumably for a non-fiction book.

On 20 December 1930 Priestley wrote to Davison informing him that he would be leaving on the liner *Olympic* on 11 February 1931 for the USA and would give ten lectures. He wanted Jane to join him in San Francisco on 4 March, after which they would spend a short time on the West Coast and then cruise to the South Seas. On their return to the USA he had arranged for them to travel home via Canada, visiting the Rockies, Winnipeg and Montreal.

However, he was to give his lectures during a slump in book sales when everyone was panicking: 'They don't seem to stand up to these crises very well. Probably the climate.' *Angel Pavement* had sold about 50,000 copies in the USA and, with Louis Bromfield's *Twenty-four Hours*, was the joint best-seller of the autumn, 'so you can see for yourself what a poor show it has been . . . three years ago I would have sold 150,000'. His most recent sales figures showed 80,000 for *Angel Pavement* and a further 125,000 for *The Good Companions*. But baby Rachel was flourishing, Jane was well – and Priestley had 'started fencing and you should see my parries in carte and sixte, my ripostes, my octaves, my doubles! Have at you! Sa, sa!' He appends a drawing of a portly Priestley, tankard in hand.

He left as planned, and shortly before he arrived in New York wrote to Jane that the voyage had been pleasant enough but rather dull and that many people had been seasick in rough weather. 'I'm looking forward terribly to seeing you again,' he told her. 'Do come out if it's humanly possible. And let me know definitely. I'm assuming of course that you are coming. The thought of your not coming is unbearable. All my love to you, sweetheart, and a kiss for the children. Your very loving – Jack.' It seems that until she sailed Jane was doubtful about leaving home and family, especially her baby, for such a long time: the Priestleys would not return home until June.

The ship docked briefly in Boston before going on to New York, and Priestley was interviewed by a young journalist from a news syndicate. The result was a story alleging that he had said that Americans suffered from collective indigestion caused by the sort of food they ate, that their country was home to 'mock culture', that London had stolen from New York the right to be known as the 'dramatic capital of the civilised world', and that the USA was in a bad way with afflictions of 'childish movies, bad plays and cheap novels'. When he reached New York his supposed views had gone before him, which hardly helped his popularity as a visiting celebrity.

Both then and later he claimed that he had not made any of the remarks attributed to him and that the interview had been a fake. Yet in the past he had expressed views not dissimilar, as his letters to Davison show. However, he immediately contacted the syndicate and was invited to meet its director, who apologised profusely for the 'flagrant misrepresentation' and withdrew the offending piece.

On 19 February he wrote again to Jane: after all his misgivings he found New York 'terrific'. It was like 'a vast mad house, though extraordinarily beautiful at times. The skyscrapers really are incredible – they take your breath away.' The Harper's directors had been kind and helpful, although he found them dull. He had arranged for one of their wives to show Jane around New York when she arrived as by that time he would be on his way across to the West Coast: 'I do hope you can come out, darling. I'm looking forward more and more anxiously to seeing you. Cable me through Hamilton if you can't. But you MUST. I'll make all the arrangements. A thousand kisses for you and hugs for the children.'

Jane joined him in San Francisco but, in spite of his eagerness to see her, during their time in the city there was friction between them, caused, it seems, by his wandering eye. Nevertheless everything proceeded as planned and they sailed off to Tahiti for their special holiday. They had much to discuss: the proposed purchase of the house in Highgate and what that would mean in terms of building, renovation and furnishing; the possibility of a second home somewhere in the country; the prospects for their children thanks to *The Good Companions*; and what Priestley planned to do next. A stage adaptation of the novel had been mooted. So much to look forward to, so many plans.

But as they say in Poland, the rats laugh when we make plans.

CHAPTER 13

'Oh she doth teach the torches to burn bright . . .'

Romeo and Juliet, Act I Scene 5

The Priestleys returned to London at the beginning of June and, according to Jane, in good spirits, looking forward to seeing their children. She was eagerly anticipating the move to Highgate, if everything went through smoothly.

Almost as soon as he had arrived in Well Walk, Priestley left for the Cotswolds with his friend Gerald Bullett as they had been working on a joint book, *I'll Tell You Everything*. Although he had his own study and Jane had plenty of help with the house and the children, he felt it would be better for him and Gerald to work in some secluded hotel. The one they found, the Lygon Arms, was in the picture-postcard village of Broadway and Priestley described it in his first letter to Jane as having a 'terrible Arts and Crafts atmosphere', although the food was good. The business of getting down to writing the book proved more difficult than he had envisaged and soon he was grumbling to Jane that he struggled to manage 5000 words a day, and while Gerald was doing his best, 'his best really isn't too good'. 'Poor Gerald', he told her, was suffering from some kind of writer's block or 'knot' which 'froze' his mind, but in spite of that the two were laughing at themselves. There is nothing in the handful of letters to Jane that foreshadowed what was to come until the last, written immediately before he returned home.

It is clear from that letter, dated 27 June 1931, that something dramatic had happened and that she had written to him about it. He begins with his practical arrangements for coming home and briefly discusses his work. Then this tone changes. In answer to her letter, he writes, he agrees that everything is wrong between them, that he's as lonely and wretched as she is, that he is no longer the man she can have fun with. He had hoped their holiday abroad would have brought them closer together but it had not done so. He goes on to tell her how fortunate she has been to find Jimmy, a man who loves her and with whom she has fallen in love, when he has had nothing as good in his own life. He realises that for a long time he has been only a 'heavy stupidish man' in her eyes and nothing to any other woman. Here, it must be said that no one within the family or who knew the Priestleys has any idea who Jimmy was or if Jane had an affair with him.

What *had* happened? It is significant that, although Priestley wrote at length to Davison about the events of the summer and autumn of 1931, Davison did not keep the correspondence, and the only account that survives is Jane's own in the long letters she wrote to Davison. In the first, she says that in the middle of June Priestley had returned briefly from Broadway to drop a bombshell: he had fallen passionately in love with a young actress. Her name was Peggy Ashcroft. Whether he had met her before leaving for the Cotswolds with Gerald or while he was there is not clear, though the latter is certainly possible for while he was in Broadway she was appearing in James Elroy Flecker's *Hassan* in Oxford. It was a true *coup de foudre*, love at first sight, for within days he was following her about declaring undying passion.

Peggy Ashcroft had shown exceptional dramatic promise right from the start of her training at the Central School of Speech and Drama. She had been picked out immediately by a London agent and cast in a revival of J. M. Barrie's play *Dear Brutus*, in which the part of the childless artist, originally written for Gerald du Maurier, was played by the young Ralph Richardson. Later, in a production of *She Stoops to Conquer*, she was cast opposite Rupert Hart-Davis, who had gone into the profession not from drama school but after taking a degree at Oxford. Subsequently, having decided being an actor was not for him, he went on to become a distinguished publisher. Within three weeks of meeting they were engaged, and on 23 December 1929, the day after Peggy's twenty-third birthday, they were married – in spite of dire warnings from professional friends that such marriages rarely last. 'It was the first romance of my life', she said later, 'the first relationship. We formed an instant bond but it was more intellectual than physical. It was a very idyllic romance which was stillborn.'

By the time she and Priestley met, her stage career was assured. In 1930 she had played Desdemona opposite Paul Robeson's Othello and followed this with a leading role in Somerset Maugham's *The Breadwinner,* in which her co-stars were Jack Hawkins and Ronald Squire. In 1931 she was Pervaneh in *Hassan* and Fanny in Marcel Pagnol's *Sea Fever.*

According to Jane there had been no warning that emotional trouble lay ahead for, contrary to what Priestley had said in his letter to her, with its implication of her involvement with another man, she told Davison that 'everything between Jack and me had always been all right. I love him as much as I ever did.' He was, though, a difficult person and she had not always been happy with his attitude to women, especially after a few drinks. Jack, she said, admitted that he did not have a very good head for alcohol and that it took only a moderate amount at a party to make him 'a little muzzy' which led, in turn, to 'a spirit of mischievous lust'. This had reared its head several times in America and had led to half a dozen quarrels between them; but, as far as she was aware, they had resolved their differences and he had been loving before he set off to Broadway with Gerald – indeed, when he had said goodbye he had told her he loved her just as much as he had when they were first married.

Jane had been devastated when Jack had suddenly told her he was passionately in love with Peggy Ashcroft, before he disappeared back to Broadway. When he returned again it was to inform her that he was going to live with Peggy. Jane, with the house to run, a family of five children and the imminent prospect of a house move, told him he had better go away on his own for a while and give careful consideration to the implications of what he proposed. Priestley immediately packed and left, and sent word a few days later through A. D. Peters that he wanted Jane to decide whether she would prefer divorce or legal separation: he favoured the latter. She replied that what he wanted to do was his decision, not hers.

There followed a highly emotional few weeks of increasingly irrational letters and messages, after which Jane collapsed with an unspecified illness. This brought Priestley hurrying home, saying he had broken off his new relationship, but within days he had disappeared again. When Jane was sufficiently recovered, she decided to contact 'that girl's husband', Rupert Hart-Davis, which she promptly did and asked to see him. Did he know what was going on? Hart-Davis replied that he knew about her husband's infatuation with his wife but that there was no need to worry. However, when he and Jane met he admitted that Priestley's relationship with Peggy was making him very unhappy, and he and Jane decided to ask their spouses if they wanted to divorce.

To her surprise, Jane was contacted the next day by Peggy herself who, according to Jane's letter to Davison, told her that while she felt an affair with Jack 'would be a valuable experience in my life and that he was obviously violently infatuated', she was not sure that she wanted one and hoped that Jane would accept her assurances that she had not been leading him on. Jane replied that if she felt what was between them was serious, then they must carry on, but if not Peggy should end it.

Peggy Ashcroft was always reticent about her private life and rarely gave interviews, even to talk about her work. She never discussed her three marriages or her children. But in 1980 I had a series of discussions with her for a book I was writing on women's roles in Shakespeare's plays, during which she referred obliquely to the events of that time. She had talked about the range of young heroines, and how she had loved them all for different reasons: Portia, Rosalind, whom she played for the last time when she was nearly fifty, Viola, Perdita, Imogen, Desdemona, Katherine. She had never, she said, played *Twelfth Night*'s Olivia 'on stage'. The Duke of Orsino is infatuated with Olivia, no matter what she does or says. 'I've always believed,' Dame Peggy said, 'that if Olivia had *really* wanted to send Orsino packing, then she could have done so straightaway. But although she wasn't in love with him, didn't want to marry him, she was deeply flattered by his constant attention and loved being the object of his adoration.' She knew what she was talking about, she said, because she had, as it were, played Olivia in real life. When she had been a young actress she was pursued by a famous writer who had fallen in love with her and, although it had not developed into a full-blown affair, she had been flattered and initially had not tried to dissuade him. However, when she had decided to end it, she had been able to do so.

Peggy must have tried to halt the romance straightaway, for later the same day Priestley stormed home and accused Jane of leaving him 'frozen in a romantic attitude', after which there was such a violent quarrel that Jane took the children and went to stay with her sister in a holiday cottage in Cornwall. Here they were soon followed by Priestley, dragging with him a sympathetic but embarrassed Hugh Walpole, who left shortly afterwards saying he 'couldn't bear it'. A brief and uneasy reconciliation took place between Priestley and his wife during the next week but at the end of it Priestley left her, saying that he had been unable to 'give up the affair in my mind'. He suggested she visit the Davisons in the USA to give them both a break. Again Jane told him to go away and decide one way or the other.

No sooner had Jane begun to pack for America than she received a telegram from Priestley telling her to stop her preparations. He was returning to London for good as Peggy had told him there was no hope of a relationship between them. He remained restless, though, and Jane suggested to Hugh Walpole that he invite him to Malvern for the Arts Festival as this might do him good. Hugh agreed, telling Jane that she should not take her husband's wild behaviour too seriously; it would pass and he would settle down again. When Priestley returned to London, he stayed with a friend and suggested to Jane that he move back into Well Walk and they resume family life, to which she replied that she would be happy to do so but needed a breathing space first. But within days he had arrived in a highly emotional state, to tell her that he had to see Peggy again. Jane said that this impossible situation could not continue and asked again if he wanted them to divorce. He replied that he didn't want either divorce or separation and left, claiming that he would make up his mind. Jane wrote to Davison again and told him that she could not stand much more of Priestley's waywardness, adding ruefully: 'What he seems to want is a love affair AND a wife!'

While all this was going on, *The Good Companions* had been adapted for the stage by Edward Knoblock, assisted by Priestley, and was going into production with Jess Oakroyd played by Edward Chapman, Inigo Jollifant by John Gielgud, Susie Dean 'by a clever young actress just making a name for herself', Adele

Dixon, and music by the popular composer Noël Gay. Plans were afoot for a Broadway version with Hugh Sinclair as Inigo, Vera Lennox as Susie and George Carney as Oakroyd. His letters are a mixture of information about the progress of his work and details of his emotional state.

Towards the end of August Davison must have been in London briefly, for in a letter to him dated 1 September Priestley apologises for having seen so little of him: 'you struck me in a crisis as I am sure you appreciate'. Priestley thought he might be seriously ill or half-way towards a nervous breakdown, and that he should leave London, but London was the only place he wanted to be. Jane had suggested sending the three older children to boarding school while they and the younger two rent a villa in the South of France and try to sort things out. 'I'm sorry you couldn't have met Peggy,' he told Davison, 'because you might have returned to New York at least feeling that your old comrade had a glorious excuse to make a fool of himself.'

It was then that the Priestleys found themselves facing a fact there was no avoiding: their brief reconciliation in Cornwall had resulted in Jane becoming pregnant, the symptoms of which she had put down to possible heart trouble, gastric problems and emotional exhaustion. In a letter to Davison, dated 3 November, Jane says that she had consulted her doctor about the possibility of an abortion and he had sent her to a specialist, who said he could do nothing without her husband's permission. She felt undecided but disliked the idea of termination and went to Holland to spend a week with friends while she made up her mind. Priestley took refuge with the long-suffering Hugh Walpole.

When Jane returned she discovered that Priestley had returned from the Lake District to Well Walk, had taken all his things and moved to Brighton where he had rented a flat for six months. Also awaiting her was a letter from Walpole in which he said that he now thought the situation between her and Priestley was hopeless.

It is symptomatic of Priestley's romantic frenzy that he had no compunction about dragging all his close friends and colleagues into the affair, including Walpole and Gerald Bullett, whether they liked it or not. A. D. Peters was in the unfortunate position of go-between to the warring couple, which culminated in his having to deliver a long typewritten letter from Priestley in Brighton to Jane saying that he saw no point in going on and wanted a legal separation, but not a divorce, and that he trusted, under these circumstances, she 'would have the operation for abortion'. Poor Peters had been told to take back an answer and had to wait as if he were a telegraph boy. Jane refused to do any such thing and told Priestley she would discuss the matter with him face to face or not at all.

In a letter to Jane from Brighton on 16 October, Priestley again referred to the question of abortion but also talked about the fall of the Labour government and his worries about the stage version of *The Good Companions*. It had done only moderate business at His Majesty's Theatre in the West End and its tour was about to open in Manchester on the Monday, but 'it looks like being a wash-out until after the Election . . . bookings which ought normally to have been enormous are consequently very poor.' In spite of everything he thought the purchase of 3 The Grove would be a sensible investment.

Jane finally decided to have her baby, regardless of what Priestley felt, and wrote to tell him so. She found it helpful that the children had to be got ready for school and there was so much to take her mind off the problem. The Priestley children remember only that 1931 was a time of great stress, when 'Daddy' kept disappearing for months on end. Within a few weeks of writing to Priestley, Jane received a long letter from him in which he suggested that he should give up the flat in Brighton and return home for the baby's birth. During this time they could talk the whole thing through quietly. He almost went so far as to admit that he had no real relationship with Peggy. As there might be gossip to the contrary he had asked Heinemann to say that he was in Brighton only for the peace and quiet in which to write, that he and Peggy were merely colleagues in a possible dramatic venture. Jane replied that if he planned to come home just to leave her again as soon as the baby was born, it was best that he stayed where he was. Priestley wrote that Peggy was not with him nor did she want to be. She had moved in with her friend and fellow actress Diana Wynyard. 'If anybody is very nosy about us tell them that Peggy and I are great friends and have some business together about a play. This is true. Ask Frere or Peters. And that's the lot!'

Jane was at her wits' end. She told Davison that Jack's letters were increasingly contradictory: he wanted to be a family man and remain married to her; he might or might not want a legal separation; he was still trying to persuade Peggy to set up a second home with him elsewhere; he was convinced Peggy fitted his temperament; she was adamant about breaking with him but he felt sure she would be happy with just part of him; he thought he might have to marry her eventually; he was appealing to his friends for *their* views. There was a pressing practical consideration apart from the coming baby: what should they do about the Highgate house? They were supposed to have moved during the autumn but the family was still in Well Walk and he was faced with the upkeep of both properties.

On 16 November Priestley wrote to Davison informing him briefly that he had finally 'broken with Peggy' – although it looks much more as if she had finally broken with him – but had still not returned to Jane. Shortly before Christmas he wrote again, saying that he had returned to Well Walk but he did not know if things could ever be the same again. However, his working life was going well: he had given up his book column on the *Evening News* and had taken over a similar slot on its rival, the *Standard*, from Arnold Bennett. He was also working on a new novel, *Faraway*.

The fever had abated, the madness was over. With the birth of a son, Tom, the following April, the reconciliation was complete. Both parents were delighted with him.

Apart from that one reference to playing Olivia, Dame Peggy never referred publicly, so far as I am aware, to her relationship with Jack Priestley. Whatever she might have felt at the outset when he presented himself on her doorstep, there are good reasons for believing what she told Jane: that she was extremely doubtful about it, that she had never led him on and, as had been implied by both of them, that she kept him at arm's length throughout.

First, she was both hardworking and extremely ambitious and, as has already been pointed out, her career was opening up in the most exciting way. Ahead of her lay that enormously prestigious London season. Second, and more to the point, was her growing involvement with 'Komis', the flamboyant Theodore Komasajevsky, who had directed her in *Take Two From One* and was shortly to do so again in *Le Cocu Magnifique*. He was, she would say later, her guru (others thought Svengali a more appropriate description), developing an enormous influence over her. He was not as good-looking as Jack at that time and was considerably older, being fifty to Peggy's twenty-three, but he was immensely attractive to young women and a dedicated womaniser nicknamed 'come-and-seduce-me' in the trade. So Peggy, whose marriage had failed in all but name largely due to physical incompatibility, found herself being courted not by just one older man with a strong physical appetite but by two. In the event she was to choose Komis, which is not surprising as he was part of her own world.

With the Old Vic season and its challenges looming ever closer, early in 1932 she moved in with him in spite of the scandal this provoked. He was her guide and mentor as well as her lover. The following year she married him, shutting her mind to the scepticism of her friends who said openly that his genius as a director was only matched by the scale of his infidelities. Their pessimism proved correct: within a year of his marriage Komis had left Peggy for a young American dancer. But in spite of the pain he caused her, she was to remain grateful to him. 'With Komis', she told Michael Billington, 'I always felt I was the pupil and he was the master and he was very inspiring. I learned from him how to approach a part, how to analyse a role, how important it was to understand the whole conception of the play. I realised from him that the whole is more important than the individual part.' Jack Priestley could not have given her that.

Sudden attraction, infatuation or passion can strike anyone at any age, but Priestley's behaviour over his romance with Peggy Ashcroft was more like that of an adolescent than of a mature adult of thirty-six – since he was eighteen he had had no time to grow up or relax. First there had been the war, then Cambridge, then marriage to his first serious girlfriend, two babies, his involvement with Jane, the birth of another child, Pat's early death and a second marriage. After that, until *The Good Companions* released him from financial anxiety, there was the endless nightmare of making enough money to keep a wife and several children. Through it all he had kept going a constant flow of essays, journalism and books.

Suddenly there was plenty of money and he did not need to rush headlong into the next piece of work; he could stop and draw breath. It was at this point that he met Peggy Ashcroft. She was good-looking, dark, fine-featured, and talented. She was a tragic Desdemona and an exquisite Juliet. Priestley's enchantment with the theatre had endured since he had fallen in love, aged eleven, with Cinderella and remained a magic world for him, a door through which he could escape into another world. When he met Peggy, he was nineteen again and she was his very own Juliet. She taught the torches to burn bright.

A strange footnote to 1931 and possibly a sign of Priestley's overwrought state comes in Graham Greene's autobiography, *Ways of Escape.* With three published novels to his name and a moderate success with one, *The Man Within,* he had set out to write 'a book to please which, with luck, might be made into a film'. It was *Stamboul Train,* the idea for which came from a journey he had made on the Orient Express. Just as he heard that the book had been chosen by the English Book Society he was informed that he was being sued for libel by J. B. Priestley.

Priestley had taken a character in the book called Savory to be a portrait of himself, as Savory was described by Greene as a popular novelist in the manner of Dickens, a phrase that had been used of Priestley. Greene writes that he was sure Priestley 'really believed that this all-but-unknown writer was attacking him: he acted in good faith'. As Greene was also published by Heinemann the matter was settled by some twenty pages being reprinted and Heinemann deducting the cost from his royalties – except that as there were none 'they were quietly added to my increasing debt to the firm'. Later he looked back on it with amusement, even generosity, but it nearly stopped his career in its tracks.

CHAPTER 14

Time and the Dramatist

In January 1932 Priestley wrote to Davison that he had broken with Peggy at the end of November and been installed back in Well Walk for Christmas, which had proved enjoyable: 'I am really very fond of Jane and she was taking it very badly. She was really wretched and ill – and then I missed the children . . . I'm not at all unhappy and Jane's been very nice since I've been back and really we're getting on better than for a year or two, though we don't talk openly yet about the events of last summer.'

Jane was now superintending the move to The Grove, which would take place at the beginning of February. Priestley thought he must be the best-paid reviewer in England for the *Standard* was giving him £60 for 1200 words. The London version of *The Good Companions* play was coming off while the tour was doing fairly well. Having his book adapted had given him a taste for writing an original play of his own. He had written one for Peggy in two weeks flat, 'but in the circumstances I could hardly proceed with it as it would only have increased the talk, of which there was plenty, so I scrapped it.' In the meantime he was finishing *Faraway*, which, most unusually for him, he had started over a year before.

The family moved into The Grove, and a photograph taken at the christening of Thomas the following April shows Jane looking serenely beautiful. 'In spite of the not-quite-healed wounds from last year, Jane and I are happy together. The arrival of young Thomas has made her even happier and has pleased me too. He's a fine lad,' Priestley wrote to Davison.

Although he did not finish *Faraway* until February 1932, Heinemann brought it out at the end of June that year. Priestley told Davison that

It will not be as much liked, I fear, as the two long novels and I'm afraid it's not as good . . . but a lot of good work went into it and there are passages here and there that seem to me better than anything else I've ever done. The fact is, I tried to do something very difficult in this novel and unfortunately somewhere in the middle I got rather bored with the whole *technique* of story-telling – if you see what I mean. By the way, DON'T – for God's sake – imagine for a moment there is anything autobiographical in this novel (I'm terribly afraid some people will think that), because I planned the whole story, including *every detail* of the final scene, long before our fuss last year.

The new house, he said, was one 'of the loveliest things you ever saw. I sit in Coleridge's old room typing this letter; I see nothing from my window but Kenwood and the slope of the Heath, and our own flower beds below, or our neighbour, Gladys Cooper, still beautiful, eating breakfast outside in pyjamas.'

Faraway suffered from its long gestation, not to mention the traumatic events that held up its progress. But one can only feel that Priestley is being ingenuous when he begs Davison not to see it as autobiographical.

Rather like the ill-fated *Adam in Moonshine*, Priestley appears to have started out to write one kind of book and ended up with another, for it begins as a treasure hunt with thriller overtones, turns into a diatribe against colonialism and the exploitation of natives, and ends up in the genre of a women's paperback romance. Its hero, William Dursley, is a conventional young man, a maltster in a small Suffolk town, a conscientious worker whose hobby is playing chess. Into his life crashes his vulgar, drunken uncle, an ex-South Seas trader, bearing a map of an uncharted island full of hidden riches. This is no pirates' treasure, however, but a source of pitchblende from which radium is extracted. To keep its whereabouts safe he has given the details of the longitude of the island to one old colleague and the latitude to another. He is then taken ill but before he dies he begs William to go and find the 'treasure', telling him the names of the two men who hold the clues, Commander Goodchild and T. E. Riley. The rest of the story deals with William's quest.

The reviewers indeed found it disappointing. So, finally, did Priestley. Hugh Walpole, though, was absorbed in it and five minutes after finishing it wrote to 'dearest Jack': 'I'm amazed at the way you've "got" the South Seas.' It was the 'picaresque and spiritual aspect' of travel that had moved him so much and 'knowing what you were going through when you wrote it makes it all so personal to me that I have no idea what I should feel if I *didn't* know. It is *rich*, full of plums and variety . . .' But he criticised the character-drawing: 'I feel that at the time your imagination was so deeply moved by actual people in your own life that you saw these people "faraway".'

Priestley finished a second, lighter novel that year, *Wonder Hero*. Charlie Habble, keen amateur footballer, works nightshifts at a factory. After a lunchtime spent in a pub with a journalist, he falls asleep at work, neglects what he is supposed to do and there is an explosion from which he inadvertently emerges as the 'wonder hero'. Taken up by the journalist, he is whisked up to London for two weeks of the high life, during which he falls in love. He is suddenly summoned north to the bedside of a dying aunt, and returns to find that the sensation-seekers have moved on; no one cares any more about the 'wonder hero'. But he has come out of it well. Hero or no, he has a cheque for £500 from the newspaper, has had a wonderful time and, in the end, he also gets the girl. Priestley described the book, somewhat grandiosely, as a deliberately polemical, journalistic social-moral fable in which he had set out to contrast the high life of London with the Depression-ridden streets of the Midlands town from which Charlie was plucked.

But the most significant event of 1932 was the production of *Dangerous Corner*, which marked Priestley's emergence as a dramatist and his entry into his magic world. As his friend the late Gareth Lloyd Evans, academic and theatre critic, wrote in his important assessment of Priestley's dramatic work, *J. B. Priestley the Dramatist* (Heinemann, 1974):

> He gives a constant impression that, even in his imaginative writing, he is never far away, in his inner mind, from a world of footlights and greasepaint, and the old fourpenny balcony on a Saturday night. The word 'magic' is never absent long from his writing . . . Even in the harsher moments, which he has often experienced, when money has frustrated a scheme, or a play has turned sour early, the deep under-swell of the romantic captive man can still be heard.

Priestley wrote thirty-nine plays. Some, like *Bees on the Boat Deck* and *The Roundabout,* have sunk without trace. Others, such as *I've Been Here Before, They Came to a City* and *Time and the Conways,* are revived from time to time. A handful, including *Dangerous Corner, When We Are Married* and *An Inspector Calls,* have rarely been out of the theatrical repertoire since they were written.

Dangerous Corner is often described as 'one of Priestley's "Time Plays" ', but although this is not strictly accurate it would seem appropriate now to set out briefly the theories that came to fascinate, indeed obsess, him. They are pertinent not only to his work but to how he viewed life from then on. The 1930s was an era of breakthroughs in scientific knowledge, in particular growing awareness of Einstein's revolutionary Theory of Relativity. The works that directly influenced Priestley were E. A. Abbott's *Flatland,* J. W. Dunne's *An Experiment with Time* and *The Serial Universe,* and P. D. Ouspensky's *The New Model of the Universe.*

In *Flatland* Abbott describes a two-dimensional world whose inhabitants can only experience anything in terms of width and length. When they see a three-dimensional person or object they cannot recognise it as being in the same time zone as themselves. A ball, for instance, appears only as a succession of concentric circles of varying diameter, a movement in time. From this Abbott infers that it is possible that our own world might have a number of dimensions which we are unable to discern. But should they exist and should we be able to perceive them, they would appear to us as movements in time.

J. W. Dunne is preoccupied not only by time but by dreams, another subject of compelling interest to Priestley which he discusses in a number of essays. By the use of complex mathematics, Dunne sets out to conduct an experiment, based on individual experiences of dreams, designed to show both the complicated nature of time itself and of an individual's experience of it. The best exposition of Priestley's understanding of this theory is to be found in *J. B. Priestley the Dramatist,* in which Lloyd Evans writes:

> Insofar as they are apposite to, and utilised in, Priestley's work they [Dunne's theories] may be simply stated. First, that in the inchoate structure and content of a dream, what are usually

termed past, present and future co-exist and are incapable of being disentangled; second, that the old distinctions between past, present and future are meaningless, and that their co-existence is a powerful and valid reality; third that there exists a *regressus ad infinitum.*

The first part of *An Experiment with Time*, he continues, is like reading a quaint account of an expedition into the interior of a dark but exciting continent. 'There is a strong *ad hoc* feeling about it but, nevertheless, his account is extremely persuasive and, at times, has an emotional vibrancy about it which strongly suggests utter mystery, intrepid exploring.'

The theory of *regressus ad infinitum* put simply is that you, the observer, can see an object in front of you; while doing so you are aware that you are observing it; so within you there must be another observer observing you while you observe the object. Taken to its logical conclusion, therefore, the conscious mind consists of an endless series of observers. However, this only applies to things on earth. According to Dunne, there is also an infinite number of dimensions and times beyond our present life, each of which contains all previous dimensions and times, which go on for ever. The sum of all these times represents real time, just as the sum of all observers represents the real Ego. At death, Man enters the fourth dimension, absorbs the sum of his three-dimensional life, and moves towards a fifth. This process, too, goes on for ever, through sixth, seventh, innumerable dimensions. The advance from one dimension to another is a new immortality: thus the infiniteness of time ensures immortality.

The third influence, that of P. D. Ouspensky, is different again. According to his initial theory, time exists around a circle so that all the happenings of a person's life are, theoretically, repeatable; with the possibility therefore that we continually relive our lives. However, later he posited that higher intelligences might not move forever in this circle but eventually begin to ascend out of it into an upward spiral until they reach a higher and different dimension. Conversely, lower intelligences, 'criminals and lunatics', move down their spiral until they cease to exist. Priestley found the possibilities of the upward spiral theory exciting for it would mean that under certain circumstances an individual might, while moving upwards, be able to look down on the lower reaches of the track on which he is travelling and so view the past. Special 'chosen people', having knowledge of this, might then actually be able to look down on another person's cycle of the spiral which would help them avoid mistakes, crises and dangers as they loom up in front of them once again.

As Lloyd Evans points out, the most obvious shared characteristic of all three writers is that they imply immortality without a deity and the consequent need for a faith combined with religious practice and doctrine. However, Priestley did not accept every aspect of the theories, recognising flaws in all three. He found in them a sense of design, pattern and survival: 'The old dreams of the alchemists, and the new dreams of the time-explorers, both enshrine an abiding human craving for controlled exploration into the unknown,' he wrote.

It says much for *Dangerous Corner* that it continues to appeal to theatre audiences. Like Ben Jonson and *The Alchemist*, Priestley wrote his first play in a week, chiefly, he said, 'to prove that a man might write long novels and yet be able to write effectively, using the strictest economy, for the stage'. In Act I he assembles his group of middle-class, comfortably-off characters for a dinner party. They are not people in the round; their function is to service the ingenious plot. During the first Act we learn that Martin Caplan, Robert's brother, shot himself to avoid the disgrace he would bring on himself when it became known that he had embezzled money from the family business. A young guest, Olwen, takes a cigarette from a box which, when opened, plays the Wedding March. She recognises the box as one she had seen in Martin's cottage, makes a casual remark to that effect, and triggers off a series of events and self-revelations which have devastating consequences.

From the revelations in Act II we learn that none of the apparently friendly relationships is as it seems, and it also becomes clear that there is more to Martin's suicide than has so far met the eye: it was not he who stole the money. In Act III comes the twist. We are where we were at the beginning of Act I. The same sequence of events occurs and the cigarette box is handed to Olwen, but this time nothing comes of it and the evening progresses as planned. The characters have successfully negotiated the dangerous corner.

In the 1930s there were no subsidised theatres at which a new play could be put on, which meant that every production was even more of a risk than it is today, not least because backers had to be found to launch any such enterprise. As Priestley had decided he wanted to start at the top, in the West End, producing *Dangerous Corner* was costly. He chose, therefore, to form his own production company, persuading several backers to join him in the enterprise.

A close involvement by the dramatist with a production would become a hallmark of a Priestley play, something he shared with Noël Coward and the actor–playwright Emlyn Williams. He was so fascinated by every aspect of it that he acquired a reputation for wanting to do everything himself. Gareth Lloyd Evans notes that some people found him difficult to work with, but his plays attracted some of the best actors and directors. The biggest 'name' in *Dangerous Corner* was Flora Robson and its director was a real star, Tyrone Guthrie, whose difficulty was not with the author but with the script. In his autobiography, *A Life in the Theatre*, he writes:

> In the original production none of the actors was over forty and all were experienced and efficient people. In a week they knew the words backwards. In two weeks we all felt we had explored the play's narrow limits of characterisation and philosophy. There was another week to go before we opened. For three more days we rehearsed, the performance at each run-through became slicker but less interesting and more perfunctory. With the author's permission we knocked off until a dress rehearsal on the night before we opened.

Dangerous Corner opened and was damned by the critics of the daily and evening papers. By the end of its first week the backers proposed pulling out. But the following Sunday, both Ivor Brown and James Agate, in the *Observer* and the *Sunday Times*, gave it favourable notices and Priestley, taking an enormous gamble, decided to risk a large proportion of his *Good Companions* profits in backing it himself. For a few more days its fate hung in the balance but then, as *The Good Companions* had before it, it took off. Audiences filled the theatre – but, in the words of the Duke of Wellington, it had been a damned close-run thing.

Commenting on this play and her stepfather's work in general, Angela Wyndham Lewis, herself an actress, agreed that Priestley was a very good dramatist and *Dangerous Corner* a clever play. She has reservations, however, about his female characters: 'He has two kinds of women in his plays: the eager, cheeky girl – you know the one – and the mysterious kind, the moon goddess who is totally unreal. Yet he had a house full of girls, five girls, girls around him all the time, but none of his women are remotely like any of us!'

Since its first production *Dangerous Corner* has never ceased to intrigue audiences, although Priestley said it had never been a favourite of his, 'for it seems to me to be merely an ingenious box of tricks'. What then, is the reason for its abiding popularity? It is not as well written as *An Inspector Calls* nor as moving as *Time and the Conways*. Gareth Lloyd Evans perhaps best answers the question:

> The greater part of English audiences has remained relatively unsophisticated, despite the proliferation of forms of entertainments and dramatic modes in the twentieth century; despite the siren calls of poetic drama, expressionism, alienism, film, television, theatre-in-the-round, the average theatre goer takes with him to the theatre a set of built-in influences which await a stimulant. It is Priestley's feeling for these reflexes which account for the success of *Dangerous Corner.*

Priestley recognised that the average theatregoer requires satisfaction of paradoxical cravings for illusion and reality. Going to the theatre is a way of escaping from day-to-day life, of relaxing and being entertained, but an audience balks at what it sees as too far-fetched or unreal. Its members do not wish to have their imaginations stretched too far.

Yet, even if this is so, as Priestley himself acknowledged, the success or failure of theatrical production is largely determined by chance and accident:

> Theatre people tend to be superstitious, and I don't blame them. Once through the stage door, you might as well believe in astrology. Some plays attract good fortune, others bad. Nothing can be done about it. By the time you realise – and this may be weeks before the London opening – that a production is heavy with doom, you are helplessly committed, surrounded by people who have contracts and you can only brace yourself to meet the next disaster. On the other hand, if the gods have decided in your favour, then everything comes right . . .

Dangerous Corner remains popular because it intrigues those who have not seen it before: they want to know what happens next. For those who revisit it, the twist in the plot never fails: by stopping time in its tracks, the playwright gives his protagonists a second chance, and who would not relish such in real life?

Certainly Priestley had the last laugh over those who criticised his first essay into stage drama. If the play had been taken off at the end of that first week it is doubtful that it would ever have been heard of again. 'It was received in Shaftesbury Avenue so tepidly that only my own insistence carried it past those five performances. It then became the most popular play I have ever written. I doubt if there is any country in the world possessing a playhouse that has not seen *Dangerous Corner*, or if any other play written during the last thirty years has had more performances.'[1]

When the play was up and running in the summer of 1932 Priestley wrote to Davison, expressing satisfaction that it was successful when plays were going down like ninepins as the slump continued. However, he thought the collapse of America was a good thing for humanity because it completely 'broke' the legend of American success and the spell of a 'mechanical material hog-philosophy'. Interestingly, in view of the present debate, Davison felt that Britain's future, both economic and political, lay in Europe.

CHAPTER 15

An English Journey

In May 1933 the Priestleys bought their 'country cottage', Billingham, a large seventeenth-century manor house on the Isle of Wight close to the picture-book village of Godshill. It stood in fifteen acres of ground and, according to legend, was haunted and had a passage running underground to Carisbrooke Castle.

In a letter to Davison dated 27 May Priestley boasted that he bought it for the bargain price of two thousand pounds, but 'I am spending a good deal of money on my two houses, furniture, pictures and so forth because these things are very cheap here now and are good investments – if prosperity returns, you have bought wisely; if all goes bust, you still have your beautiful things instead of worthless bits of paper.' He also said that he was not offended by what Davison had said about *Faraway* (unlike Walpole, he did not think it worked), 'but I still think it better than most of you do'. He hoped *Wonder Hero*, which was about to be published, would go down better with his friend and everyone else.

For the next six years the Priestleys divided their time between Highgate and Billingham. The family remember both as exquisitely decorated and furnished. The daughters recall vividly that when it came to interior design Jane was an artist. 'We had these beautiful, beautiful houses,' Angela said. 'My mother made the most beautiful houses I've ever seen. This was, of course, after my stepfather began to make money but when she had an interest in something she would make it her business to learn as much as she could about it. For example, when she wanted to know about really good furniture she got to know people at the absolute top, the experts at the Victoria and Albert Museum, and went to them for advice and guidance.[1]

'They weren't House-and-Garden, they weren't trendy or

fashionable or in a "look-at-this" style, not at all. They had her own special stamp on them.' She went on, 'She was also a marvellous housekeeper. She was not, I have to say, a very good cook but she was a brilliant teacher of other people and we had the most fabulous food.' According to Barbara,[2] Jane knew all about French cooking from spending time in France and Angela remembers that when they were in the Isle of Wight, Jane 'got to know all the fishermen and they brought her really good fresh fish, lobsters and so on which they caught for her specially. It was like that with everything. When she wanted some special quilts for the beds, she found ladies in Wales who could make them for her. That's how she functioned. And she always had the most marvellous clothes. She used to go to Molyneux for them and when we were older we were sent there too.'

Barbara said that people loved working for Jane: 'She had a sort of Welsh friendliness with the people who worked for her. Our cook, Miss Pudduck, must have come to Mummy when she was only about nineteen or twenty and Mummy taught her right from the beginning. In my opinion Miss Pudduck became one of the best cooks in England.'

There is no doubt in the minds of the Priestleys' children that Jane contributed substantially to their father's success, a point emphasised by Barbara, in spite of the fact that both she and Sylvia still feel that much of their childhood was far from happy. Jane, Sylvia said, was immensely hospitable and well organised: 'During those years a huge number of people came to stay at Billingham, people like Basil Dean, the Gollanczes, a wonderful sculptor called Maurice Lambert, brother of the composer Constant Lambert, and, of course, Hugh Walpole. We all liked him so much as he was always so kind to us children. He'd buy us wonderful presents at the Medici Gallery or somewhere like that, pictures and things, which were rather grown up for children but which we've all still got. He was a lovely, lovely man.'[3]

From the early days at College House Jane had provided for her husband what Mary Priestley described as a 'rhythm', which enabled him to work as he did.[4] Unless he was travelling or on holiday, Priestley's day followed the same pattern from his marriage to Jane until almost the end of his life. After breakfast he would work until shortly before lunch when he would pause for a drink. After lunch he would have a break during which, if the weather was suitable, he would go for a walk. He would then have a light tea before returning to his study to work until – at least in the old days – it was time to change for dinner. He would pound away at his ancient typewriter facing a wall, with cotton wool stuffed in his ears to keep out the world.

As the girls reached the age of around nine, they were sent to boarding schools, indeed to a succession of them. Sylvia found it deeply unsettling: 'We seemed to go from school to school rather on Jane's whim. As there was so little difference between Mary and I in age, we tended to be sent together and we went to schools in Hampstead, Highgate, then Bedales – I actually enjoyed it there – then to Moreton Green, which I really loved but I'd no sooner settled in than I was moved again, to Langford. We were never asked what we thought about it. Of course by the time I was coming up for exams the war was on and our school was evacuated to Shropshire.'[5]

They all remember emotional tension in the home. Throughout his marriage to Jane, Priestley was unfaithful to her. He was quite frank about it with close friends and, later, with his children. The enormous energy that produced the constant flow of creative work also encompassed sex. Could he ever have been faithful, his friend Diana Collins once asked him. He doubted it. 'I was always looking for something,' he told her, 'but I never found it.' But he had had 'a lot of fun with a lot of nice women'.

'Jack', Diana Collins wrote, 'was a deeply sensual man but always gentle and personal. "Sex", he would say, "is a psychological act."' On another occasion she told him she truly believed he could *talk* a woman into bed, he had such a richly seductive voice. 'He agreed, rather pleased.'[6]

Sylvia felt that 'Escapism was the name of the game. He had an eye for the ladies without a doubt and I think if you're a very successful author they throw themselves at you. I've seen it myself at parties, how people would come up to him and suck up like mad. I remember being absolutely astonished at the sort of ladies that came on like vampires. I don't know, but I think my father just thought it was lovely and I can see it was very flattering. And he did have that very strong sex drive but then you've only got to read about half the classic writers to see he wasn't alone in that.' He was, he admitted once to Barbara, a weak man where women were concerned.

There were other problems, too. Unlike Pat Jane never

found herself at a loss in literary company or at the lunches, dinner-parties and country weekends she arranged for their friends, but nevertheless she had to live with the knowledge that it was Priestley most of them came to see. Years later she told Angela: 'My trouble was that I loved reading and always thought writers would be like their books. But neither Bevan [Wyndham Lewis] nor Jack were the least like what they wrote.' A clever, gifted woman in her own right, she was continually sidelined. 'Sometimes, you know,' she told Angela, 'we'd go to a party and I'm standing there and someone comes rushing over to me with a great smile on their face. Then they say, "Oh, hello, Mrs Priestley, I've always wanted to meet your husband," and it doesn't help to know that this happens to the wives of lots of famous husbands.'

She also had to deal with Priestley's moods, especially the bouts of depression that were concealed so well from the world. Mary Priestley suggested that they might have stemmed from his experiences in the First World War 'and I think possibly also it was to do with the time when his first wife died and he was never able properly to mourn her. There was never a time when he could truly go into his sad feelings, because he immediately had to care for three children and another on the way. What he did was to force himself to write that book about English comic characters. He said it was mostly for financial reasons, but I'm sure it was really because he couldn't allow himself time for his sadness or to mourn or to try and find peace in himself that these depressions kept coming back.'

There were spectacular rows, especially, the daughters remembered, at Christmas, that notorious season of supposed goodwill from which few families emerge unscathed, but Priestley never lost the ability to play enchanting games with his children and encourage them in any interest they took up. 'He was a great one for clowning,' Sylvia recalled. 'I remember we were at some kind of music festival once, everyone being *very* cultural, when Dad appeared and said to everyone, "The party's been invaded by mad dwarfs." Then he disappeared only to reappear again shortly after, all twisted up as a mad dwarf!'

In the autumn of 1933 Priestley set out on the journey that formed the basis, in the opinion of many, of his best non-fiction book, *English Journey*. Its lengthy sub-title is: 'Being a rambling but truthful account of what one man saw and heard and felt and thought during a journey through England during the autumn of the year 1933'. He dedicated it to Jane, 'who has shared so much of this England with me', and baby Tom, 'whose England this is', adding 'with the Author's love'. 'Full of amusing characters, unexpected happenings, shrewd, humorous and racy comments', says the blurb on the most recent edition, quoting a review from *Harper's Bazaar* that must have been written in 1934 in an attempt to present the book as a light-weight travel journal, a meander through the England of Shakespeare, Wordsworth and cream teas.

It is not at all like that. In the early 1990s when it was read on BBC Radio 4, it became a talking point everywhere. It was, said listeners, so topical. 'It's just like now,' was a comment heard again and again.

Jack Priestley's odyssey begins in sunlight with his journey by motor coach to Southampton. His driving skills had improved little since the days when Pat had written exasperatedly that they never seemed to be able to go out without some mishap or another, and the previous year he had been involved in a minor accident in Newport. His problem, he would say, was that he found it difficult to concentrate sufficiently on what he was doing and on that occasion, lost in thought, he had driven into a lamp-post. After that he relied on either public transport or his chauffeur-driven Daimler. He found the new motor coaches an admirable way of getting around.

As he climbed aboard in London with the minimum of clothes, his beloved portable typewriter, 'the usual paraphernalia of pipes, note-books, rubbers, paper fasteners, razor blades, pencils, Muirhead's *Blue Guide to England,* Stamp and Beaver's *Geographic and Economic Survey* and, for reading in bed, the tiny thin paper edition of *The Oxford Book of English Prose*', he marvelled at the luxury of this means of transport:

> It was the first motor coach I had ever travelled in and I was astonished at its speed and comfort. I never wish to go any faster. And as for comfort, I doubt if even the most expensive motors – those gigantic, three-thousand-pound machines – are as determinedly and ruthlessly comfortable as these new motor coaches. They are voluptuous, sybaritic, of doubtful morality. This is how the ancient Persian monarchs would have travelled,

if they'd known the trick of it . . . they have annihilated the old
distinction between rich and poor travellers.

His journey takes him from Southampton to Salisbury, to Bristol
and through the Cotswolds to the industrial heartlands of the
Midlands and the north, to Bradford and finally, through East
Anglia, home. As the journey progresses small shadows appear,
then periods of light and shade, and finally he enters darkness
from which emerges what must be among the most savage, bitter
writing on the state of the nation in the 1930s that has ever been
published.

The first small cloud appears when he approaches Salisbury
through a countryside that has reminded him of the old
landscape artists, of Hazlitt,

> of the mediaeval England that must have looked like this through
> county after county . . . it reached its peak when we crossed the
> spur of the Downs, looked into the distant vale and saw, far
> away in the autumnal haze, the spire of Salisbury Cathedral
> like a pointed finger, faintly luminous. This is a noble view
> of England, and Constable himself could not have contrived
> a better light for it. You have before you a Shakespearean
> landscape, with shreds of Arden all about, glimpses of parks
> of Navarre and Illyrian distances. So we descended upon
> Salisbury.

Then the mood changes abruptly: 'Once in the city, I could
not see the Cathedral: but I saw the Labour Exchange and,
outside it, as pitiful a little crowd of the unemployed as ever
I have seen. No building cathedrals for them, poor devils: they
would think themselves lucky if they were given a job helping
to build rabbit-hutches.'

In Bristol he wanders round the docks and quays, musing on
the city's great past, when Cabot and Hakluyt sailed on their epic
voyages, and its associations with writers, Coleridge, Chatterton,
Southey and Savage, and the slave trade, on whose evil proceeds
Bristol once flourished 'and is now only a reminder of man's
cruelty; the port, depending on the shallow, twisting Avon,
is only a shadow of its former self'. But Bristol, he writes,
optimistically, lives on and he lists its attractions: the new

university, the pleasant villas on its outskirts, Bristol Milk sherry
by the glass, the Spanish Main richness of the streets of a city
which is also a port. Then he walks straight into a meeting
being held by Oswald Mosley's Fascist blackshirt movement.
He goes to a meeting of the unemployed in a Labour Hall
and watches an elderly speaker rouse an apathetic audience to
enthusiasm and hope. Our class, the working class, the speaker
says, 'have become nothing but donkeys'. He describes the latest
'pettifogging' welfare scheme for giving out tiny strips of land
for growing vegetables and breeding rabbits. ' "Radicalism," he
bellowed. "Talk about radicalism. I remember it fifty years ago.
And they were real Radicals then. Jesse Collins. He wanted three
acres for every man – and a cow. Now they've cut the three acres
down to inches, and instead of a cow it's rabbits." At which they all
roared.' And the son of Jonathan Priestley, the Bradford radical,
roared with them.

The Cotswolds provided pleasant relief. At Broadway, which
must have brought back memories of that extraordinary summer,
he visits Snowshill Manor, now owned by the National Trust.

> The house itself had a Gothic craziness. There was no sense,
> though an infinite antique charm in its assembled oddity of
> roofs, gables, windows and doorways. It might have been plucked
> straight out of *Hoffmann's Tales* . . . There was a tiny courtyard
> between the house proper and a large outhouse, which had on
> its wall a painted wooden knight whose hand was waiting to
> strike a big bell. In this courtyard were a score or so of white
> pigeons that rose and fluttered at our approach, so that for a
> second there seemed to be a blizzard raging.
>
> When the last pigeon had gone creaking to the roof, the
> courtyard and the manor house, the whole valley sank again
> into the deep quiet. Not a mouse stirred. Round the walls were
> coats-of-arms and painted inscriptions. Beyond the outhouse
> were descending squares of garden, where a stream wandered
> from one clear carp pond to another, slipping past clumps of
> miniature box, marjoram and rue and thyme, and the shadow
> of yews. Olivia and Malvolio would have been at home anywhere
> in this garden.

He was fortunate that the owner *was* at home, 'one of the last
of a famous company, the eccentric English country gentry, the

odd and delightful fellows who have lived just as they pleased, who have built Follies, held fantastic beliefs, and laid mad wagers. But why English? Was there not Don Quixote? You could have settled *him* into this house in a jiffy. I half expected to meet him.'

The owner showed him round the house with its crazy, fascinating collection of old clothes, model toys, ancient musical instruments, spinning wheels, sedan chairs, dozens of clocks and much, much more. It is all there to this day and still looks as he described it, 'like the early illustrations to *The Old Curiosity Shop*, with its shelves of tools, painted saints, tomes of plainsong, swords, daggers, wooden platters and I know not what else'. The Cotswold interlude is the last in the book where the sun shines for any length of time. Gloucestershire and Oxfordshire have not escaped the Depression, Priestley considers, but at least most of the people in the villages seem to be getting by with just about enough to live on.

Coventry and Birmingham provide an opportunity for him to discuss their industrial past and their place in the economy of the country. Priestley visits Cadbury's model village at Bournville and notes it as an example of what can be achieved by a moral manufacturer who had thought it only his duty to provide his employees with good housing, decent schools, access to health care and a wide variety of social facilities. A booklet provides him with some interesting statistics:

They are taken from an average of seven years ending 1931. Death-rate per thousand: England and Wales 12.1; Birmingham 11.6; Bournville 6.5. Infantile mortality per 1000 live births: England and Wales 69; Birmingham 72; Bournville 56. Some years ago, the heights and weights, age for age, of Bournville children and children from one of the bad areas of Birmingham were compared, and the Bournville children were from two to four inches taller and between four and nine pounds heavier. And the Estate [Bournville] is flourishing.

When he resumes his journey and travels on to the Black Country, we descend into the pit. It is Sunday. The weather is cold and raw, everything permeated by dripping fog. He has been visiting and lunching with businessmen in West Bromwich, one of whom takes him to his warehouse in a street Priestley calls 'Rusty Lane'. It is this passage that had such a marked effect on 1990s' radio listeners:

He keeps sheets of steel there, and no doubt any place is good enough to keep sheets of steel in; but I do not think I could let even a sheet of steel stay long in Rusty Lane. I have never seen such a picture of grimy desolation as that street offered me. If you put it, brick for brick, into a novel people would not accept it, would condemn you as a caricaturist and talk about Dickens. The whole neighbourhood is mean and squalid, but this particular street seemed the worst of all. It would not matter very much – though it would matter – if only metal were kept there; but it happens that people live there, children are born there and grow up there. I saw some of them. I was being shown one of the warehouses where steel plates were stacked in chill gloom, and we heard a bang and rattle on the roof. The boys, it seems, were throwing stones again. They were always throwing stones on that roof. We went out to find them, but only found three frightened little girls, who looked at us with round eyes in wet smudgy faces. No, they hadn't done it, the boys had done it and the boys had just run away. Where they could run to, I cannot imagine. They need not have run away for me, because I could not blame them if they threw stones and stones and smashed every pane of glass for miles. There ought to be no more of those lunches and dinners, at which political and financial and industrial gentlemen congratulate one another until something is done about Rusty Lane, West Bromwich. While they still exist in their present foul shape, it is idle to congratulate ourselves about anything. They make the whole pomp of government a miserable farce. The Crown, Lords and Commons are the Crown, Lords and Commons of Rusty Lane, West Bromwich. In the heart of the great empire on which the sun never sets, in the land of hope and glory, Mother of the Free, is Rusty Lane, West Bromwich. What do they know of England who only England know? The answer must be Rusty Lane, West Bromwich. And if there is ever another economic conference, let it meet there, in one of the warehouses, and be fed with bread and margarine and slabs of brawn. The delegates have seen one England, Mayfair in the season. Let them see another England next time, West

Bromwich out of season. Out of all seasons except the winter of our discontent.

He progresses slowly through the Black Country, Leicester and Nottingham until he reaches his beloved West Riding. Here we learn that what prompted the visit, indeed almost the whole journey, was a battalion reunion in Bradford. He explains at some length the unusual make-up of Bradford's 'German quarter' and not only the financial but cultural riches that Germans and German Jews had brought it. But the war had changed everything and the immigrants had vanished almost without trace. Without them Bradford was the poorer. Such exchanges, he writes, are good for everyone. In another disturbing echo of today, he goes on:

> Just lately, when we offered hospitality to some distinguished German-Jews who had been exiled by the Nazis, the leader-writers in the cheap Press began yelping again about keeping the Foreigner Out. Apart from the miserable meanness of the attitude itself – for the great England, the England admired throughout the world, is the England that keeps open house, the refuge of Mazzini, Marx, Lenin – history shows us that the countries that have opened their doors have gained, just as the countries that have driven out large numbers of their citizens, for racial, religious or political reasons, have always paid dearly for their intolerance.

He moves on to Saturday night, the battalion reunion and his first piece of writing on the war since his letters from the trenches. He tells how the various battalions of the Bradford PALS, full of young men of above average intelligence, physique and enthusiasm, were all sent to the attack on the Somme in 1916 'where they were butchered with remarkable efficiency'. He remembers the gangs of lads with whom he used to roam as a boy, and how it might be thought he would look them up to talk over old times, but he cannot 'for the men who were boys when I was a boy are dead. They were slaughtered in their youth', killed 'by greed and muddle and monstrous cross purposes, by old men gobbling and roaring in clubs, by diplomats working underground like monocled moles, by journalists wanting a good story, by hysterical women waving flags, by grumbling debenture-holders, by strong, silent, be-ribboned asses, by fear, or apathy or downright lack of imagination'.

Men pour into the upstairs room of the tavern where the reunion is being held and he finds himself searching for familiar faces, 'but I knew I would not see the ones who had been closest to me in friendship for they had all been killed'. For a moment he forgets the cruelty of life and believes they will all be there, the dead and the living, and that if he had climbed the stairs and found Irving Ellis and Herbert Waddington and Charlie Burns waiting for him, pint in hand, 'I would not have been shocked nor even surprised, would not have remembered that they had returned from distant graves ... I have many vivid dreams and the dead move casually through them.'

The emotional evening wears on. There is a dinner, speeches, the men 'sweat like bulls' over their roast beef and apple tart. Eventually he finds a handful of comrades. Scenes from the front, frozen in time, appear before his eyes, as clear as if they had happened yesterday. The ex-soldiers drink the Loyal Toast, then a toast to the Dead. He meets the survivors of his own platoon in a small room downstairs. Among them is that 'little Padd O', whom he had sent off with the rations before the world blew up on him. 'Nay, Jack,' Paddy stammers, 'I wasn't gone more than t-ten minutes, and when I c-come back, where you'd been, Jack lad, was nobbut a bloody big hole and I n-never set eyes on you again until tonight.'

Gradually Priestley becomes aware that something is missing. He goes back upstairs and looks around him, searching. He was one of a number of the better-off survivors who had offered to pay for the tickets of any veterans who had been unable to afford the cost of the dinner. But the secretary tells him that the men had been unable to attend even with a free ticket: their clothes were so shabby that they felt ashamed. Priestley is appalled: surely they knew they would have been welcomed if they had turned up in rags? But their pride had not allowed them to come. 'We could drink to the tragedy of the dead; but we could only stare at one another, in pitiful embarrassment, over this tragi-comedy of the living, who had fought for a world that did not want them, who had come back to exchange their uniforms for rags. And who shall restore to them the years that the locust hath eaten?'

He leaves Bradford for the Potteries where he describes visits to factories, including Wedgwood, then to Manchester and Liverpool, the latter with its exotic dockside area inhabited by people from every continent, then north to Tyneside and Teesside and ravaged Jarrow:

> The whole town looked as if it had entered a penniless, bleak Sabbath. The men wore the drawn masks of prisoners of war. A stranger from a distant civilisation, observing the condition of the place and its people, would have arrived at once at the conclusion that Jarrow had offended some celestial emperor of the island and was now being punished. He would never believe us if we told him that in theory this town was as good as any other and that its inhabitants were not criminals but citizens with votes.

Finally, after a less harrowing visit to East Anglia, he returns home and ponders what he has seen and experienced and what it says about the society in which he lives and what it had inflicted on so much of the nation.

> For generations the blackened North toiled and moiled so that England should be rich and the City of London a great power in the world. But now this North is half derelict, and its people, living on in queer ugly places, are shabby, bewildered, unhappy. And I told myself that I would prefer – if somebody must be miserable – to see the people of the City all shabby bewildered and unhappy . . . If Germans had been threatening these towns instead of Want, Disease, Hopelessness and Misery, something would have been done quickly enough. The Dole is part of no plan; it is a mere declaration of intellectual bankruptcy . . . The Labour Exchanges stink of defeated humanity.

It is not difficult to see why, in the 1990s, readings from *English Journey* resonate today. It is, of course, easy to point up the irony of a best-selling writer – who owned a large house in Highgate and a mansion in the Isle of Wight, whose wife was dressed by Molyneux and whose usual means of travel was by chauffeur-driven Daimler – speaking up for the poverty-stricken, hopeless and dispossessed. J. B. Priestley the writer had travelled a long way from the young Jack who had turned the handle of the mangle for his stepmother on washdays in the basement of the house in Manningham, and there is no doubt that he had taken to the upper-middle-class way of life like a duck to water. But every word of *English Journey* had been wrung from his heart and he used all his expertise to put across his case as clearly and effectively as he could: and what carried weight was that he *was* a best-selling writer. Of all the books 'J. B. Priestley' wrote, Jonathan Priestley would surely have been most proud of this one.

CHAPTER 16

Theatre,
Hollywood and Arizona

During the six years between Priestley's completion of *English Journey* and the outbreak of the Second World War, he and Jane seem rarely to have stayed in one place for long. They moved constantly between 3 The Grove and Billingham, and during the winters of 1935–6 and 1937–8 the entire family were in Arizona. The Priestleys spent much of the intervening winter in Egypt. They went abroad for the sake of Jane's health. Now some family members consider it possible that her illnesses were psychosomatic, but the real problems seem to date from shortly after Thomas's birth: he recalled having been told that she had suffered from a severe viral infection. If this is so then her symptoms were similar to those experienced by sufferers from myalgic encephalomyelitis or ME, which develops after severe viral infections such as influenza or hepatitis.

In spite of the wealth and security that he now enjoyed, Priestley's flow of work did not abate, but both it and his journeyings took place in the shadow of forthcoming war. His earnings insulated him from the effects of the Depression but not against the threat posed by the rising tide of fascism in Europe, of which he was all too aware.

However, the pattern of his work changed: between 1933 and 1939 Priestley wrote only three novels but fourteen plays, which included most of his best, though not *An Inspector Calls* which came later. He had learned much from his experience with *Dangerous Corner* and now set up a production company, English Plays Limited. He became co-director of the Duchess Theatre, which gave him a permanent venue for any play he wanted to put on in the West End.

Two major productions followed *Dangerous Corner*: *Laburnum Grove* and the elegiac *Eden End. Laburnum Grove*, written in

1933, was directed by Cedric Hardwicke and opened at the Palace Theatre, Manchester, on 18 November, then, after a brief northern tour, went to the Duchess Theatre. The play is a comedy but, again, has a twist at the end. The setting is the respectable, dull suburban home of the Redferns in Shooter's Green. George Redfern, who works in the paper industry in a job that frequently takes him abroad, has a kindly wife and a daughter with an unpleasant fiancé who is on the make. Also part of the household are two relatives, recently returned from abroad and sponging off George. George is *very* ordinary, considered a soft touch where money is concerned by his daughter, the fiancé and the relatives. Into this placid ménage a bombshell falls. George is not, after all, primarily involved in the paper industry: he is, he informs his family, an international counterfeiter and forger.

Everyone reacts with horror and the fiancé immediately decides to jettison the daughter, while the greedy relations make plans to leave immediately. George's view is pragmatic: he is not only doing what capitalist big business does all the time but is actually helping the country through the Depression:

> Well, a lot of people think this depression in trade is chiefly due to the fact there isn't enough money in circulation. Like playing a game with counters and finding you haven't enough counters to go round. Our organisation – my associates and myself – have been quietly busy these last few years trying to remedy this unhappy state of things.

On the arrival of Inspector Stark from Scotland Yard all of the family, except George's loyal wife, are prepared to save their own skins by informing on him and seeing him go to jail. At which point his wife steps in and explains it has all been a joke. She produces a detective novel in which, she says, they will find the plot that gave George the whole idea. There is much relief all round. Then Inspector Stark returns . . .

Jane had not liked the first act when she read it (which did not please Priestley) but it is interesting that the *Times* critic did not care for it either.[1] However, he found the play improved steadily during Act II and by Act III had become 'entrancing'. Writing after he had seen a much later production, Gareth Lloyd Evans considered George Redfern one of the most attractive characters Priestley created in his whole canon of plays. Audiences loved

Laburnum Grove, there were relatively few production problems and it ran for the rest of the year and a considerable time afterwards.

The spring of 1934 saw Priestley involving himself in yet another medium: film. He had been unhappy not to have been allowed any say in the cinema adaptation of *Benighted,* released under the American title of the novel *The Old Dark House.* Interestingly, this is now considered by film buffs to be a connnoisseur's horror film not least for its star-studded cast, directed by James Whale, which includes Charles Laughton, Ernest Thesiger, Eva Moor, Melvyn Day and Boris Karloff as the sinister servant. (A later remake by Hammer in 1963 flopped.) Now the producer Basil Dean had invited Priestley to write an original film script for the popular Lancashire comedy actress and singer Gracie Fields. In April 1934 he had 'to dash off to Capri with Basil Dean', where the star had a magnificent villa, to gain her approval of his script. The weather was beautiful, there was much lying around on beaches and in gardens and, according to Dean, Priestley and Fields immediately hit it off and were 'very close'.[2] Just how close is a moot point: the notorious eye may have wandered but she was famous for giving over-enthusiastic admirers the brush-off, as the actor Gerald du Maurier had discovered to his chagrin a couple of years earlier. Du Maurier, who could truly have been described as a mateneé idol, had a charismatic effect on most of the young actresses with whom he played and his long-suffering wife put up with a string of fleeting affairs. He always excused his little adventures on the grounds that at heart he remained true to his wife. But Gracie Fields was one of the few on whom the famous du Maurier charm did not work. When he suggested that their relationship became closer, she laughed at him, telling him, in public, that he was far too old.[3]

In a letter to Hugh Walpole on his return from Capri,[4] Priestley informed his friend that he was rushed off his feet. First he had had to meet Jane in Barbados, where she was having a brief holiday, then he had had to go north to Blackpool as much of the story of the film was set there. As a result, there had been no time to see his friends, heaps of letters demanded answers, he had to finish his film script and 'the minute that's done, I have another one to do, for Gaumont-British, to say nothing of the two plays I've promised to do after that'. Presumably the second film, which was to have starred Charles Laughton and to be directed by Alexander Korda, came to nothing as there is no trace of it.

The Gracie Fields film, *Sing As We Go*, was a considerable popular success. The plot is slight. Fields, as a young mill girl, loses her job and goes off to Blackpool in search of work, thus giving plenty of scope for adventures in the famous northern holiday resort. Priestley never rated it but it is interesting that Halliwell's *Filmgoers' Companion* says of it: 'You can almost smell the tripe and onions in this cheerful Gracie Fields' film scripted by J. B. Priestley. As things have happened, it also preserves the most authentic flavour on film of Britain's industrial north in the 1930s.'

The two plays to which he referred were *The Roundabout* and *Eden End*. He recognised early on that the former was simply not going to work, but *Eden End* remained one of his favourite plays. In his note to the published edition he writes of having lived for months in tranquillity with the characters, a departure from the rushed creation of both *Dangerous Corner* and *Laburnum Grove*. 'I found myself wondering how I came to write this particular play, because everything in it is imagined – I have never known any people like the Kirby family – and I know nothing in my own life that would suggest to me this particular theme of the pathetic prodigal daughter. But it gave me great satisfaction to write it.'[5]

It is set in 1912, a period to which he returned a number of times, and is the first of his plays to be permeated with nostalgia and sadness for that lost golden age before the First World War. Like *The Cherry Orchard*, with which it is sometimes compared, it is a play of mood rather than plot. A widowed doctor, who lives with his plain, embittered younger daughter, Lilian, and a son who has been in the colonial service, is unexpectedly visited by his elder daughter, Stella, a supposedly successful actress. She has not been home for many years, not even on the death of her mother. Lilian is hoping to marry the man with whom Stella was involved before she went on the stage and, frightened that she might now lose him, invites Stella's estranged husband, Charles Appleby, to make up the party. Charles is an actor who has never realised his potential, due to his weakness for drink. Gradually we discover the reason Stella has never come home: she could not face telling her family that she is a failure. At the end, she and Charles leave together, resigned to a future of third-rate touring companies and penury, leaving the others to count the cost of her visit.

Eden End went on at the Duchess almost immediately *Laburnum Grove* came off, and marked the beginning of a fruitful and happy collaboration between Priestley and the actor Ralph Richardson. Their friendship lasted throughout their lives. Priestley wrote of Richardson:

> We worked together in five plays, two of which I wrote for him. He has said in print that mine were the speeches which pleased him most, and I am not returning cutlet for cutlet when I say as much about his acting. Just as I am not the 'plain-down-to-earth writer' that many people have called me, Richardson is not, as I have so often seen him described, the ordinary Englishman enlarged. And not simply because of his unusual range and flexibility of tone. His was the only Falstaff of our time. Mixed with his large helping of ordinary elements is one that never came out of the earth. He is a kind of Bully Bottom providing his own enchanted glade. For a while he may seem as commonplace as some familiar town, but then suddenly, above that town, a strange moon is rising. He can be a bank clerk, an insurance agent, a dentist, but very soon mysterious lights and shadows, tones of anguish and ecstasy are discovered in banking, insurance and dentistry.[6]

Richardson's relaxed stage manner belied his perfectionism, and Fabia Drake, who played Stella in that production of *Eden End*, remembered him preparing himself as Charles Appleby before the first night: '. . . a figure in the gloom which rose from a table, moved unsteadily towards a door up-stage and passed, or rather tottered, through it. I reached the box office where there was a sizeable queue and after about half an hour collected my tickets, and, returning through the pass door again, crossed the stage. The figure was still there, still moving unsteadily across the room, still "weaving" unsteadily out of the door.'[7]

Neither of Priestley's next two plays was as successful as *Eden End. Cornelius*, which followed *Eden End* at the Duchess, had Ralph Richardson in the leading role and the play was dedicated to him. Described by Priestley as a satire, it ran for only seven weeks. It was directed by Basil Dean who, as well as working in films, was one of the earliest proponents of what is now described as 'director's theatre'. Priestley admired him but wrote of him that 'actors hated his guts for he could be very sharp-tongued and sarcastic'. Richardson, however, wrote to Dean after the opening night to say how much he had appreciated his direction, that it had taught him a great deal and he hoped they would work together again. They remained firm friends, not least because they shared an interest in vintage cars and powerful motorcycles.[8]

Priestley was disappointed by the reception of *Cornelius*. Shortly after it opened, the writer and critic E. V. Lucas wrote to him suggesting that it might work better if the characters were used again in a sequel and the two plays performed on successive nights. Priestley thought this an interesting idea but doubted that people's memories would carry them through a second play: 'It is really rather a subtle tribute that you and other people should feel that the characters could step out of a particular dramatic frame that encloses them.' But others seemed to think that while he created vivid characters, he put them on stage to do nothing. Priestley refuted this: 'This is quite untrue. My characters, like those of any other dramatist, are conceived quite strictly in relation to the particular action of a particular play and have not really for me any life independent of that action.'

Bees on the Boat Deck, put on the following year, is similarly flawed: as in *Cornelius* the satire is heavy-handed and the characters two-dimensional. The good ship SS *Gloriana*, beached in a creek and representing England, is looked after by two ex-seamen who sailed with her in her great days. She is to be either broken up or used in an experiment to test a new explosive, which will make its inventor rich. A host of other characters appear and disappear, divided roughly into good people who are dull and crooks straight out of Victorian melodrama. In his preface to the published edition of the play Priestley insisted that, while he intended *Bees on the Boat Deck* to be humorous, it was also concerned with the iniquity of present-day society; but it fails on both counts.

Throughout the mid-1930s Priestley was dogged by depression, his 'black moods' as Jane called them. Whether it was due to the failure of his poor plays or some unexplained estrangement between himself and Edward Davison, on 26 October 1934 he sent his old friend a distinctly strange letter, after an unusually lengthy gap in their correspondence. It is not written in his usual relaxed, chatty style but is a formal and stilted résumé of the last year, its tone that of a writer on automatic pilot. The family was well but Mary had given them cause for concern over a year earlier when she had developed paratyphoid. Jane was at Droitwich Spa recovering from 'a mysterious infection, possibly the result of the last two children, which began giving her a constant temperature at the beginning of this year, making her continually feel tired and faint'. He had recovered from his own tonsillectomy during the summer and 'I have put in some colossal spells of work and not felt much the worse for them'. What is truly odd is the way in which he goes on to detail his work: hitherto Davison had been kept regularly informed of the progress of every novel and play.

> These days I am more a dramatist than a novelist. My last book was called *English Journey*, which created a great (and good) stir here and has done pretty well for itself . . . Then I wrote a comedy called *Laburnum Grove* which I put on myself and it has done very well indeed. It has been running a year here, and comes to New York in the New Year. My new play – and my best so far – a serious play about 1912 called *Eden End* – is proving so far even a bigger success, almost a smash hit. I am now joint director of a theatre, the Duchess, which we have made into the prettiest small theatre in London. For the time being, I am only interested in the theatre (and a little in films) and in general social questions.

He had now published twenty-five books and 'In about two years I have forced myself into the theatre, made a lot of money out of it, been played all over the world, and have a rapidly growing reputation . . . that's not bad going, is it?'

A sour round-up follows of what has happened to their various acquaintances in the last twelve months. J. C. Squire had made 'a silly attack' on *Wonder Hero*, 'which obviously touched up some of his growing Tory and Fascist prejudices', and had finally lost his job with the *Mercury* and his reviewing slot in the *Sunday Times*. 'He does not live with his wife and family, who are terribly hard up, and altogether is a mysterious, pathetic figure.' He and Gerald Bullett had drifted apart. He had decided that Bullett considered him vulgar while he thought Bullett little more than a dilettante. The Lynds, supposedly so liberal, were upset because their daughter had become a Communist and moved in with a Jewish refugee from Germany. England, he added, was a queer place. Most of it was badly off but literary London was 'the gayest city in the world'. However, he warns Davison, there were no literary jobs going 'or I would have mentioned them to you'. Indeed he seems deliberately to be putting Davison off coming home: 'Actually, the market for literary articles, serious reviewing, must be rapidly dwindling, I am afraid.' He ends on an unusually prejudiced note: 'The new young poets, Auden, Day-Lewis, etc., have brains but do not seem to be quite poets – all a little cold and conceited. Somebody told me the other day that the whole lot of them are homosexual which doesn't help in my opinion.'

The reviews of *English Journey* were good, with the exception of that in *The Times*, which drove Priestley to explode to Walpole: 'What am I to do about *The Times*? For ten years now every book I've ever brought out, they've dismissed with a sneer. Even *English Journey* is dismissed like that. It is obviously the same man and somebody who very much dislikes me. What can a man do about it? Not send them the books?'

At the beginning of October he received a bundle of American reviews of *English Journey*. Most were appreciative but their overall content impelled him to write an annoyed letter to Eugene Saxton at Harper's. He had been pleased, he told him, that the critics had enjoyed the book, but he took exception to their dismissal of the rest of his work. Worse, where he himself was concerned, they were factually inaccurate: 'These fellows say, in effect, "Here is Priestley who became popular (undeservedly) by writing a lot of sentimental novels, watery imitations of Dickens; he's a bovine, hearty sort of ass; but about a third of the way through this book he suddenly discovers all is not well with the world."' He did not care, he said, if his other work was not mentioned, but if it was, then they had no right to make such sweeping generalisations. What of *Wonder Hero*, which painted a true picture of northern dereliction? Not to mention *Angel Pavement*, which vividly presented the country's social conditions without 'a glimmer of sentimentality'. It really would not do, he continued. Would it be possible to find space for either him or a friendly journalist to put his side of the story? Something that would show that his novels and plays were serious pieces of work.

An opportunity would arise when he returned to America: there was a strong possibility of a Broadway production of *Eden End.*

In spite of his involvement in the theatre, 1935 was not a happy year for either Priestley or Jane. In the early part of the summer her frail sister, Bubbles, had died, followed in August by Amy Priestley. His stepmother's death from cancer affected Priestley deeply for she had, he wrote to Walpole, 'been a mother to me since I was a small child'.

In the autumn of that year the Priestleys and their children went to America, their destination a 'dude' ranch, a kind of ranch hotel, in the dry climate of Arizona. Priestley went ahead to spend time in New York as, much later than originally anticipated, *Eden End* was to play on Broadway. Jane, the six children and their nanny went first to the West Coast via the Panama Canal. There they met up with Priestley and planned to spend two weeks in California before going to Arizona for the rest of the winter.

Priestley made the crossing in the luxury liner *Aquitania.* He usually enjoyed sea voyages, whatever the weather, but this time he was full of foreboding. The weather during the voyage was far from good and the political situation in Europe exacerbated his depression. 'Nothing was wrong,' he writes in *Midnight on the Desert,* the collection of autobiographical essays that resulted from this trip, 'with what Americans call "the set up". Yet everything was wrong. I felt depressed, perhaps, by the state of the world [Italy had just invaded Abyssinia], perhaps by the state of my liver when we left Southampton . . .' Perhaps he had a premonition that *Eden End,* so heavily dependent for its success on the mood of pre-war England, would not translate to the brash theatrical world of New York.

He had already put up the backs of the New York theatrical fraternity by saying publicly that the reason his previous three plays had flopped on Broadway was that they had not been properly done. This time, therefore, he was coming in person to supervise the production. The preliminaries did not augur well. It took an interminable time for the production process to get started and, as week followed week, he could no longer enjoy New York: its strange architecture palled, there was little to entertain him and, as he wrote later, he did not console himself with romantic interludes. It was also unseasonably hot and he found it impossible even to walk the streets in comfort. It took three weeks just to cast the play, which went into rehearsal in a bleak old warehouse.

Today's long rehearsal periods of our major national companies, and the even longer ones common in Europe, were unknown in the 1930s. Three or four weeks was the norm even for a major West End or Broadway production, but even by these standards the rehearsal period for *Eden End* was short – too short. The day before it opened Priestley faced a stark choice. He was expected to attend the first night but it coincided with the arrival of Jane and the children in California. And although he did not say so, he must have known that the American production was not going to work. He left for the West Coast. Susan Cooper, Priestley's early biographer, wrote,

> *Eden End* sank without trace on Broadway, after a few weeks of struggling survival. By the time Priestley read the glum telegrams reporting its poor reception on the opening night, he was a long way from Broadway, standing on the platform of Albuquerque railway station, New Mexico, a windy place where civilisation seems to have been swallowed up by a great embrace of open sky . . .[9]

Nevertheless, the Priestleys' sojourn in Arizona was one of the best times they ever spent together as a family and is still remembered as such by the children. Angela said it was 'the happiest time of our entire childhood. We were all together, all happy, doing things, getting out and about with none of the tension there was at home.' Life at home, either in London or the Isle of Wight, was formal. Here, in the desert, they had tremendous freedom. Angela and Barbara, wearing jeans, checked shirts and sombreros, spent their days riding and visiting rodeos. Sylvia and Mary became 'entranced tomboys, for when they were not riding cow ponies, they turned themselves into ponies, galloping about on all fours, while the two babies [Rachel and Tom] have played solemnly for hours with "stick horses", taking the bits of wood out for a lope and them corralling them again in "stick horse ranch", a messy little place among the sandhills just beyond the bunk-house.'[10]

If there had been a period of coolness between Priestley and Edward Davison, it was over, for both he and Jane sent a constant stream of letters to both Davisons and looked forward to being joined for several weeks by Teddy, Natalie and their children. As some point Natalie must have asked Jane what she should wear during the holiday, to which Jane responded, 'We all wear Levis, sort of blue dungaree trousers worn with check shirts. The trousers cost about a dollar and a quarter and the shirts a dollar. We don't wear evening dress ever.' She and Priestley changed for dinner into casual wear, he in a sports jacket, she in a silk dress, and that would be quite sufficient. Natalie should also bring some warm clothes with her as the evenings were so cold that Rachel and Tom had to wear bedsocks, but there were wood stoves in all the bedrooms. They were having a wonderful time, spending all day on horseback – except for Jack 'who hardly rides at all', and the riding was easy, the horses marvellous. She was writing her letter sitting in the sun in a cotton dress and straw hat, 'not bad for December 1!'.

The time passed pleasantly. Jane taught the four older children as far as she could, then rode with them in the desert. Her health had improved substantially. Meanwhile Priestley, in spite of having said that he was turning his back on novel writing for the time being, began another, *They Walk in the City*. He also made regular trips to Hollywood: 'With nine of us to keep there, I could motor in a day to Hollywood and there pick up odds and ends of script work which I could do back at the ranch, taking the magic money away before it could turn into dead leaves. An inspection of credit titles in the middle and late 1930s will not reveal my name, for I surprised and gratified my scriptwriting colleagues by demanding to be left out of the credits.' The work was undertaken on a purely freelance basis without even a contract.

In both *Midnight on the Desert* and the later *Margin Released*, Priestley writes at length the Hollywood of his day and how he met more stars than he could even recall. The place was 'daft but not boring'. Men arrived at parties fashionably unshaven, clad in open-necked shirts, while their women wore full evening dress and glittered with jewels. His happiest days there were spent playing tennis, 'the best evenings with Chaplin and Groucho Marx'. A week just before Christmas had been particularly memorable:

H. G. Wells had suddenly popped up, and we had an entrancing evening with him and Charles Chaplin. Our old friend Hugh

Walpole, whom we had met off and on all winter, was also there, a rosy piece of England. There was a droll evening of dining and boxing in the company of two of the Marx brothers ... And that week the place was looking its best for Christmas with illuminated trees all along Hollywood Boulevard ... so charmingly spangled under clear night skies, and with every shop window stuffed with gifts and brilliantly illuminated all night, Hollywood did, for once, look the fairy-tale place that it appears to be in the imagination of thousands of youngsters all over the world.[11]

They were due home at the beginning of April and it was decided that at the end of their stay in Arizona they would visit the Grand Canyon. Afterwards Jane would take the four older children on to Death Valley and Rainbow Bridge while Priestley went to Santa Barbara with the two little ones and their nanny. In a letter to Natalie on 3 April, Jane waxed lyrical about her 'heavenly month with the four children'. After visiting the Grand Canyon they had all stayed for a time at Phantom Ranch, then Priestley had left for Santa Barbara to work on correcting his new novel, while she and the children set off for the Navaho reservation 'and saw the most heavenly country and met some of the nicest people'. They had stayed in Indian trading posts in spite of 'various discomforts, sometimes no beds!' but it had all been the most tremendous fun – this from the woman who is sometimes said to have been unable to cope without every comfort and convenience.

Rainbow Bridge, she wrote, 'was the most beautiful thing I ever saw'. They had continued to Boulder Dam and Death Valley before visiting Yosemite National Park, 'but it was too civilised and so we cleared off to San Francisco'. She and the children were loath to leave, but not so Priestley. In his last letter to Davison before he left for England he said he was tired of America and had much to do at home. He was also concerned about the ever-darkening political situation. He had reason to be: that summer Spain exploded into the civil war, the terrible rehearsal for what came later and which, in the small town of Guernica, introduced the world to the horrors of saturation bombing.

CHAPTER 17

Aspects of Time

Reticent as Priestley is about Hollywood in *Midnight on the Desert*, it is clear from a letter he wrote to Hugh Walpole before he returned to England that he had been busy there. He had been commissioned to produce a treatment for Paramount for a film starring the comedian W. C. Fields, whom he had admired from music-hall days, and had been 'working against time', but whether or not he would be asked to write the entire script he did not know 'as he [Fields] may not like it, as he is a queer old cuss and they never know what suits him'. But neither this nor a western to star Gracie Fields, who was no relation to W. C., came to anything. He told Walpole that on his return home he had 'to do the dialogue and revision for *National Velvet*', but the film, which starred the young Elizabeth Taylor as the girl who rides in the Grand National in Enid Bagnold's popular novel, did not appear until 1944 and Priestley's name is not in the credits. However, there had been a film of *Dangerous Corner*, starring Ronald Colman, and Tom Priestley remembers a photograph taken in Hollywood showing his parents with the popular romantic actor. Priestley's agent for film work in the states was Zeppo Marx, who appeared in the early Paramount films but left the screen when his brothers signed for MGM.

Almost as soon as he returned Priestley was caught up in his production of *Bees on the Boat Deck*. He hoped to have had the play on before going to America but this had not been possible for several reasons, not least the casting. Ralph Richardson had agreed straightaway to play one of the two seamen in charge of the beached SS *Gloriana*, but for the second Jack wanted a young actor who had had a considerable success in *Romeo and Juliet* but who was not yet free: Laurence Olivier. Neither was it possible to put the play on at the Duchess, so *Bees on the Boat Deck* went on, instead, at the Lyric Theatre. As well as Richardson and Olivier the production boasted a string of other well-known names, Richard Goolden, John Laurie, René Ray and Raymond Huntley, but even so starry a cast could not make the play a success.

In America, Priestley had been approached by Herman Ould, secretary of the international writers' organisation the PEN Club, inviting him to become president of the English branch. He had written back, expressing reservations as to his suitability for the position, in part because Jane's health precluded him from spending the winter at home, but said that he was willing to have his name put forward. He was keen on PEN as a force for international goodwill and a guard against intolerance aimed at writers. He also felt there should be a strong drive to attract to the club distinguished English writers who did not already belong and who he thought might have been put off by the dinners and the personality of the late Mrs Dawson Scott, who had been one of its leading lights:

> I would like to see the Association getting out a report, combined from reports from its correspondents in various countries, showing exactly what freedom of expression writers have throughout the world . . . This would be work of extreme importance. My own political sympathies are Left wing, but I am, like you I imagine, anxious that the PEN should not be used by Communists, who are themselves opposed to freedom of expression, simply to oppose the repressive measures of Fascism.

On his return home, however, he took on what turned out to be a short-lived presidency.

The reception of *They Walk in the City* did not ease his black moods. That he had had his own doubts and reservations about it is clear from his account in *Midnight on the Desert* of how, one night, he had gone to the hut built for his use as a study with the specific intention of stuffing a substantial portion of the manuscript into the stove. But, after a whole night of looking at the sky and puffing on his pipe, his spirits had risen and he had reapplied himself to it with enthusiasm. But the novel is not one of his best. Like *Cornelius* and *Bees on the Boat Deck*, it had been planned as an allegory of the times. According to his own account, he had set out to write the story of two young working-class people who, after many difficulties, come together 'in the fashion of the oldest love stories'. Rose and Edward first meet on the Yorkshire moors, are drawn to each other and arrange to see each other again at a specific time and place in the future; but, due to a foolish mishap, Edward misses the appointment whereupon Rose leaves for London with a friend. They search the streets of London for each other without success until they both attend a political demonstration and are reunited, only to be parted again when Rose is injured in a riot. The plot then descends into melodrama as Rose falls prey to a procuress looking for new girls to service her clients, a fate from which she is rescued at the eleventh hour by the doughty Edward.

Priestley was hurt by the reaction of critics and of his friends. He felt haunted by *The Good Companions* and the fear that reviewers were always looking for more of the same. The *Times Literary Supplement* was typical of other reviews. Offering faint praise for his ability to compose 'descriptive reports, genial and satirical, of the daily round of wage earners of both sexes', it went on: 'His wares are excellent of their kind, and if close scrutiny does not associate them all with the hand-made, all the more credit to the hand that devised the machine.'[1] When even the loyal Hugh Walpole wrote saying that he had found the book a problem, Dear Old Jack was so upset that his emotion spilled over into his writing:[2]

I'm sorry my book has been such a nuisance and that my night letter wakened you up, etc., etc. But why rage and storm so much? Why the accusations of conceit, bogus mysticism and what not?

Mysticism doesn't come into this matter at all. I said the symbolism was political. You tell me to stick to the JBP of *English Journey*. But this novel is – in part – *English Journey* dramatised, especially the last third. The two young people become symbolic figures of the exploited classes, threatened by various forces – some old, like capitalist imperialism, etc., others new, like the Fascists and the Communists. In order to show what I am getting at, I deliberately break the narrative thread, and show these various forces personified. The rest is melodrama, if you like, but then so is this morning's newspaper.

We are living in a melodramatic world. You seem to me – in your letter about it – to have misunderstood the nature of my novel, but I didn't mind that much. But when I found you were reviewing it for one of the very few newspapers that could be sympathetic towards the political side, and at the same time did not seem to notice that it had a political side, naturally I was a bit worried. After all, you know, I have certain quite strong political convictions, and I tend more and more to bring them into my writing. It's quite possible that this way of doing it – that is, instead of making a novel or a play a debate as Wells and Shaw did – trying to find some figures and action symbolic of the questions at issue (as I did in *Bees on the Boat Deck* as well as in this novel) – may be all wrong, not come off at all. (It's certainly not an easy way to work out.) That's an arguable point. But all this stuff of yours about my symbolism being nonsense because I'm no mystic and comparisons with the Bennett of 'The Glimpse' is simply beside the point.

Strict realism bored him, he told Walpole; he had always liked an admixture of 'the fantastic, the philosophical, the symbolical', as found in *Don Quixote*. 'I am always trying to grapple with it. On the other hand, I was *NEVER* a great Bennett fan; and apart from both being rather cocky chaps from the provinces, we have little in common.' *Of course*, he was not a mystic, did not pretend to have a religious nature and would not attempt to compete with Hugh in this field 'that cloudy vision of the battle of good and evil you do so well . . . but I refuse to be imprisoned for the rest of my life in a strict naturalism for your sake or anybody else's.' Whether as a result of this outpouring or the bonds of friendship Priestley's attitude must have softened, because a week later he wrote again to thank his friend for his 'kind review'.

In January 1937 Priestley set off with Jane for Egypt. She needed to spend the winter in a dry climate and both wanted to visit the antiquities. Also it was supposed to be a complete break for Priestley from continual work: 'I had promised for the first time for years really not to do any work at all during the next two months. This was to be a genuine holiday.' It went wrong almost from the start. The voyage was 'wretched' with hardly a glimmer of sunshine, they hated the ship, both went down with colds and their first sight of Port Said roused no enthusiasm.

However, primed with Professor Breasted's *History of Egypt*, they visited all the ancient sites. 'The expense seemed fabulous. I have never before or since paid out so much, and, here and now, I announce that never again shall it happen. Every visitor to Egypt is regarded as a triumphant conqueror who should be distributing largesse. They have a technique there of extracting money from the tourist that is thousands of years old . . .'[3]

During this time in the desert, Priestley had not only found the time to pursue the philosophies of both Dunne and Ouspensky in more detail and at greater length, but he had also now become fascinated by the work of Carl Gustav Jung. As with the work of the other two, it is impossible to go into Jung's various theories in detail, but suffice it to say that there were three main areas which were to engage Priestley until the end of his life. First, that mankind has a collective unconscious, a reservoir of energy and ideas from which individuals could draw inspiration and which was the origin of, as he writes in his book of essays *Rain Upon Godshill*, 'the sudden arrival of what seems to us "wonderful ideas".' Second, that the masculine and feminine principles must be evenly balanced if human society is to remain healthy. The masculine principles encompass sensation and intellect, the feminine, intuition and emotion. Third and last was the part played by dreams. Jung's theories on this subject were first published in Britain in 1961 in his book *Memories, Dreams and Reflections*. It was Jung's view of the place of dreams in personal consciousness which particularly drew Priestley, for it was a subject that had always fascinated him and almost all his published collections of essays have at least one in which a dream or dreams are the subject.

Sometimes they are charmingly ridiculous, such as the episode of the *Berkshire Beasts*, huge, green, elephant-like creatures who, he is told by his dream companion, are kept for their beautiful singing voices; on other occasions they are the true stuff of nightmare such as that in which he believed himself to be inside the persona of another man, in an unknown city, possibly a spy or agent, who is shot by pursuers. He felt his life draining away from him and became convinced that somehow he had, in that dream world, and within the circles of Time, actually experienced the physical death of another man. Jung meant a great deal to him and one of his favourite quotations from his work, according to Diana Collins, was: 'A man at peace with himself, who accepts himself, contributes an infinitesimal amount to the good of the universe. Attend to your own private and personal conflicts, and you will be reducing by one millionth millionth the world conflict.'

Steeped in Dunne and Ouspensky, Priestley expected to feel great things when faced with the wonders of ancient Egypt, but the Pyramids and the Sphinx, Karnak and the Valley of the Kings left him unmoved. Ouspensky had waxed lyrical about his first visit to Egypt, but not so Jack Priestley: 'No strange emotions, no magical memories of other existences, disturbed my mind . . . if I have ever lived before, it certainly was not in Egypt, unless I had a brief existence during the short and stormy reign of Ikhnaton . . .' Only that reign, its art and its queen, Nefertiti ('one of the loveliest women's faces I have ever seen'), appealed to him. Neither the expanses of desert nor the sunsets were as spectacular as he had seen in Arizona, and the only aspect of the holiday he enjoyed was a river trip up the White Nile, planned by Jane so that she could visit one of the world's major bird reserves. She was becoming increasingly interested in ornithology and was developing considerable expertise, which would later result in her writing extensively on the subject. Even this had caused considerable contention between them.

When she said that it was what she would like to do, he told her he wanted to go home. He had things to do. But, writing later, he had recognised that he represented the 'negative current' on their holiday: 'If her tendency was to say *Yes* to every suggestion, mine was – and still is – to say *No*. Hers is the irresistible force, mine the immovable body. It makes a good balance.' The reason why he was so unenterprising in travel, he groused, was that unlike his wife he was no longer romantic about it, convinced that any proposed journey would be uncomfortable, tedious and not worth the alternating spells of waiting about and fuss.

Although afterwards he admitted that he would like to do the steamer trip again, he wrote grumblingly to Walpole from Khartoum that Egypt 'swarmed with touts, parasites and scoundrels and . . . its flyblown charm soon palls . . . it is also very hot and seems a long way from everywhere.' However, Khartoum was better than anywhere else they had been and 'there is a little zoo next door and I am making friends with a gigantic sad hippo for whom I have a profound fellow-feeling.

I shall feed him with sugar. Somebody ought to try feeding me with sugar . . .' He does not mention the magnificent birdlife except to say that on their return, looking at the notes Jane had kept of their trip, he saw that she had listed red-breasted shrike, Abyssinian roller and green parakeet, 'but I do not remember a single flash of their wings'.

As they travelled back to the coast to take ship for home the outside temperature fell as his rose inwardly. 'At every stage of the journey I lost more and more of my temper, for you cannot travel in Egypt without a great deal of fuss and no man suffers it less gladly than I do.' He almost went berserk when, just as they were about to leave one destination, their luggage was lost briefly and as they looked for it they were accosted by an old woman trying to sell them hard-boiled eggs. 'When we finally arrived at Port Said, after a packed and suffocating train, I felt like a homicidal bankrupt.' When at last they boarded their ship he roared and stamped until presented with a large English breakfast, 'after which I gradually subsided into being an ordinary sensible man'.

They arrived in England to sleet. The popular press was obsessed with the new Royal Family and the coming Coronation of George VI and Queen Elizabeth, but Priestley was cheered briefly by the reviews for *Midnight on the Desert*. Within days he was in Liverpool, working on a production of his latest play, *The Bad Samaritan*, which, he recognised almost immediately, did not work. He was annoyed because he had written the play in textbook fashion, starting with a detailed synopsis, then clothing each scene with dialogue: 'The result was that my imagination never got to work anywhere; it was all done with the surface of the mind, like a film script; so craftily and coldly put together that nowhere was there any life in it.'[4]

His next two plays were critical and popular successes. One he wrote with considerable difficulty, the other with ease. Both were 'time plays'. In April 1937 Angela, who was studying in Paris, became ill during a trip to Italy. Jane went out to her at once, found that she had measles, and immediately contacted Priestley, asking him to join them at the nursing home in Fiesole where Angela was, and to bring with him drugs unobtainable in Italy. He did so, only to become ill almost at once with some influenza-type complaint. As he and Angela recovered, he began to work on the draft of a play he had put aside some time earlier,

I Have Been Here Before. He had had considerable difficulties with it and in his preface to *Two Time Plays,* published in 1937, he says that it was 'laboriously composed and re-written five or six times'.

He felt so unsure of it that he submitted one of the early drafts to J. M. Barrie, who had become a family friend. On the whole Barrie liked it, praising in particular Act II and the end. But Priestley was still dissatisfied.

Back at The Grove, he had just embarked on yet another draft when he had an extraordinary interlude with a Hollywood producer.[5] He had become accustomed to the crazed world of Hollywood and had written in *Midnight on the Desert* of the difficulty of getting a film into production, the apparently intense enthusiasm of film producers that can vanish like mist, and the fanatical dedication needed by a director to drive a project through to filming. (His description of the process is as apposite today as it was in 1935.) He had also learned from painful experience the arcane methods of American theatrical production. But even this did not prepare him for the man who combined all of it, Jed Harris, 'the brilliant New York producer and director, who had been responsible for some of the most sensational theatrical successes of that sensational and theatrical city. (You can almost see the neon lights going up in my prose.)'

Harris arrived unannounced in Highgate, having heard that Priestley had just finished another play. He talked all day without stopping, leaving with a copy of the script. He returned the next day. *I Have Been Here Before* was one of the worst and best scripts he had ever seen. He bombarded Priestley with suggestions for cuts and improvements, many of which Priestley took on board. He could no longer view it objectively, and knew that although Harris was a ruthless editor he had a touch of theatrical genius 'and was just the man to have no patience with my lumbering attempts to suggest rather subtle ideas in dramatic form. Thus the present shape of the play owes a good deal to him.'

Then came what he describes as the most astonishing incident of his entire theatrical life. Harris returned to New York with the amended script, proposing to stage it on Broadway. Time passed. In the summer Priestley wrote to him saying that he was now planning to put the play on in England, whereupon he received a cable from Harris, aboard the liner *Berengaria,* telling

Priestley to hold everything until he arrived in a couple of days' time. Priestley waited . . . and waited. Days passed without any communication. He, his secretary, his play agent A. D. Peters and *his* secretary all tried to track Harris down but to no avail. He had vanished. Finally Harris returned to New York without exchanging a word with Priestley. 'Months afterwards I learned that he considered that I had treated him badly. Certainly I had neglected to use bloodhounds to trace him, after he had crossed the Atlantic to see me, but short of that I had employed all the usual methods, whereas he had only to pick up a telephone and talk to me.'

Why Harris had changed his mind about the play after coming three thousand miles to discuss it, why he never told Priestley that he had altered his plans, why 'after behaving so discourteously and mysteriously' he had imagined he had been badly treated, was never revealed. Priestley was told later that this brilliant young man had a passion for startling people. Harris would remain in his memory as '*The Great Broadway Enigma*, the whole sign picked out in flashing lights'.

The plot of *I Have Been Here Before* is simple, although heavily influenced by Ouspensky's theory of the time spiral. A strange man, Dr Gortler, arrives at an inn on the moors and asks first if he can have a room, then if the landlady is expecting three visitors, a married couple and a young single man. The answer to both questions is no. She is expecting three single ladies from Manchester and all the rooms are booked. Dr Gortler goes away but almost at once there is a call from Manchester to say that the three ladies are unable to come. Then three unexpected guests arrive, a married couple, the husband a businessman much older than his wife, and a young headmaster recovering from an illness. Dr Gortler returns and is accommodated in the third room.

The young wife, Janet, is overwhelmed by a feeling of *déjà vu*, which Dr Gortler recognises. He is one of Ouspensky's 'chosen' ones: he has been here before and has seen events unfold in which adultery between Janet and the young teacher has tragic consequences, leading to the suicide of her husband, Ormund. He is determined to break the cycle and set all three on the path to the next level. In Act I we are presented with the protagonists; in Act II they begin to follow the predestined course of action but in Act III, following the intervention of

Gortler and mainly through a series of long exchanges with Ormund, the outcome is changed. Although it is a contrived play it is saved dramatically by the relationship between Gortler and Ormund, which contains some of Priestley's finest writing for the stage.

However, as Gareth Lloyd Evans writes, the play diminishes as it progresses because it is tied to the demands of Ouspensky's theory:

> Thrill and ingenuity, explicit statement, replace the powerful sense of truth and depth with which the play begins. But, like so many others of Priestley's plays, it haunts the imagination and in no other play has he created a character which steps so firmly along the tragic path (only to lose his way) as Ormund. He does not seem at any point to be a modern Everyman, but he might well have been a modern Hamlet, had his creator shown the faith in him that he displays in the first Act and the first part of the second Act. The spiral reduces Ormund and confounds Priestley.

While he had been battling with *I Have Been Here Before*, Priestley had also written *Time and the Conways*. The idea for it had come while he was working on a short play, *Duets in Floodlight*, he had been commissioned to write for an amateur play competition, but this time the influence was Dunne, not Ouspensky. He had written it out of sequence, beginning with Act II. Once again the play is set in an era heavily influenced by the First World War, but this time it is not about the shades of things to come but the loss of innocence in its aftermath. We first meet the Conway family and three acquaintances in 1919 at Kay Conway's twenty-first birthday party. The young people are looking forward to a new order, new ideas, a better life.

In Act II, nearly twenty years have passed and we learn what has become of all the young hopefuls. One is dead, another has become a feckless con man, and of them all only two retain some part of their ideals. In Act III we return to the end of Act I and the action continues where it left off, but the audience now knows what the outcome will be for the Conways. Only Alan and Kay, the most perceptive of them, are at all aware of what might be in store.

By June 1937 Priestley was casting it, making only a handful of alterations in rehearsal to a hundred-page script. He had planned originally to put on *I Have Been Here Before* first, but things had gone so well with *Time and the Conways* that he changed his mind. He had the 'right' theatre, the Duchess, the 'right' producer, Irene Hentschel, and his 'right' cast included Jean Forbes-Robertson, Molly Rankin, Raymond Huntley, Mervyn Johns and Wilfred Babbage.

It opened on 26 August 1937 and was an immediate success. In spite of this he felt impelled in the published version to tackle various criticisms that had been levelled at it: first that it was 'pessimistic' and second that he had loaded the dice against the Conways. He disagreed with his critics: the Conways, he said, only seemed so unfortunate when compared with the characters currently peopling the English comedy scene 'in which handsome creatures in expensive new clothes philander gracefully in eternal bright sunshine'. Everything that happened to them could have happened to any other family which had suffered misfortune. As for the play's pessimism, he had hoped to show by the attitudes of Alan and Kay that, given only a marginal change of events, the outcome might have been different and that, in another timescale, it perhaps would be. What he had written was, after all, a play of ideas.

I Have Been Here Before opened less than a month after *Time and the Conways* at the Royalty Theatre, with Lewis Casson as Dr Gortler and Wilfred Lawson as Ormund. Then Priestley and his family left for Arizona, via Manchester and California. In a letter written to Walpole shortly before both plays opened Priestley is in full theatrical mode.[6] There had been a hitch in finding a theatre for one play, he told his friend, but this had now been resolved. *I Have Been Here Before* was 'a very rum piece'. The cast of *Time and the Conways* was 'the nicest I've ever had so far'. He explained the structure of the play and confessed to doubts as to how it would be received by audiences, but hoped for the best. He was also, he said, finishing a third play while adapting a fourth, an American play, *Blind Alley*, for possible production in London.

On 10 September, four days after his second first night, the Priestleys sailed from Manchester. When they arrived, Priestley had to give a series of lectures before he could join his family on what was to be the last holiday they would spend together.

CHAPTER 18

America Again

For a month before the family's departure, Priestley led a life of such frantic activity that it nearly overwhelmed him. He found himself 'doing five men's work' to meet the deadline of the coming lecture tour. There were three plays in hand in Britain, two up and running and *People at Sea* about to go into rehearsal, an American production of *Time and the Conways* due to open in New York around Christmas, which had to be cast with English actors, a promised series of articles for the *Sunday Express* to finish before he left, the lectures to prepare, and 'letters that demanded immediate replies came in blizzards'. He said, 'I've known dramatists and producers who felt they had to have a good holiday after doing one play. They should try doing three!'

Always a poor sleeper, he was turned by this regimen into an insomniac. He would rise to face a day of work, letters, rehearsals, snatched lunches, more rehearsals, more work, then, 'with eyes heavy and hot and a mind rattling round like an old Ford engine, to retire to bed only to remember fifteen important things that ought to have been done that day and would certainly have to be done in the morning. Nothing less than the certain salvation of the human race would justify such an existence and until I am called upon to save my species I do not propose to work like that again.'[1]

As his son, Tom, pointed out in conversation with me, one can only ask why on earth such frantic activity was necessary. He did not *have* to work like that, for either financial or any other reasons, and his son can only suppose he was now unable to stop driving himself and had become, in fashionable parlance, a workaholic. He also, of course, loved a good grumble and posing, as always, being hard done by.

It is hardly surprising that *People at Sea* was a failure. Priestley put this down not so much to mistakes in writing and casting as to his being in America when it went into full rehearsal. It is unlikely that he could have saved it even if he had stayed in England because it is not a good play: pressure of work had resulted in a tired script. Again we are on board a ship, the SS *Zillah, en route* for Central America. A fire breaks out, the ship is in danger of sinking and the survival of all depends on the efforts of each: the moral hardly needs pointing out. It might just have worked had the characters been plausible, but they are merely a collection of mouthpieces for stereotypical attitudes from the capitalist financier who finds himself by cooking, to the token representative of the bolshie working class, Boyne the stoker. Both, as one critic put it, 'stumble out of their creator's imagination half-made up . . .'[2]

Priestley experienced another bad Atlantic crossing, this time on the *Queen Mary*. He had left behind a country facing the new real possibility of war, the conflict in Spain was drawing towards its conclusion and the death of the country's democracy, and the papers were full of what might be to come. On shipboard those passengers who were not seasick were discussing the prospect of war.

Priestley's arrival in New York was almost a replay of what had happened two years earlier when exhilaration had been followed swiftly by desolation and fatigue. He found the American theatre scene no easier to cope with, dominated by the word 'success, success, success'. If you had it you were the new wonder man, if not you were nothing.

Most celebrity lecturers were happy to spend several months on a leisurely tour of the USA, but Priestley had stipulated that his should last only a month, in spite of warnings that this would mean a punishing schedule. As he felt the need of a short holiday before he started the tour he arranged to meet Jane in New Orleans. Neither had visited the city before and it 'seemed to offer the perfect rendezvous'. The train journey from New York to New Orleans is supposedly one of the world's great railway experiences, but Priestley did not enjoy it. He left early on a Saturday morning and by the time the train reached Washington everyone was coughing. There followed one of 'the longest Sundays I can remember. In Georgia there was thick cloud and mist, in Alabama rain. The men's room was filled

with men even fatter than myself; the books I had with me
had no more savour than the train's food; even dozing was
hard work and seemed to consume no time at all.'

When he arrived in New Orleans it was raining heavily, the
station was black and wet, and he presumed the porters had all
drowned as there were none to be had and he was left to lug his
heavy suitcases through the downpour in search of a taxi to the
Carling Dinkler Hotel. There, Jane was waiting for him, which
was as well because the first thing he saw out of a window was an
illuminated time signal that pointed an arrow at every passing
minute 'and seemed to be conjuring your very life away'. In
spite of its dismal start, the holiday was a great success. The
sun came out, the telephone never stopped ringing, showering
them with offers of hospitality, and the food was wonderful. 'We
drowned in Sazerac cocktails and were smothered in delicious
seafood. If there is a city in England where a wandering American
author and his wife would be instantly received with such warm
hospitality, I am afraid I do not know where it is.' Together he
and Jane explored the old French quarter, dined in magnificent
restaurants, shivered in the grisly cemeteries. Priestley mused
on the city's past, the southern belles with their gardenias and
orchids and their handsome, indolent beaux, a world that had
died on the battlefields of the American Civil War.

One morning he was shown a letter in which an old lady
described the young men in their Confederate grey marching
down to the wharf to embark for the war. The girls pelted them
with red roses, the bonnie blue flag fluttered in the wind, the
older women waved their parasols and as the boat pulled away
a band played 'The Girl I Left Behind Me'. None came back.
In the bookshops of New Orleans paperback copies of *Gone With
The Wind* were piled high.

In a letter to Natalie Davison from New Orleans Jane writes of
the concentrated tour Jack was facing, but hoped that she and
Teddy would visit them in Arizona, possibly for Thanksgiving,
by which time Jack would briefly be back before returning to
New York to rehearse *Time and the Conways*. She also mentions
the likelihood of *I Have Been Here Before,* under its American title
I'm a Stranger Here, also being produced on Broadway. Once one
or both were playing, she thought neither she nor Jack would
be in Arizona as they intended to visit the Navaho reservations
that had so enchanted her when she had been there previously

with the children. Then they would have to return home. This visit, she wrote, was causing far more problems than their last; in January Barbara, Sylvia and Mary should go back to school and Angela, to whom the entrance papers for Newnham College were being sent out to Arizona, would, if she were accepted, be going up to Cambridge. She signed off by saying that while she had enjoyed her week in New Orleans, she had now had enough of it as being in a 'hotel in the middle of noise gets me down after a few days. I wish we could have had a quiet time together.'[3]

A few days later she went to the ranch in Arizona while Priestley returned to New York to deliver a lecture at Columbia University, then, most unusually, to act as the presenter of a programme of English documentary films brought over by Paul Roth for the film archive of the Metropolitan Museum of Modern Art. Roth had asked him to do this because he had worked on one of the films, *We Live in Two Worlds*. It was unusual in that, rather than having been made from an existing narrative or story line, film left over from other projects was shown to Priestley, from which he produced a narrative. It was about Switzerland 'and anybody who would like to meet in a film a gigantic and apoplectic frog talking with a broad Yorkshire accent, should have a look at me in *We Live in Two Worlds*'. He introduced this and other short documentaries, some directed by the great John Grierson, then head of the GPO Film Unit, including the famous *Night Mail*, and *Drifters*. The evening was a great success.

Then the tour proper began. Almost as soon as he set off Priestley realised why his American lecture agent had tried to dissuade him from doing twenty lectures in four weeks: the travelling alone was a nightmare. The itinerary looked as if someone had been trying to map 'the adventures of a crazy giant in seven-league boots, reeling around the Middle West': from Battle Creek, Michigan, to Tulsa, Oklahoma, for instance, 'was rather like being told after Danzig that your next lecture would be in Avignon'. Life was reduced to interminable journeys in pullman coaches, where sleepless nights were followed by formal lunches and much hand-shaking. The various towns dissolved into a blur: 'Not that they were absolutely all alike. There was only one I really disliked and that was . . . a smallish, cranky, puritanical town, where nobody was allowed to drink or smoke or eat meat or produce children or do anything. They were not only the gloomiest people I have ever talked to (as well they might be) but also the stupidest.' Day and night and the endless vast tracts of country merged into each other until, tired as he was from his hectic summer, he could hardly differentiate one from another. 'I do not think I have ever felt so far removed from any sensible reality as I did during all that month.' A hurried note to Davison, written on the tour and dated 3 November but without any address, expresses Priestley's hope that they can meet soon 'after I have done my plays and by the by if they won't have these plays this time, I give them up, for I've seen nearly everything on Broadway (including that dreadful job of Anderson's) and if I can't give them better dramatic writing, producing, acting than what I've seen, I walk out of the Theatre forever'.

The one brief interlude of sanity came when Priestley was in Cedar Rapids, Iowa, and learned from another English writer, Gerald Heard, that Aldous Huxley, who was on a similar lecture circuit, was laid up nearby with an injured arm and shoulder, having fallen on an icy pavement. The three had not met before but they talked away a morning 'like shipwrecked sailors suddenly meeting on their island', although in temperament, capacity and background they were all different. Heard asked about the two time plays, and when Priestley had described them the three men realised that Heard's book *Third Morality*, Huxley's *Ends and Means* and Priestley's *Midnight on the Desert* and the time plays 'were all moving in the same direction'. They parted, planning to meet again on their return to England, but only Priestley went home. Huxley and Heard settled in California when war broke out.

As the tour progressed Priestley found one consolation: during the endless journeying and the wakeful nights the idea for another play took hold, perhaps prompted by that intense discussion about time. Odd scenes and fragments of dialogue began to drift through his head, enabling him, when he reached Arizona, to begin the first draft of *Johnson Over Jordan*.

In a letter to Natalie on 10 November Jane told the Davisons that she was no longer sure of their plans as Jack's kept changing, but that he had now signed the contract for *Time and the Conways* and expected it to open in New York in either late December or early January.

He'll be here by Thanksgiving and the most I can do at the moment is to ask you to keep Christmas tentatively in case we can

do something about it. I'm longing to see Jack again. He seems to
be getting along pretty well with his lectures. He's changed a lot,
I think, in the last two years and has become more serious and
more deeply himself. I think his work is improving tremendously
and for a man who wrote a best seller like 'Good Companions',
I think that's tremendous. The 'Conways' and 'I'm a Stranger
Here' are in the 'Eden End' class only better and I know you
thought well of 'Midnight on the Desert'. Jack's career is very
exciting to watch.

While the family waited for him, they had a pleasant time.
The children were doing lessons with Jane in the mornings –
'I'm being interrupted by Mary – struggling with simultaneous
equations, Barbara's geometry and Angela's French literature.'
In the afternoons they went riding and Jane also went out
on bird expeditions. Only then did she mention her own
not inconsiderable success. ('By the way, Gollancz have just
published my bird anthology and Macmillan are doing it here
in the spring.') They had all started painting and 'I occasionally
spend an afternoon daubing away with horrid results but great
amusement.'
Priestley was so relieved to return to Arizona with the tour
behind him that he felt as if he were coming home. Eagerly he
walked around his small domain: the ranch had not changed,
the little shack in which he worked had been restored to its
former modest order – indeed, it looked as if he had only left
it for a day or two rather than two years. Tired though he was,
the sight of his chair and the little table with its typewriter set his
fingers itching to start work and so, stopping only for intervals of
tennis-playing with the children in the afternoons and banging
away on an old piano in the evenings, he began work on the
first draft of *Johnson Over Jordan*: 'Restored to my family and
a sensible life, no longer badgered by managers and agents
and reporters, eating at meal-times and sleeping at bedtimes,
warmed by the Arizona sunlight and healthily cooled by the
chill crisp nights, I felt a nobler human being and tried to write
like one.'[4]
But the idyll was short-lived, for by the end of December he
had to be back in New York for rehearsals of *Time and the Conways*.
They had all expected to return to London in the early New Year
but, as this was now looking unlikely, it was decided that Priestley,

Jane and the two older girls should all go to New York for the opening of the play, after which Barbara, who was eager to go back to school, would sail for home while Angela visited friends in New York. The quartet set off on the afternoon of Christmas Day, leaving the four younger children with their much-loved Yorkshire nanny in Arizona. Unlike the journey from New York to New Orleans, this was a splendid trip even though it meant catching three different trains, beginning with a local one from their nearest railhead which was followed by journeys on two of the 'greats', first 'The Chief' from Ashfork to Chicago, then 'The Twentieth Century' from Chicago to New York. 'Within three days of eating our Christmas pudding on the ranch we were comfortably installed at the Algonquin Hotel.'

The Algonquin, famous for its literary clientele, suited Priestley down to the ground, not least because it was entirely unlike the gadget-ridden sanitised boxes in which he usually stayed, marvels of efficiency though they were – '. . . I cannot imagine anyone but Arnold Bennett enjoying a stay in them'.

But as had been the case with *Eden End*, staying *Time and the Conways* proved a frustrating, depressing process, involving predatory financiers, bad management and ludicrous backstage union rules and regulations. Rehearsals moved with irritating and expensive slowness. The play eventually opened early in January 1938. The company was excellent, with Sybil Thorndike and Jessica Tandy proving the equal of their counterparts in London. Jessica Tandy, wrote Priestley, interpreted her role differently from Jean Forbes-Robertson but 'I think the last few minutes of the play were more moving in the New York production than in London'. But not to the New York audience, it seemed. Even those Americans who had enjoyed the London production did not seem to care for it when it was transferred to their home ground and, once again, a play that had been so successful in London failed in New York. The New York critics, then as now, could make or break a play and they did just that. Even one who admitted to enjoying Priestley's books wrote that it seemed to him that Priestley underestimated theatre audiences and wrote down to them, 'negligently lowering his voice'. Later, in England, Priestley thought he should consider the possibility that the difference between the two cultures was such that it was virtually impossible for any play to transfer successfully.[5] (However, a National Theatre production of *An Inspector Calls* in the early 1990s was a tremendous hit on Broadway and, indeed, all over the world.)

Time and the Conways lasted only a month and never paid for itself. Priestley thought about trying to keep it going with his own money but there were too many contractual difficulties. Writing to Davison early in February after he and Jane had returned to Arizona, he blamed the press for killing *Time and the Conways* with their savage notices: 'You didn't see the really bad ones. The evening papers, with one exception, were downright malicious. Even Watts of the *Herald Tribune*, who did praise the play, did it grudgingly and almost admitted he hated to say anything in favour of me.' The notorious interview given in Boston all those years ago was dredged up once again 'and I was almost called a liar for having denied having given it'. Yet the American comedy *You Can't Take It With You*, 'which these boys had thought the last word in fun and wisdom, has come a nasty cropper in London . . .' But after so much hard work, he was bitter: 'There is an America – the smart-alecky, Broadway, Hollywood, Newyorker-Time America – that doesn't like me and I don't like it; and unfortunately that small America almost controls opinion.'

By now Priestley had written a second draft of *Johnson Over Jordan*. He had met Thomas Wolfe and liked him, had run into Thornton Wilder, had lunched with Edna Ferber and was also toying with the idea of a longish novel set somewhere in Central Europe around the beginning of the nineteenth century, but everything was overshadowed by politics:

> To my mind the news gets steadily worse. I have just been reading a book published by Harpers called *The House that Hitler Built* . . . and it's terrifying, and as it happens the most recent news from Germany makes it more terrifying still. The Germans of 1914 were quiet, sane, sensible, reasonable people compared with this lot. These people *must make war*; they cannot organise for permanent peace, only for approaching war, therefore it is inevitable that they will make war and that pretty soon.

March found the Priestleys still in Arizona. In a letter to Natalie dated 1 March, Jane explained that they would not be able to visit the Davisons in Colorado before their delayed return home. After squeezing in a hurried trip with her to Rainbow Bridge and the Navaho reservations, Jack was now in the throes of a new novel. It was not set either in Central Europe or in the nineteenth century but in America in the present day. 'He has been writing an adventure story, "The Doomsday Men". He has written it at colossal speed, 80,000 words in three weeks! It's a great lark.' She, too, found the news from home frightful: 'They all seem to have gone mad.' She was sorry for poor Chamberlain and it made her feel sick to see in the headlines 'England Preparing for War'. On 11 April, Priestley had finished the new novel and he and his wife sailed for England on the *Britannic.*

CHAPTER 19

The Dogs of War

In the run-up to the outbreak of war in 1939 Priestley produced three books: *Rain Upon Godshill*, a second fine collection of autobiographical essays that began where *Midnight on the Desert* left off, *The Doomsday Men* and a short, lively novel, *Let The People Sing*, whose title was used for a catchy number in a Charles Cochrane revue and became a popular song of the early 1940s.

The Doomsday Men does not pretend to any great depth or meaning: three men, a fanatic, a millionaire and a mad scientist, meet up in a fantasy castle in the middle of the Arizona desert to plot how best to blow up the world. It's a good romp and it is surprising, in view of the film options taken on other Priestley books, that it did not appeal to Hollywood.

There is a hint of sadness in *Rain Upon Godshill* as well as comedy. It opens with an idyllic description of Priestley's Billingham study, built into the roof of the old house, its row of five huge windows giving a spectacular view across a quarter of the island to the sea. '. . . I tell myself all over again this is the best workroom I have ever had, and probably the best I shall ever have.'

Although his energy and enthusiasm for what he was doing never flagged, it seems that Priestley was aware that he was racing against the clock: the ever-growing likelihood of war is a constant theme in his letters during this period.

While he continued to struggle with *Johnson Over Jordan* he wrote two other plays, *Music at Night*, specially commissioned for the Malvern Festival of 1938, and *When We Are Married*, one of the all-time greats of classic comedy. He also produced the first Act of another, which he called *The Linden Tree* although it is not clear whether this was the same play as the one of that title produced later.

He found *Music at Night* a far more difficult task than he had anticipated when he accepted the commission. As the deadline for casting it and starting rehearsals drew inexorably nearer, he was struggling to finish it. In fact, it had to be cast even before the characters were clear in his mind. At one point he contacted the organisers of the Festival, H. K. Ayliff and Roy Limbert, to say that he did not think he could finish it on time, but he was pressed to honour his contract. Right up to the day before rehearsals began, he was rewriting and making major changes. While this is not uncommon today, sixty years ago it was almost unheard-of.

In some ways *Music at Night* prefigures *Johnson Over Jordan* in that it is a brave and experimental piece of theatre. In his programme note for the Festival, Priestley acknowledges this and admits that he will be happily surprised if more than half the audience like it. 'But even if everybody at Malvern heartily dislikes it, I shall not apologise . . . this is not because I do not enjoy success or think there is something rather fine about failure . . . No, I shall be unrepentant because I shall feel that I have done my duty.' Such a festival, he continues, should be, among other things, a laboratory for new and experimental work.

The storyline is simple. A group of people assemble in a house to hear a new piece of music. Like those trapped on the SS *Zillah* they have been devised to portray types and attitudes, but in *Music at Night* they are more rounded and include a gossip columnist, an ageing politician, a businessman, a society woman and two musicians. In Act I each of the four protagonists reveals the worst side of themselves: the journalist is looking for scandal to feed the public appetite, the society woman has ruthlessly used sex as a means of supporting her elegant lifestyle, the politician has wheeled, dealt and prevaricated, and the businessman has sacrificed everything to success and profit.

The action takes place while they are listening to music, which gradually draws them together. In Act II, they consider what they might have been, the lost opportunities, the failure of human relationships, how they have all put material things first. In Act III their individual consciousness and personalities become subsumed into one whole.

Describing it himself, Priestley says: 'The progress throughout the play is from the surface of the mind to deeper and deeper levels of consciousness. The strange happenings in Act III arise from my belief that at these depths we are not the separate beings we imagine ourselves to be.' The inspiration for the play had been drawn from his experience of visiting the Painted Desert and the Navaho reservation, the extraordinary peaceful landscape, the Indians with their song prayers to the Black, Blue, Yellow and Iridescent Winds and their cry, 'That it may be peaceful before me, That it may be peaceful behind me. All is peace, All is peace.' Nobody, he wrote, understood or believed him when he said he wished he had been born a Navaho woman to wander with her sheep in those lost canyons, under a burning empty sky and crying to the Blue and Yellow Winds. 'They wouldn't believe me . . . yet it was true . . . it was true.'

Music at Night failed with the critics and, as Priestley had forecast, with a proportion of the audience as well. The critic Ashley Dukes said of its characters that 'an evening in their company on the plane of realist convention would be just terrible'.

Meanwhile Priestley was not neglecting his role as entrepreneur. He was associated with a number of production companies over the years but the best known is the Mask Theatre Company, which operated from before the Second World War and for a short time afterwards. One of the company's main aims was to present good theatre at the lowest possible prices: the cinema, with cheaper seats, was encroaching rapidly on live theatre, especially in London's West End.

In 1938–9 the Mask Theatre Company ran a season of plays at the Westminster Theatre and included Bernard Shaw's *Candida*. Priestley wrote in the programme that the company's previous Shaw production, *The Doctor's Dilemma*, had successfully transferred to the Whitehall Theatre:

> The experiment of presenting Shaw at prices reduced to half the normal figure has certainly been interesting. It has been found that many of the audience are visiting a theatre *for the first time* and they tell us they are enjoying the experience. Previously, the high prices had compelled them, if they wanted to sit in comfortable seats, to patronise the cinema. Shaw has always been a stickler for reasonable prices. It is therefore right and proper that he should be prominent in the 'war' against conditions which are

not economic for theatre or playgoer. Whilst we are on this price question, it is worth mentioning that the Westminster might almost be described as the modern pioneer of cheap prices. Our seats have never been higher than 8s. 6d.

It was an interesting season, offering Shakespeare's *Troilus and Cressida*, now rarely performed, *Dangerous Corner*, Eugene O'Neill's *Marco Millions*, Strindberg's *Miss Julie*, J. M. Barrie's *The Will* and, significantly, T. S. Eliot's *The Family Reunion*. Priestley had begun work on *When We Are Married* even before *Music at Night* had opened, and had none of the difficulties with it that he had experienced with *Music at Night*. Once again he turned to Basil Dean as director and it was a towering success. Three middle-aged couples meet to celebrate their silver wedding anniversaries as they had all been married on the same day by the same minister in the same chapel. In the middle of the festivities, however, they learn from a drunken photographer employed to record the event that in fact they have never been married because the minister who performed the ceremonies had not been licensed to do so.

The play opened at the Manchester Opera House on 19 September 1938 to packed houses (and has been packing in audiences ever since). Then it toured in Blackpool during the town's famous Illuminations Week when coach parties from all over the north poured into the town 'to see the lights'.

Shortly afterwards Neville Chamberlain returned from Munich, promising 'peace in our time', and Priestley was quoted in a local newspaper as having said that he did not think there would be a war. It is clear from his correspondence, though, that this did not reflect his real opinion. In a letter to Jane, he ruminated on what might happen to theatres if war broke out. While he felt that 'people will want entertaining more than ever, I can't believe they'll allow people, especially in London, to congregate in non bomb-proof buildings like theatres'. He promised Jane that if war was declared he would return to her at once: 'I must see you soon, my love, and I'm thinking of you all the time and admiring you more than ever . . .'

Shortly after *When We Are Married* opened in London at the St Martin's Theatre, Frank Pettingell, who played the part of the drunken photographer, was taken ill. He had no understudy and, as no other actor could be found to take his place, Priestley played the part for twelve performances until Pettingell recovered. Initially he found it hard, struggling to remember the lines that he had written, waking sweating in the night for fear he might forget them, and enduring the strange, desolate sense of anticlimax at the end of every performance. But he received rave reviews and the publicity his appearance provoked brought even bigger queues to the box office.

On 4 November 1938, Jane wrote a long letter to Edward Davison. He had written to the Priestleys expressing his concern at the situation in Europe and, as he saw it, Chamberlain's capitulation to Hitler: Jane replied that she believed Chamberlain had gone to Munich as 'an honest broker with a definite policy', albeit one with which a great number of people did not agree. The country, she reminded Davison, was in a weak position as successive governments had refused to re-arm. She reserved her main scorn not for the Conservative appeasers but for the previous Labour government which she believed had brought the country to this pass, even though 'people like Jack and the intelligent middle-brows and high-brows were in sympathy with the Labour Party'. On a practical note, when she had heard that the London County Council were planning to move children out of London, she had offered Billingham to the London school attended by Tom and Rachel and they had taken up the offer: 'We have twenty-four children and four staff down there and Tom and Rachel love it.' If war came, Jane wrote, Jack had been asked to join the Ministry of Information and would have to stay in London, but she would keep Billingham going and find some war work. As for the children, she told Davison that Angela was now at RADA, Barbara in the throes of School Certificate and Mary home for half term. Apparently there had been a production of *I Have Been Here Before* in New York but it had failed dismally, which had upset Jack deeply.

For *Johnson Over Jordan* Priestley drew on all his theatrical expertise, his thoughts on time, his reading of Jung, Dunne and Ouspensky and his desire to experiment with what are now known as multimedia theatrical forms, but which were new to theatre in the late 1930s. Most of the play's critics described it as 'expressionistic', an adjective Priestley considered totally inaccurate. He was right, for it could have been used of almost anything from the work of serious German dramatists to the early films of Orson Welles. *Johnson Over Jordan* was 'experimental', yes, 'expressionistic', no.

In it, Priestley moves on from time seen as a circle or a spiral or even as a serial dimension, for when the play opens his protagonist/hero Johnson has died and, in showing what happens afterwards, Priestley attempts to offer an alternative to Christian belief. In Act I the newly dead Johnson faces an inquisition at the hands of the mysterious Examiners, who confront him with his earthly actions. In Act II Johnson is in a nightmare world of lust and violence where, in a surrealistic nightclub, he is overcome with desire for a young veiled woman and stabs the young man he assumes is her lover. When he tears the veil from her face, though, he discovers she is his own daughter and the young man his son. Faced with the kind of man he really is, Johnson asks if he might return to earth to put right all that he has done wrong, but this is refused. Instead he is sent to an inn, described by Gareth Lloyd Evans as a sort of clearing-house where residents discover 'what it is that, beneath the coruscating surface of the world, has been the reality that meant most but which went unregarded'. At the inn Johnson rediscovers pleasure in simple things, experiences better relationships with his family and the joys of friendship. Throughout the play he has been accompanied by a masked figure which he sees at first as death and corruption but finally as a spiritual guide. At the end Johnson and the figure are standing at the foot of a staircase. The figure tells him it is time to go. 'Is it a long way?' asks Johnson. 'I don't know, Robert,' it replies, and both it and the staircase vanish, leaving Johnson alone on a great bridge preparing to set off into the unknown.

A tremendous amount of talent was brought together for *Johnson*. The young Benjamin Britten was commissioned to write the score, the designer was the great Edward Gordon Craig, who used the new design technique of cycloramas, and the director was Basil Dean. Ralph Richardson played Johnson, heading a cast of twenty-three actors and dancers. In his preface to the published edition of the play Priestley writes that he wanted to make use of every modern theatrical technique and resource. However the project failed in production – not least because it broke such new ground. Neither those involved in putting it on nor the audiences that went to see it had experienced anything like it before, and although it contains some fine writing, it does not live up to the grandeur of its theme.

All those who saw and wrote about it said that Richardson gave one of the best, possibly even *the* best performance of his entire professional life and that no one who saw that last exit could leave the theatre unmoved. Standing at the back of the auditorium on the first night, Basil Dean was moved to tears, while the young Harold Hobson wrote that Richardson's voice alone made him want to cry. The press was mixed, some reviewers at least recognising that they had witnessed a remarkable theatrical experience. The *Times* critic wrote that it was 'a deeply conscious, impassioned and charitable attack upon a great subject and that in the theatre is more than half the world'. On the other hand, James Agate, who had helped to save *Dangerous Corner*, upset Priestley by saying he had disliked it 'not because the presentation was new but because, while pretending to be new, it was, or seemed to be, a mish-mash of *Outward Bound* and *Liliom* done in the demoded Elmer Rice manner'.

It had opened at the New Theatre on 22 February 1939, and after only a few weeks it was clear that it could not continue: audiences were thin and it was losing money hand over fist. Priestley ended its run in May, hired the smaller Saville Theatre and persuaded Dean to take only half a royalty. Richardson agreed to continue on no salary for the first few weeks, to be followed thereafter by a fifty-fifty split of the box office receipts, after deduction of production costs. Priestley reworked some of it, spicing up Act II with more sex, which provoked the Lord Chamberlain, the official censor, to demand the removal of the line 'as the bishop said to the actress'. The play was relaunched with seats at reduced prices and fresh publicity.

However, Ralph Richardson had sunk into the depths of despair: Basil Dean, who had other commitments, had had to leave the production. After one matinée Richardson wrote to Dean in desperation, pleading with him to find time 'before you go away to help us with our second act. It is terrible as it is – it all wants setting and pulling together – we are sunk unless this is done. You did say you would help us with the alterations we would make. I never wanted help more than now.'

But Hugh Walpole wrote to Priestley saying that after he had seen the play he had been so moved he could hardly speak. He said he had been staggered at the difference between the play he had seen and that described by the critics: 'The critics are absurdly wrong.' The playwright Clifford Bax had also written congratulating Priestley on his

> brave, skilful, big-minded work which ought, if people had more sense, to be a landmark in our theatre. The fascination of the play never stopped for me, nor shall I ever forget the moving and beautiful end (superbly played, I thought, by Richardson). This was indeed the best evening which I have had in the theatre for a very long time. The fine sincerity of both author and actors made upon me a deep impression.

But in spite of Dean's skill, Richardson's devotion and the author's belief in it, nothing could save the play that Priestley then considered the best thing he had ever written for the stage.

On Sunday, 3 September Jane was driving her husband to the BBC in London. *Let the People Sing* had been adapted for radio and he was to read the first instalment. It was a lovely day, the sky was blue and the sun shining. As they came down the hill from Bagshot they were suddenly aware of cars, loaded with people and luggage, racing past in the opposite direction. Then, out of the quiet blue, came the scream of sirens. 'Beneath the astonished noonday sun, people in steel helmets came hurrying, shouting and gesticulating. It was then I learned we had been at war for the last hour.'[9]

CHAPTER 20

Postscripts

If the journey into London had seemed unreal, the rest of the day resembled a slow-motion silent film. The usually busy roads of Camden Town and Kentish Town were as empty as if the plague had struck. Jane was to remain in Highgate while after his broadcast Priestley had another engagement. On arrival at the BBC he was ushered into a basement studio, which immediately resurrected memories of the trenches: 'At any moment I felt I might be told to crawl out to a listening post up towards Regent's Park.'[1]

Afterwards, as he drove to Paddington, he thought he had never seen the streets so empty: 'It was like going in a taxi through an immense deserted film set of a city, still illuminated by great yellow lights. Through this unreality I carried within me a companion feeling of unreality, not unlike that I remember having on my way to a Nursing Home for an operation.' But his westbound train was crowded with people fleeing London, '. . . the place reeked of weary humanity. The platforms thick with waste paper, half-eaten buns and empty bottles, and everywhere mothers appeared to be feeding their young. The trains, you felt, had no longer the old particular destinations. They were simply going perhaps never to return.' The dreamlike feeling continued when he looked up into the evening sky as the train emerged into the countryside and saw a curious cloud formation like a 'rampant dragon, etched in fire . . . The beast had been trapped inside the vast azure bowl.' Whatever the outcome of the conflict, he felt nothing would ever be the same again.

Priestley had readily agreed to work for the Ministry of Information and his enormous output of books fell sharply during the war years. There were two novels, both with a war theme, *Blackout in*

Gretley and *Daylight on Saturday*, and four official commissions on topics such as *British Women Go to War* and *Out of the People*. But he produced five plays, the best-known being *They Came to a City*. He also started work on *An Inspector Calls*.

Two letters to the Davisons written in October 1939, the first from Jane, the second from Priestley, describe how they were learning to live with the new situation.[2] 'Life has changed drastically for us,' wrote Jane, 'but not so far unpleasantly.' Priestley was away writing a series of '*English Journey*-type' articles for the Ministry of Information to be published in Britain, America and 'the Dominions'. The change from peace to war had come fast for the civilian population, yet 'there is such a queer silence about the war itself'. Everything was thrown into confusion. Normally the Priestleys, except for Angela, would have been in London, the children at school. Barbara and Mary had been evacuated to Dorset and the two girls were joined there by their sister Sylvia, who had been at a different school in Gerrard's Cross. The three girls were due to leave shortly and when they did Barbara went on to study architecture, Mary enrolled at the Royal College of Music and Sylvia joined the WRNS as a despatch rider. Angela had just left RADA and was to have gone into a play at the Westminster Theatre but in the early stages of the war theatres were being closed.

However, the war did not stop her becoming a débutante. Exquisitely gowned by Molyneux, she had been presented at Court by Jane and went on to do the Season. What her father thought of this is not known. 'I gave a dance for her in July,' Jane wrote, 'but now *all* her young male friends have vanished – some are in the Navy, some in the army – none are left.' Soon Angela, too, was gone, to train as a volunteer nurse. She was sent immediately to an understaffed cottage hospital where, in the course of her first week, she dealt with a woman who vomited continually, another with dysentery and a third who died. Jane returned to Billingham, taking Rachel and Tom with her. Petrol was now rationed and as she could not get them to school she taught them at home as she had in Arizona.

The war impinged on everything. There was a blackout now in the evenings at Billingham. Its use as a school had been short-lived, only a matter of weeks, and it had now reverted to use by the family who found themselves having to manage with oil lamps as there was no petrol for the generator. The

upkeep of the house had required a substantial staff, many of
whom were now being called up, and Priestley's secretary left
'to take part in the war effort'. At least this meant less expense
and the Priestleys had already decided that their household
budget should be cut by half: they felt his income was bound
to decrease. The future for plays was in doubt and there was
no way of knowing if Jack's books would continue to sell.

Jane told the Davisons that the most positive thing to have
resulted from the outbreak of war was that people had become
more friendly: they talked to each other in a way that previously
they never had. There did not seem to be mass hatred of
Germans, just of Hitler and the German government. Davison,
who was ex-Navy, had immediately written to the Royal Navy
Volunteer Reserve, asking if there was anything he could do if
he returned to England, but Jane, in a hastily added, rather odd
note, told him that there weren't enough jobs in the services for
the British, let alone Americans!

Priestley echoed his wife's view of attitudes to Germans and
the war a week later in his letter to Davison:

> . . . the whole atmosphere is quite different from 1914 – no
> jingoism or flag-waving, no bands, none of that hysterical Bank
> Holiday feeling, no romantic exaltation. This is a complete
> refutation of the charge that human nature doesn't change,
> for I never saw such a change. Apart from some young Nazis,
> if they haven't already learnt better, nobody even pretends to
> like war. It's just a damned nuisance, like having to tackle a
> huge raving drunk who threatens to set your house on fire.

He was desperately busy. His series of Ministry of Information
articles was appearing in the *News Chronicle* but he had found
the Ministry badly organised, with too few journalists and too
many civil servants. It did not have the power to decide what the
public should be told and when. The older ministries were 'still
exercising their right of censorship. The truth is the people in
power have not yet fully understood that this war depends more
on public opinion and morale than on anything else. Deep down
they have the mandarin's contempt for the general public.'

By January 1940 Priestley's great spate of war writing had
already entailed travelling over 3000 miles, after which he
returned to Billingham to get on with some work of his own.

He had been approached to write a film script for propaganda purposes, showing how valuable freedom was and what might happen if Britain lost it, but at that stage, he wrote to Davison, it was 'still in the air'. The film, *The Foreman Went to France*, was finally made in 1941, directed by Alberto Cavalcanti. Based on a real-life incident, it followed the adventures of a Welsh factory foreman who was sent to France on a sabotage mission before Dunkirk, and starred Tommy Trinder, Robert Morley and Gordon Jackson. But Priestley was finding it harder to write than ever before because of his anxieties 'over the world's madhouse'. Even at this early stage, he was giving considerable thought to what would happen when the war was over: 'I anticipate great changes here, much greater than after the last war . . . I see an opportunity for liberal socialism of the type towards which the Scandinavian countries have been moving.'

In March 1940 he wrote enthusiastically to Eugene Saxton of Harper's that he had just embarked on 'an actor novel, which I have entitled *These Are Actors* – the familiar phrase from Prospero's speech, of course'. After their reaction to *The Good Companions* he was well aware of how prospective publishers viewed stage novels, but he felt there was a place for 'a serious intelligent novel about an actor'. His hero would be an intelligent fellow 'modelled, to some extent, on my friend, Ralph Richardson'. He was writing the book, he said, 'to get a lot of stuff out of my system, just as I wrote the autobiographical books – and *not* as I've written novels these last few years – and my attitude is LIKE IT OR LUMP IT. But I believe you will like it very much . . .' However, a month later Priestley told Harper's that he was abandoning the novel. He had come to the conclusion, he said, that its subject matter was too narrow and technical for the great majority of readers and that the theatre itself was too small a world to have universal appeal. 'So it's off. And you can imagine that after doing 30,000 words in blood and sweat and tears at a time like this, I don't abandon them lightly.'[3]

Early in the war Jane had considered sending all the children except Angela to America for the duration, the three older ones to Springfield in Massachusetts, where Walter Gropius had offered 'hospitality' to their boarding school, and the younger two with their nanny to friends. In April 1940, though, as Jane wrote to the Davisons, she was beginning to think it was already too late to risk the crossing: she had been told that the earliest

possible date would be mid-August. She continued to worry
about the younger children's safety and Tom Priestley has
vague memories of time spent in the Welsh seaside town of
Criccieth, in a cottage in Snowdonia belonging to Jane's sister
Ena, and, during the first year of the war, in a house owned
by the writer Joyce Cary in Oxford.

Jane herself continued to divide her time between London
and Billingham, but spent most of it in London with her husband.
She wrote to Natalie Davison on 30 June 1940 that 'Jack is doing
simply magnificent work broadcasting on Sundays at 9.15 p.m
and any other evening he is asked to, to the Dominions and USA
on short wave. The English broadcasts are an abnormal success.
They are a "Good Companions" success.' The realisation that
Britain was now standing alone against Germany had led to a
curious atmosphere in the country of exhilaration and uplift.
'Everyone feels it, most of all in the labouring classes . . .' There
was plenty of work, still plenty of food in spite of rationing, and
'a lot of improvisation'. She could not say where she would be
or what she would be doing in the future but felt strongly that
she must use her organising ability. Currently she was running
a Red Cross Supplies Depot, dealing with Polish refugees and
their problems, 'getting them registered through the police,
getting them identity cards, ration cards and gas masks, then
to their billets'. One young girl stayed in her mind: she was
barely out of her teens and had 'an adorable baby' of only
three months.

During this period Jane's letters are written in a racy
'Britain-can-take-it' style and it is in this way that she described
an event that in fact distressed her greatly. On returning with
Miss Pudduck from a visit to the Isle of Wight, she was informed
that Billingham had been requisitioned for immediate use by the
Army. This was most unusual as house owners were supposed to
be given forty-eight hours' notice. 'I was glad to know it was to
be used,' she wrote gamely, but this was far from the truth. In
an unpublished manuscript written towards the end of her life,
she recorded that she had returned to London to be told by
a friend that she must ring Billingham as 'something frightful
has happened'. She did so and was surprised to be answered by
a man's voice; he said he was sorry to have to tell her but that
the Army had taken over the house and the Priestleys were not
to return to the island. For fear of raids on London many of

their valuables had been taken to Billingham from The Grove for safety and most of their personal possessions were there too. 'I said, "You can't do that. I've just come away for two weeks and I have clothes with me for that amount of time and nothing else. Everything I have is now on the island. You can't take over a house with all our private belongings." He replied that he was afraid he could and that I must abide by what he said.'

Shortly afterwards she had a message from Billingham to the effect that it had become the Army's General Headquarters on the island and would she please come down at once, empty it of furniture and remove all the family's possessions. Seventeen different regiments passed through Billingham during the first six months of the war.

In that same June letter to the Davisons, she remembered how, shortly before she left Billingham, there had been a minor air raid and, against all the orders, she had stood in the window of Jack's rooftop study and watched the dog fights in the sky above. 'I saw two planes brought down on different nights.' But now it was Sunday in London, a lovely sunny day, Jack was playing tennis with some neighbours and she could hear the ping of the balls down the hill. They felt at any moment that 'things would start here so every hour of a day like this, every meeting with a friend is doubly precious. We pray and hope and are determined to sacrifice everything, if necessary, rather than give in. It's not a bad moment to be alive in and I can't tell you now exalted and consecrated one feels England to be.' Jack was being 'simply magnificent. All he is doing – and he is at it eighteen hours a day – in articles, films, broadcasts is inspired and if I'd never been proud of him before, I'd be most proud now.'

The broadcasts that had drawn the 'abnormal audiences' and were proving as popular as *The Good Companions* were the famous *Postscripts*. For nineteen weeks, between 5 June and 20 October, Priestley had a regular slot at peak listening time following the nine o'clock news on the BBC's Home Service, and millions of people listened to him; official audience research put the figure at 29 per cent of the adult population.

Almost immediately after the outbreak of war, he had approached the BBC and asked if he could do some broadcasting. After Dunkirk, prodded by Jane, he contacted them again and was asked to go in to see an executive. Jane remembered him coming back from his interview and saying, 'What a ridiculous idea! They want me to do a Sunday talk after the news at nine o'clock. Nobody will ever want to listen to that.'[4]

The first *Postscript* was seen as a pilot, and its theme was the gallantry and bravery of everyone concerned with the Dunkirk evacuation, but particularly that of the captains of the pleasure boats and steamers that had played such a crucial role. Picked out for special mention was the pride of the Isle of Wight ferry service, the paddle steamer *Gracie Fields* on which Priestley had eaten many an egg-and-bacon breakfast – and which had sailed to Dunkirk never to return. But Priestley also pointed out that Dunkirk had happened because serious mistakes had been made, that this had been acknowledged and should be freely discussed. 'We have gone sadly wrong like this before; and here and now we must resolve never, never to do it again.' The first *Postscript* remained for ever in his mind, for as he was leaving the recording studio he bumped into 'a prominent broadcaster', who was weeping.

Priestley turned out to be a consummate broadcaster. The *Postscripts* were a brilliant mixture of sturdy uplift, personal anecdote, honesty, humour, and excursions into English literature with quotations from Shakespeare, Dickens and Chesterfield. He was heartening and rousing but without a trace of jingoism. Several editions stand out. There is a haunting description of 'some fantastic dream of a day trip to Margate'.[5] It required passes and permits, tin hats and gas masks, and a journey in Army vehicles through country lanes lined with Bren guns. Priestley and his companions had almost reached the promenade before he realised that they had arrived in the town 'even though *I* was actually holding the map!' The sun came out, it was boiling hot, and everything was there: bathing pools, bandstands, gardens blazing with flowers, the lido, theatres and miles of golden sand spread out beneath the July sun.

But no people – not a soul. Of all those hundreds of thousands of holiday-makers, of entertainers and hawkers and boatmen – not a soul! And no sound – not the very ghost of an echo of all that cheerful hullabaloo – children shouting and laughing, bands playing, concert parties singing, men selling ice-cream, whelks and peppermint rock, which I'd remembered hearing along this shore. No, not even an echo. Silence.

But gradually a subtext began to creep into the *Postscripts*. The young Jack Priestley who had left the Army in 1919 had seen what had happened to so many servicemen who had survived the carnage of the First World War. Not for them Cambridge University and a successful career. All that 'the land fit for heroes', for which they had fought, offered them was unemployment, starvation wages – if a job could be found – and nowhere to live. He had never forgotten the pathetic army of white-faced men who knocked on doors trying to sell brooms, vacuum cleaners or doubtful insurance policies on commission, or the veterans who had been unable to attend his battalion reunion in 1934.

Within the confines of the *Postscripts*, he asked what would happen after the war was over and Hitler defeated. Winning the war was not enough: it should herald a brighter dawn and a better future for all who had taken part in it. We must, he told his listeners on 21 July, stop thinking in terms of property and power and begin to think in terms of community and creation. Property is

that old-fashioned way of thinking of a country as a thing, and a collection of things on that thing, all owned by certain people and constituting property; instead of thinking of a country as a living society, and considering the welfare of that society, the community itself, as the first test . . . I tell you, there is stirring in us now, a desire which could soon become a controlled but passionate determination to remodel and re-create this life of ours, to make it the glorious beginning of a new world order, so that we might soon be so fully and happily engrossed in our great task that if Hitler and his gang suddenly disappeared we'd hardly notice they'd gone. We're even now the hope of free men everywhere but soon we could be the hope and lovely dawn of the whole wide world.

Nor was it enough to salute the young men and women of the armed services for their courage and bravery if, at the end of it all, they had to return to a re-run of the 1930s: 'I felt we had no right to praise them in wartime without assuring them we would improve their working and living conditions in peacetime. To thank a man publicly, with tears in your eyes and voice, while conveniently forgetting that his fo'castle was a hell-hole and his wife and children lived in a slum, seemed to be a job for Pecksniff.'[6]

The *Postscripts* were written under increasingly difficult conditions yet, a true professional, he always delivered them on time. Every Sunday he would arrive at Broadcasting House carrying his battered portable typewriter and, with cotton wool in his ears, would sit down at seven thirty p.m. and write the next *Postscript.* After he had finished that, he would do a script for the USA, then the Home Service broadcast, to be followed by that for America at two a.m.

By the beginning of September the Priestleys had decided to shut up the Highgate house for the time being. In a letter to the Davisons, headed 'The British Trust for Ornithology (Hon Treasurer Mrs J.B. Priestley)', Jane described the scene at The Grove. She was sitting on a mattress in the basement, the others being occupied respectively by the cook, the parlourmaid, the housemaid and 'the master of the house'. The ceiling was shored up with timber and it was very dark, as the blackened window looked out only on to the area steps, but she had hung her Navaho rugs on the walls to make it look more cheerful. An air-raid was going on and German planes were droning overhead to the steady rhythm of ack-ack guns. 'Jack keeps going into the next room where there is a typewriter – he has a half-written article. Every time he sits down to the typewriter our nearest guns start and make a terrific noise. At the moment he's given it up and is back on his mattress.' The previous night she had slept under the kitchen stairs: the raids seemed to have gone on for hours and she was on her own as Jack had been broadcasting and had been unable to get home until six in the morning.

Jane went to the children in Wales and Priestley booked into the Langham Hotel next door to the BBC. The raids had been so bad one night that he was unable to leave the BBC's cellars. News bulletins were carrying a report that a large London hotel had been hit. At dawn as the all-clear sounded, Priestley went out into the street to see that the Langham had been bombed and his own room had disappeared in a mound of rubble.

*   *   *

Nothing else on radio had quite the same impact as the *Postscripts*. People broke their necks to get home from their day shifts to listen, while nightworkers would gather round their firm's radio. Hours before the broadcast, those in remote parts of the country started trying to tune their old valve radios to the right station. NAAFI canteens fell silent as servicemen listened to what J. B. Priestley had to say in that rich, full and, above all, comforting Yorkshire voice.

Letters poured in to the BBC from listeners. Newspapers wrote that the voice of J. B. Priestley was now as well-known as that of Churchill. (It was, of course, not known then that Churchill's speeches were read by an actor.) At the beginning almost all the letters praised him but a few did not and, gradually, a steady flow accused him, of being insufficiently patriotic or, worse still, peddling left-wing political notions. As early as the beginning of September some influential people began to make their views felt and among them were Colonel Scorgie, of the Ministry of Information, and Lord Davison, ex-chairman of the Conservative Party. When he was told of their complaints, Priestley wrote to the BBC's director-general pointing out that the majority of the letters he received supported his views and only a few accused him of bias. Other big guns joined the opposition, not least the BBC's head of talks, Sir Richard Maconachie. In a letter to A. P. Ryan, the Home Office adviser on broadcasting, Maconachie wrote that Priestley had 'definite social and political views which he puts over in his broadcasts and through these broadcasts is, I think, exercising an important influence on what people are thinking'. This, of course, would never do: '. . . the question I wish to raise is whether any single person should be given the opportunity of acquiring such an influence to the exclusion of others who differ from him merely on the grounds of his merits as a broadcaster which are, of course, very great'.

But this growing hostility was not why the first series ceased on 20 October – indeed, Priestley went out of his way to emphasise his good relationship with the BBC. It had ended because he felt that he had had enough for the time being and thought his audience would appreciate a change. But, he said,

Stupid persons have frequently accused me in public of – I use their own words – taking advantage of my position to bring party politics into my talks. This is extremely ironical because I am not a member of any particular party. I've no close personal relations with any prominent members of any party, and no expectations from the success of any particular party, whereas it is obvious that these critics of mine are members of a political party and that their criticism comes from taking a narrow party line. It is not I, but they, who put party before country for I've never even learned to think in terms of a political party. And the most I've asked for in these talks is that we should mean what we say; be really democratic while fighting for democracy; and that we should make some attempt to discover the deeper causes of this war and to try and find a remedy for them . . . if all this together with certain obvious elements of social justice and decency seems to you Socialism, Communism or Anarchy, then you are at liberty to call me a Socialist, a Communist or an Anarchist, though I would implore you to stop pasting on labels and instead to think a little.

Various other writers took their turn in the Priestleys' slot – Clemence Dane, A. P. Herbert and Emlyn Williams among them – but none commanded the listening figures or the loyalty inspired by Priestley. He had become a household name. Finally, on 26 January 1941, he was brought back for a second series. Immediately the popular right-wing press were gunning for him, the *Daily Mail* of 3 March declaring that out of 816 letters they had received about the Priestley *Postscripts*, 529 were against them.

On 22 March *Picture Post* decided to make the *Postscripts* its major feature in a lengthy article written by Charles Fenby. A huge portrait of Priestley dominated the front cover and the caption read: 'Do listeners like Priestley?' According to *Picture Post* they did, some 3000 having written to him between 26 January and the beginning of March to tell him so. Against this, he had received only around 300 letters of complaint. As the *Mail*'s columnist, Charles Graves, had assured his readership that those who were sympathetic were all socialists, it must follow, Fenby wrote, that of the millions of people who listened to Priestley about 14 million were socialists 'or, at any rate, this is the conclusion to which we are led by the ingenious correspondence test of Mr Graves. And a very remarkable conclusion it must appear to the Socialist party . . .'

At first, Fenby said, it had seemed that Priestley's enemies had been acting independently of each other, but now it was beginning to look like a concerted attack led publicly by the *Mail*, the London *Evening Standard* and the *Weekly Review*, and orchestrated by the then Minister of Information, the Conservative MP Brendan Bracken. The *Review*, Fenby reminded his readers, had supported Mussolini before the war. Yet another weekly, *Truth*, had dismissed Priestley's pleas for a better Britain: 'Is it not merely a coincidence that the majority vote in this country has been given again and again to a party which – except in the emergency conditions of war – favours the least possible interference by the Government in private affairs?' Could this possibly be, asked Fenby, the same *Conservative* party that had brought in tariffs, the means tests and marketing boards? Not to mention the Depression.

Next the *Post* aimed its spotlight on Brendan Bracken and how, in his book *Men, Martyrs and Mountebanks*, published as late as January 1940, he had deplored the unwillingness of Adolf Hitler to become 'one of the great constructive figures of history, reverenced by his own people and respected by others'; how in November 1936 he had told the Holborn Chamber of Commerce that within twelve months there would be internal trouble in Nazi Germany and that Japan would be forced to co-operate with the democracies; how, after Munich, he had written in the *Sunday Graphic*, 'At last we have a chance to secure peace for this troubled world ... I do not believe there will be a war'; and how, in July 1938, he had told the House of Commons, 'I think we are very foolish in this House sometimes, those of us who refuse to believe that there is any good in National Socialism or that there is no unselfishness in men like Hitler and Goering.' Mr Bracken, Fenby wrote, had taken it upon himself to criticise Priestley's past. It was only fair, therefore, that his own political judgements should be resurrected for the enlightenment of those 14 million people who did not agree with him. Could it be, he mused finally, that those who attacked Priestley and all who agreed with him were moved by a desire to cover up the part they had played in leading the country towards its present crisis? 'We have lived through ghastly years. Ghastly years of appeasement, non-intervention, timidity, pretence, hypocrisy, lies. Men who liked that pre-war atmosphere dislike the man who has done so much to dispel it. But they have had their day and it is over now. "Thank you, sir!" said a postcard to Priestley. "You have begun to show us the Englishman."' Game, set and match to *Picture Post*.

But Priestley found it hard to accept that Hugh Walpole could be among his critics. Whether he had told Priestley personally what he thought or whether it was in a missing letter is not clear, but whatever Walpole had said provoked a strong response from Priestley:

> I did not realise that you sat so firmly on the other side of the fence . . . you say that in the summer the whole country followed me because I was a patriot. But the fact remains that a determined effort was made by a small but very influential group even then to get me off the air and the only reason I wasn't stopped was because the BBC was afraid of the public. It was the *News Chronicle* – and I wrote a long article myself about it – that before the war demanded that Churchill should immediately be given a place in the Cabinet. It was the Progressive press that, together with the Labour Party, brought about the downfall of the Chamberlain government which would have *undoubtedly lost us the war*.

He hoped that the same influences would not weaken the country's effort further and that 'we really fight for what we say we are fighting for'. People like him only asked that the incompetent and suspect should no longer be allowed to decide policy: 'Believe me, it is not the progressives who are not "playing the game" but the reactionaries who quietly break the so-called political truce all the time. I hope you enjoy your Christmas. Yours. J.B.P.'

Shortly after the *Picture Post* feature, the Priestley *Postscripts* stopped for good. 'This time I really was taken off the air,' he wrote later in *Margin Released*. It had infuriated him because

> I dislike being pushed around, especially when I can discover who is doing the pushing. I received two letters . . . one was from the Ministry of Information telling me that the BBC was responsible for the decision to take me off the air, and the other was from the BBC saying that a directive had come from the Ministry of Information to end my broadcasts. While blaming each other, I think both of them were concealing the essential fact – that the order to shut me up had come from elsewhere.

It has often been suggested that the order to stop the *Postscripts* had come from the highest possible source, Churchill himself, although there is no proof of this.

It seems that little has changed since Priestley wrote of the incident:

I don't know how other people feel about this stealthy hocus-pocus, but to my mind it is one of the most contemptible features of British public life. Power is exercised in such a way – a nod here, a wink there – that it can't be challenged. We are democratic and free in theory but not in practice. Work may be censored as it is elsewhere, but not openly, through a censor's office that everyone knows about; it is quietly shuffled and conjured away. Men are squeezed out of public jobs, not for political reasons – oh, dear no! – but because they are discovered to be not quite the right type, not sound, old boy. This is the British way, slimy with self-deception and cant, and the older I get, the more I dislike it.

CHAPTER 21

Through the War

By the end of September 1940, 3 The Grove was finally packed up, and the family never again lived there permanently. Later it was badly damaged when a land mine hit the nearby church, and at some stage in the course of the war it was sold. During the early war years Priestley lived mostly in London hotels, then in a service flat off Whitehall, but in 1943, wanting a permanent base, he leased two small flats in the exclusive Albany complex just off Piccadilly.

As Priestley himself constantly reiterated, he had never been a joiner of organisations, and his brief tenure of the presidency of PEN had ended in acrimony following an international conference. Yet in the early days of the war he became involved with three organisations. The first, the Authors' Planning Committee, had been set up in 1938 after the invasion of Poland and Priestley had been asked to support it – not least because his own books were banned in Nazi Germany. The original committee was made up of the writers A. P. Herbert and Dorothy Sayers, Priestley's agent A. D. Peters, the politician Richard Crossman and the academic Denys Kilham Rogers, under the chairmanship of the distinguished lawyer Raymond Needham. By May 1940, it had achieved so little that it was disbanded. Priestley formed a new group, the Authors' National Committee, to encourage writers to take an active role in the war effort, and he set about rounding up as many 'names' as possible. He met with a degree of success but one of his failures was Bernard Shaw. Priestley was not surprised: he had got to know Shaw quite well during the pre-war Malvern Festivals of which Shaw had always seen himself as the doyen. 'There was a kind of innocent vanity about Shaw,' Priestley said later. 'He just naturally assumed he was at the centre of things. Once when I was in Malvern I thought of hiring six tall character actors, giving them beards and dressing them all as Shaw and having one in every street . . .'[1] But neither vanity nor patriotism moved Shaw to join Priestley's committee: presumably, he wrote, Jack had never had to sit on an Authors' Committee. Shaw had, and that of the Society of Authors had put him off it for life; however delightful authors might be socially, 'in committee, to call them hogs would be an insult to a comparatively co-operative animal'. Outside literature he felt he had no special abilities that the Government could employ. He added that there were enough duffers in national service already 'and I am the prince of duffers except when I am doing what terrifies the Government and confirms its "strange prejudice" (surely a very natural one) against an ungovernable profession. So don't put my name down.' He recognised the need for the war and the effort involved, hoped it would soon be over and then 'we shall have some fun, you and I'. He ended in a particularly Shavian way: 'The broadcasts are a waste of your time; but they are very enjoyable.'[2]

The Authors' National Committee failed in what Priestley had seen as its prime task, to persuade the Ministry of Information to commission writers to cover aspects of the war in greater depth than could be expected of journalists. It descended into constant wrangling, divided for much the same reasons that had brought about the demise of the *Postscripts*. Priestley's views on what people deserved after the conflict were considered too left-wing by some committee members, including Denys Kilham Roberts, Professor John MacMurray and the novelist Storm Jameson. It staggered on for a while but was eventually disbanded.

On the other hand the 1941 Committee, of which Priestley was chairman, came about directly as a result of the *Postscripts* in general and the one that dealt with the theme of property in particular. That broadcast had struck an immediate chord with Sir Richard Acland, then a young, radical and independent MP. He had already embraced the idea of common ownership and had even divested himself of large family estates in Devon and Somerset, which he made over to the National Trust. Immediately after he heard Priestley's *Postscript* of 21 July 1940 Acland contacted him, suggesting that between them he was sure they could gather together a powerful team devoted to social reform. The 1941 Committee met for the first time at the home of Edward Hulton, publisher of *Picture Post*. Financial support came from Alan Good, a wealthy Midlands industrialist, and economic advice from the academic economist Thomas Balogh, later Baron Balogh. Members were drawn from a wide variety of backgrounds and included publishers, journalists, writers, novelists, artists, sociologists and those in public life. As Diana Collins pointed out, several of them, Acland, Kingsley Martin (editor of the *New Statesman*), the publisher Victor Gollancz and journalist Ritchie Calder, not to mention Priestley himself, later stood shoulder-to-shoulder in the Campaign for Nuclear Disarmament. The Secretary of the new Committee was Raymond Gauntlett.[3]

The 1941 Committee produced a number of pamphlets and short books, putting forward proposals such as joint industrial councils of men and management, national insurance, family allowances, and a basic minimum wage, much of which was later either incorporated into the Beveridge Report or became part of Labour Party policy, leading on to the founding of the Welfare State.

Priestley's own contribution to the social debate, *Out of the People*, sold over 41,000 copies in a year. In it he set out his own political credo. Democracy, he wrote, meant devolution of power, not centralisation. It required local activity and responsibility, especially in more remote areas. To this end support should be given to the trade unions, the Co-operative movement and cultural, professional and charitable organisations, because these were the sinews of democracy: 'Parliament should not drain away all the political life of the country.' He favoured a mixed economy: 'All large-scale and absolutely essential utilities and services should be taken over by the community. But the main bulk of production would not be a State affair, because private enterprise permits more experiment, flexibility and efficiency . . . a rigidly planned State economy means dragooning the people.' In a paper she gave on 'Priestley as Citizen and Social Critic', Diana Collins wrote that although he was a socialist, 'Jack was never in favour of State Socialism. [He said] "I do not want to see people's lives arranged for them, I want to see them re-creating their own society." It might be described as moderate, common-sense socialism, she continues, 'the kind we now call Social Democratic and which he had imbibed in his

Bradford youth, and though his ideas were radical, he was always a moderate and democratic reformer, not a revolutionary'.

But soon the 1941 Committee was not enough for Acland: he wanted to found an entirely new political party and invited both Priestley and H. G. Wells to join it. Wells disagreed fundamentally with Acland on so many points that he refused point blank, but Priestley gave it his cautious support. He told Acland, though, that he had severe doubts about it as a strategy, and refused his request to speak at a series of meetings even though they would not be sponsored by any political organisations. Priestley saw one of his main tasks as holding together the disparate membership of the 1941 Committee, many of whom would consider the founding of a new political party harmful to the Labour Party's chances of forming a post-war government.

Acland, however, went ahead and on 26 July 1941 set up his new party, the Common Wealth, its aims based on ideas he had put forward in a booklet of his own, *The Forward March.* Priestley was far from happy. He and Richard Acland, says Diana Collins, were 'too temperamentally different to be able to work together for long'. The Aclands were good friends of hers 'and we knew Richard to be an honourable, sweet-natured and lovable man; his lively, clever and practical wife, Anne, described her marriage to him as like holding on to the string of a gas-filled balloon, and trying to keep it tethered to the ground as it dragged her along . . .' Priestley tried to bring him back to earth, pointing out that people would find many of his ideas, such as common ownership, hard to accept, and asked how he proposed to bring it about. By dictatorship? As for making a clean break with all international capitalism, how could such an overcrowded island, unable to support itself, afford to do such a thing? Eventually Priestley withdrew his support from Common Wealth and resigned his chairmanship of the 1941 Committee, although afterwards he spoke several times on its behalf. Years later Acland told John and Diana Collins that, 'Despite our agreement on many issues it would, I suppose, have needed a miracle to keep us together in a fighting organisation.' Acland wanted political power; Priestley wanted influence. Such partnerships can prove successful but in theirs the aims proved incompatible.

Perhaps there was another possible reason for Priestley to have lost heart for a fight: in 1941 Hugh Walpole died. He was only fifty-seven but for some years he had suffered increasing ill health. It is clear from their correspondence that he and Priestley had overcome their disagreement over the *Postscripts*: their friendship was too strong and long-standing for it to have been otherwise. There are no surviving letters to Davison from the middle years of the war, although the correspondence must have continued, so we have no revelation to any other friend of how Walpole's death had affected him; but in a letter to Eugene Saxton of Harper's in June 1942 there is a strong inference that he was only then turning his attention again to some of his literary activities following Walpole's death.

Throughout the war, Priestley continued to broadcast to the USA and the Dominions. He wrote to Cass Canfield, a director of Harper's, that the only country unable any longer to hear his views on the radio was Great Britain. He kept up a constant flow of newspaper and magazine articles, continued to write official or semi-official publications and produced the two wartime novels. In 1940, he adapted for the stage *The Long Mirror*, a novel by Jane's sister Ena about a psychic long-distance love affair and its effect on the wife of its leading character, a famous composer. *Good Night Children* appeared in 1942 and is a satire based on Priestley's experiences in broadcasting. In 1943 he wrote two plays, *Desert Highway* and *They Came to a City*. The first, very much a play of its time, he wrote for, and dedicated to, the Army, presenting it to them 'as a small tribute from a soldier of the last war'. Now it rarely sees the light of day, but the second has remained in repertoire ever since.

They Came to a City shows the influence of the 1941 Committee in its portrayal of Utopian socialism. In it, nine people find themselves outside the huge gate of a mysterious city. When the gate suddenly opens they walk through it – and into situations in which each is tested. We never know what the City is like, only that it has its own set of values and that the experience of those who visit it is coloured by their own beliefs and prejudices. The atmosphere of suspense and mystery lasts throughout and the play is both moving and highly comic.

It was directed by Irene Hentschel and rehearsals started in London, although they had to stop from time to time because of air raids. It opened in January 1943 at the Palace Theatre, Bradford, with a cast that included the venerable A. E. Matthews, John Clements, Googie Withers and Raymond Huntley, then transferred to the Globe Theatre in London. Despite the views of some critics it was a great success. Yet again Priestley could not please James Agate, who described it as 'sermonising'. The play that followed, *How Are They At Home?*, produced in 1944, lacked the sure touch Priestley had rediscovered in *They Came to a City*. However, by the end of the war he had completed what many feel is the best play he ever wrote: *An Inspector Calls*.

During the war Priestley's domestic life was chaotic and he must have looked back longingly on those carefully ordered pre-war days, the time set aside for writing, the lack of distractions, the beautiful houses and lavish entertaining.

Jane was busy on her own account. She had continued her search for a serious war job and had contacted Stella Reading, the founder of the Women's Voluntary Service (WVS), who told her that a hostel was urgently need for young mothers who had been bombed out of their homes where they could keep their children with them. 'That,' wrote Jane, 'was the only thing I ever heard from her!' She was put in touch with the Duchess of Marlborough, who suggested that the Home Farm at Blenheim might be converted into a hostel. Jane looked at it, agreed that it was suitable and arranged for some of the furniture that had been in The Grove to be taken out of store. An opening date, a Monday, was set and three young mothers and their families were booked in. Then, on the Friday before the hostel was to be occupied, the Duke's agent arrived to tell Jane that the Government was taking over Blenheim and the Home Farm.[4]

While she was wondering what on earth to do – her furniture and the families were all *en route* to Home Farm – the War Office contacted her and said they could offer instead Broxwood Court, which was ten miles on the Shropshire side of Hereford. Its female owner had gone to the South of France for a fortnight in 1939 and had been unable to get back. The War Office had requisitioned the house but discovered it had insufficient water for the needs of the regiment they had planned to billet there. Jane set off at once to organise the storage of the owner's belongings. She locked the wine safely away in the cellar and, as Broxwood boasted a private chapel, asked permission of a local priest to use it as a furniture store.

Jane's cook, Miss Pudduck, and the parlourmaid, Gertrude,

joined her in Herefordshire, and the Broxwood gardener with one of the manservants agreed to work at the hostel. Jane was also fortunate in having acquired the services of an experienced matron and her friend, both of whom had worked 'as social people' in London's East End. The hostel was still not quite straight when the first family arrived, consisting of a shell-shocked young soldier, his wife and their two small children. 'The father wandered around every hour of the day and night calling for his wife. I can still remember his pathetic voice calling, "Wife! Wife? Where are you, wife?" '

When the mothers arrived, Jane asked them how much money they had and what they could afford to contribute to their upkeep. The hostel was heavily subsidised, and the most any family was charged was a pound a week. If that was beyond their means, they stayed for nothing. She also asked what work they could do: everyone was expected to help keep the household going but they could choose what they did. Most wanted to scrub: 'I could have had that house scrubbed three times a day from roof to basement.' But she persuaded them that other things needed doing, such as cooking, laundry, assisting in the school. An elderly laundress had been brought in to supervise the washing. It was the one job the women did not like and the only one that Jane had to pay them to undertake.

Outside the hostel's grounds, she was treated with great suspicion: 'The local ladies of the county were very cross with me. They got it into their heads that I had taken over Broxwood on my own initiative; that I had taken over the owner's wine for my own consumption.' When the huge Priestley library arrived and Jane weeded out some of the books for the Red Cross, 'the rumour went around that I was disposing of the owner's books from her own library'. The steady stream of families built up to such an extent that the staff had to expand. Soon there were so many children of nursery age that a school was opened with a trained Macmillan nursery school teacher in charge.

Priestley was proud of what Jane had achieved, and wrote to Cass Canfield at Harper's telling him how the hostel had been all her own idea and how successful she was. He spent what time he could with her but his visits were erratic, and in a letter to the Davisons in 1942 Jane said that she could not even rely on his being there for Christmas. Rachel and Tom would be with her, and Mary would come home at the end of the term, but

Barbara was now in an ack-ack unit, Sylvia in the WRNS, and Angela in ENSA.

Running Broxwood Court liberated Jane, although she had to work seven days a week from seven in the morning until ten at night. But it must have suited her because illness was more or less a thing of the past. When Priestley was there he took a personal interest in her protégées. Shortly after his father's death Tom Priestley received a touching letter from a woman who had been at Broxwood. She had been only seventeen when she arrived, the mother of twin sons, her young husband officially 'missing'. She had been bombed out and lost everything.

> One evening, after I'd been there about a week, this gentleman came and said come to my study so as we can talk. I thought he was a farmer and only later I learnt who he was. I was only a child myself with my two babies and my husband missing. I was at my wits' end. We talked and I cried my eyes out. My sanity was saved thanks to your father. My son stayed at the nursery till it closed down and I got a job with the American Red Cross. Your father saved my life and he and your mother will always be in my memory.[5]

Her husband did finally return.

On another occasion, Jane remembered that the Zorian String Quartet had played at Broxwood *en route* for an engagement in the area and had suggested an evening of light music as suitable entertainment. But Jane had asked them to play what they usually did and the women had listened spellbound to Mozart and Schubert; it was the first time most of them had heard live music, apart from bands. The following day, as the quartet rehearsed for their next concert, one young woman from Liverpool crept in and sat at the back of the room, her eyes full of tears.[6]

It is hardly surprising that, with Priestley spending so much time apart from Jane, and her exhaustion when he came to Broxwood, he was propelled into the arms of another woman, with whom he had an affair that lasted several years.

According to Vincent Brome, she was Mary Hope Allen, one of his BBC producers.[7] Although his children were well aware of the Ashcroft interlude, none had heard of Miss Allen, even from Jane, although they all agree that, knowing their father's proclivities, an affair was likely. Miss Allen seems to have been happy to talk about it to Brome. According to her the liaison began in 1941 when she met Priestley in the lift at the BBC in Manchester where her department had been evacuated. He told her he remembered her face from before the war when he had seen her being squired to London first nights by various celebrities, her face 'blazing like a lighthouse'. According to Brome, she told him that over the years Priestley wrote her hundreds of letters, 'a river of love', some even from Broxwood Court, but that throughout their relationship he had never discussed his wife with her, she had not even known her name, and he only rarely mentioned his children. Apparently there had been no suggestion that the relationship would become permanent.

At the same time, Priestley was also writing loving letters to Jane. As well as keeping her up to date with his work, it looks as if she had a good idea of what else he was up to, for in one letter he thanked her for her letter, which was full of 'love, steadiness and good sense', and continued that 'in a few weeks we will try to get a real solid basis of understanding. I have a very deep real feeling for you which operates all the time – and not only when we've quarrelled and I see you unhappy – and though you may not believe this, it is a fact that I always put you first.'

Later, when she briefly became ill with a recurrence of her old gall-bladder trouble, he wrote to her about his disappointment that she could not come to Bradford for the opening of *They Came to a City*, how he felt she had had so much undeserved bad luck.

I've hurt you and you've done nothing to hurt me, though I certainly didn't want to hurt you and was feeling very close to you. It's true I'm sometimes afraid of you – I suppose it's my conscience – but I do know that when I'm with you and you're happy, then I'm happy and when I know you are suffering, I suffer too. And that seems to me genuine love. I am always thinking about you and talking about you and am proud of you. I think you're a magnificent person, very brave, very intelligent and fundamentally nice and generous. And I hate thinking of you in any other terms than those. If you could look into my heart you would see an image of yourself which would please and comfort you.

Sometimes, he told her, he felt that his personal relationships had become complicated by the largely unconscious one he had with the public. Jane had obviously wanted him to talk things over as he ended by saying that he was ready to try it, that he was afraid not of talk but of emotional scenes as they could do so much damage. The following letters were more cheerful and equally loving. On one occasion he and Barbara had spent the evening together in the Albany, eating salmon kedgeree and peas 'and wishing very much you were with us . . . I think of you continually, hope you are thinking of me not unkindly and believe too that with some patience and essential tenderness we can make something better than we've had for a long time.' He realised, he said, that he had made a poor visitor to Broxwood, frequently tired and worried.

From time to time they took a cottage near the seaside for two or three weeks. A Dr Charles Lack wrote to Tom Priestley remembering his father on just such a holiday in Tintagel in Cornwall. He had presented himself at the doctor's surgery suffering from fibrositis. A friendship developed that lasted many years, but Dr Lack recalled one incident from their first encounter particularly clearly. He had been called to the King Arthur's Castle Hotel to visit Mary, who was suffering from some mild illness, and

as I entered the lobby a child of about ten was crying because he could not find his parents. Jack walked across to him and by entertaining him with some brilliant miming, which included Jack stooping, then winding himself round, then straightening up a little as he tugged at an imaginary string, then saying to the child, 'Do you know what that is? That's an old man flying a kite!', he had him in tears of laughter within minutes.

During other visits to Tintagel, Priestley talked to the villagers and discussed their problems with Lack: 'I soon realised that he had learnt more about them than I had, though I was their G.P.'[8]

In 1944 he was suggested by a number of people to the BBC as a possible speaker for a new series entitled *Questions for Tomorrow*.

The Conservative Party immediately swung into action, three of their new MPs putting a motion to Parliament that 'in the opinion of this House the continuing practice of the BBC in giving excessive preference to left-wing speakers such as Mr Priestley calls for censure'. But this time the BBC stuck to its guns, saying that it gave air-time to speakers of all schools of thought, a statement seized on by the Labour MP John Silkin, who immediately put forward an opposing motion congratulating the BBC on the revival of broadcasts by Mr J. B. Priestley.

Nineteen forty-five saw the publication of another unexceptional novel, *Three Men in New Suits*, and a pamphlet detailing Priestley's view of what should happen next, *Letter to a Returning Serviceman*. He had finished *An Inspector Calls* and was planning to put it into production the following year. But he had one more thing to do first. He decided to stand as an independent candidate in the 1945 general election.

CHAPTER 22

Post-War

Priestley's decision to stand for Parliament caused much surprise among those who knew him. Quite why he chose to do so, given his general opinion of politicians and his decision to distance himself from Acland's party, is difficult to understand; nor did he write about it later except in passing. He took an easy route. Until the incoming Labour Government abolished this privilege, graduates of the universities of Oxford and Cambridge were entitled to two votes, one for a candidate representing their university and the other in whichever constituency they happened to live; so, as a graduate of Cambridge University, Priestley put himself up for its seat.

Without a constituency to worry about, he had little to do in the way of ordinary electioneering and campaigning. His election manifesto was broadly that of the Labour Party, but he also suggested that there should be a Ministry for the Arts, an Arts Council to decide national policy, and that money should be set aside to subsidise theatres, art galleries and libraries. He spoke little on his own account, touring the political circuit on behalf of the Labour Party. But the tide that swept Labour into power with 394 seats, a majority of 197, and almost wiped out the Liberal Party, passed by Cambridge University. It returned its sitting member, Kenneth Pickthorn, a senior tutor, history lecturer and ex-junior Conservative minister, by a massive 73,641 votes, leaving Priestley limping in a poor third behind another independent, with only 5,746.

Some time during the winter of 1944–5 he had written, in one week flat, *An Inspector Calls*. Unable to find a vacant theatre in London straightaway, he sent the script to his Russian translator in the USSR where it was immediately taken up by two theatre companies – the Kamerny in Moscow and the Leningrad Theatre

Company – and had its first performance in two cities at the same time. A number of Priestley's books had been translated into Russian and had proved popular, so there was no reason to doubt that the play would be a success. Needless to say, this brought opprobrium from the right, along with suggestions that the play had not been considered good enough for the West End.

The idea for a play about a mysterious stranger, an 'Inspector', who suddenly appears at a family gathering, dated from before the war when Priestley had discussed it with theatre director Michael McOwen. When the two met again in 1944 McOwen reminded him of it, which prompted Priestley to dig out an old notebook, in which he had jotted down the idea, to see if there might be something in it.

An Inspector Calls is a fine play, a classic of the twentieth century. Its theme is that of human responsibility: we have to recognise that we are responsible not only for our own actions, but also for one another. We are, in the Biblical phrase, our brother's keeper. For Gareth Lloyd Evans it was a play about both social responsibility and guilt.[1]

With *An Inspector Calls* Priestley returns to his favourite period, that immediately preceding the First World War. The play has been described variously as a well-constructed thriller, a time play and a morality play, but there are overtones of all three. The scene is the Birling family home where an engagement party is taking place. Into this happy, complacent family gathering comes a supposed police inspector, making enquiries into the death of a young girl, Eva Smith, who had committed suicide by drinking disinfectant. At first everyone present denies any knowledge of her but gradually the Inspector elicits from everyone present that they have, to a greater or lesser extent, been responsible for the sequence of events leading up to her death. The trigger for her slide into destitution and despair was her sacking from his factory by Mr Birling for fomenting a strike, which was then compounded by his daughter who, on discovering that the girl was working in her favourite dress shop, had had her dismissed. The final event leading to her suicide was her seduction by the Birling son, who abandoned her when she told him she was pregnant.

All the characters react differently but eventually turn on each other in recrimination. When the Inspector leaves, to everyone's relief, all but the Birling son and daughter revert to their previous style of behaviour. Towards the end of the play most of the characters have convinced themselves that the Inspector was a practical joker, and telephone the police station and the local hospital to discover that no such Inspector is known to the local force and no girl is lying dead in a mortuary. Relieved, the characters return to their celebration – and the telephone rings. It is the police station: a young girl has died in the local hospital and a police inspector is on his way to make some enquiries.

Who is the Inspector? Priestley leaves the question unanswered. The distinguished critic the late J. C. Trewin considered him to be a member of 'the Celestial Watch Committee'. Gareth Lloyd Evans wrote that he was 'not Christ but conscience', which makes cowards, hypocrites, liars, bombasts and contrites of us all. It is, he said, one of Priestley's most 'warning' plays, but the warning is all the more acceptable because it is thrillingly communicated: 'It makes no large statements about the state of society, does not pronounce on class or the monetary system, it ignores the politicians and does not sentimentalise the exploited or caricature the exploiters.'

When the play reached the London stage in 1946, with Ralph Richardson as the Inspector, it was not a success. 'Finally,' Priestley wrote in his introduction to the published script, 'to the city who liked it least – London.' It had a splendid cast 'which could hardly be bettered' and included Alec Guinness, Margaret Leighton and Julian Mitchell as well as Richardson, and a fine set which gave different views of the same room, but 'Although it was greeted with enthusiasm by many people including some who were not easy to please, it was most sourly noticed and barely maintained a most modest place in the Old Vic's repertoire that season.'

Ironically it has never been out of the regional and amateur circuit since and has been produced all over the world. In the early 1990s it was 'rediscovered' as a national and international box-office smash hit. Stephen Daldry's production for the National Theatre was so successful that it played for years in London's West End and on Broadway. Angela saw the National Theatre production and said that she had gone in some trepidation as she had gathered 'some peculiar things had been done with it and I thought I should hate it, but it was the most wonderful production. People who saw it just couldn't stop talking about it.'

There was to be one other fine play, *The Linden Tree*. It is a story of subtle relationships centred around a university professor who finds he is losing touch with the times and that the magic circle of his life is disintegrating around him as all his family, apart from one daughter, try to persuade him to retire. There is no happy resolution. He is left, supported only by that daughter, to hang on to the bitter end, convinced that without tolerance and understanding life is not worth living. The play, directed by Michael McOwen, was backed by Priestley with his own money under the banner of the Mask Theatre Company, and went on at the old Duchess with a star-studded cast which included Sir Lewis Casson and Dame Sybil Thorndike. Priestley had to wait sixteen years before he had another West End success, with his co-adaptation of Iris Murdoch's novel *A Severed Head*. Yet so strong was the pull of the theatre that, apart from magazine and journal articles, Priestley devoted himself almost entirely to it in the immediate post-war years. The one major exception is the novel *Bright Day*, written late in 1945 and one of his best. He said on numerous occasions that it was *not* autobiographical, but it is impossible not to recognise much of the young Jack Priestley in Gregory Dawson. Dawson lives where Priestley lived, works in an office almost identical to that in the Swan Arcade, shares his creator's interests. His later experiences, too, owe much to Priestley's own, for when we first meet him he is a cynical, established Hollywood scriptwriter working on changes to a screenplay in a Cornish hotel.

It is a haunting tale. In a letter to Davison on its publication Priestley says he is sure that it is his best novel 'and has a special poignancy for people of our generation, many of whom – writers and the like – have written to me about it'.

At the 1945 Cheltenham Festival Priestley met the composer Sir Arthur Bliss. The two men got on well and it was during one of their conversations that Bliss mentioned his germ of an idea for an opera based on the legend that, after the old gods of the Greeks and Romans had been overthrown by Christianity, they had been exiled from Mount Olympus, condemned to walk the roads of the world for ever. Once a year, on Midsummer's Eve, they were allowed to recover their powers and intervene in human affairs. Adapting the story for the stage was not a new idea – indeed, in 1934 Dame Ninette de Valois had choreographed a ballet, *The Gods Go A-begging*, on the same theme, using music by Handel in an arrangement by Sir Thomas Beecham.

Within a few weeks Priestley had sent Bliss a rough draft of the plot for what became the opera *The Olympians*. He had set his story in eighteenth-century France where the gods, now a troupe of strolling players, arrive in a Provençal village on Midsummer's Eve. He found the role of librettist difficult, although Bliss later described him as the perfect collaborator. The opera was completed by 1947 and accepted for production at Covent Garden, although it was not staged for another two years.

With the end of the war, it was time for the Priestleys to try to return to something like normality. The Albany flat remained their London base and Billingham had reverted to them shortly before the Japanese surrender. It was in poor shape and with many things missing. The boiler and heating system had been wrecked, most of the beds and bedding had to be burned as they were filthy, and much of their crockery and glassware, carefully stored in the attics, had disappeared, along with treasures belonging to the children. All she could say, Jane wrote to Natalie Davison, was that she supposed it might have been worse.

Rachel was now working towards her School Certificate, and Tom was at Bryanston, while Barbara and Sylvia had returned to studying respectively architecture and fabric design. Mary was finishing her studies at the Royal Academy of Music and had become an accomplished violinist, while Angela was still working in the theatre. She had been in her stepfather's production of *How Are They at Home?* and was to have appeared in *Ever Since Paradise*, but she had become involved with the Priestleys' Dutch playwright neighbour on the Isle of Wight, Jan der Hartog. 'He said I must either marry him and give up the theatre or we must stop seeing each other. I was a very timid and mousy child then so I did. Now I'd have said I wouldn't do any such thing but then I thought, Oh, God, no, so I was never in the second play. I gave up the theatre for years and years.' Angela was the first of the girls to marry, followed quite quickly by Barbara and Sylvia. Soon afterwards, Priestley remarked in a letter to Edward Davison that for one who had had much to say in public about over-population, his family seemed to be snowing grandchildren.

During the summer of 1945, Priestley was invited to visit the USSR in September. He accepted enthusiastically. Jane, with her flair for languages, managed to learn sufficient Russian at least to enable them to get by, which proved useful. Priestley had been commissioned to write a series of articles on the trip for the *Sunday Express*, but Jane wrote regular letters back to the family in the form of a diary, beginning with their flight from Croydon to Hamburg in a Dakota aircraft full of military personnel. Their stopover in Germany enabled them to see the ruined cities, the blasted landscape, the camps full of refugees, and to visit an orphanage of starving children who tried to sing for the visitors, a sight that brought Priestley to tears.

Later Priestley was intensely criticised for the *Sunday Express* commentaries. Indeed, for the next twenty or thirty years *any* writer who visited the USSR and failed to excoriate every aspect of its life was subjected to streams of abuse. Priestley had never believed in Communism, did not equate it in any way with the liberal socialism in which he had been brought up and not only saw its flaws with clarity but, even in 1945, recognised the Stalinist regime for what it was: a reign of terror. But he also understood the suffering that the Russian people had undergone and the triumph of the human spirit over it, the kindness of the ordinary people towards whom he felt deeply sympathetic, and the superhuman efforts being made to rebuild life from the ruins.

The USSR of 1945 had been devastated by the war, which cost the lives of as many of its citizens as were killed in total on the Western Front during the First World War. Food was scarce, though sufficient was found for visitors, accommodation limited, public utilities primitive, women of forty looked seventy, queues for goods of any kind snaked down the streets. However, the Priestleys also saw magnificent productions of *Prince Igor* and *The Cherry Orchard*, in theatres that were full of ordinary people in cheap seats, and met a wide cross-section of the population both in the country and in the towns. They visited Tolstoy's house, met Soviet writers such as Sholokhov, author of *And Quiet Flows the Don*, argued with some over the writer's freedom to say what he wanted, and put right others who were convinced that nothing had changed in Britain since the days of Dickens. Just before they left Leningrad Priestley was honoured with a farewell lunch to which writers, poets, theatre people and government officials had been invited, one of whom recalled how moved he had been by the *Postscripts* when he had been Russian ambassador in London in 1940. But all around was desolation and the results of nine hundred days of starvation, and the Priestleys found it almost unbearable to talk to families who had had to choose which of their children should be fed and so survive. Interestingly, it is Jane's account of the visit written for her children which is the more detailed and vivid. It deserves publication even now.[2]

In January 1946 Priestley went down with pneumonia from which he took some time to recover. Once he was over it, he and Jane took up their usual routine of dividing their time between London and the Isle of Wight, but things were now different. Billingham was costly to restore and increasingly difficult to keep up. While the faithful Miss Pudduck and Gertrude had returned with Jane, there was no chance of employing the large staff of pre-war days. Fuel was in short supply, which meant that the electricity generator could only run for short periods and the house was permanently cold. Evening activity had to take place by the light of oil lamps.

But it was not only buildings and a way of life that were proving difficult to restore; so was the relationship between the Priestleys. They had spent too long living separate lives during the war to settle down easily again with each other, although it seemed at first that both were prepared to make a fresh start and there is nothing in their existing personal correspondence to friends to give a hint that it was not working out. Chatty letters from both partners to the Davisons are full of continual requests for consumer goods, and Priestley arranged to pay for them from income generated by books or magazine pieces published in the States. For years the Davisons – whose own marriage was now rocky – sent across the Atlantic a steady stream of bedlinen, towels, pyjamas and underwear for Tom and Rachel, nylon stockings, hams, tins of meat and Hershey toffees.

Once relieved of her war-time responsibilities, Jane began again to suffer from the illnesses that had plagued her before the war. She knew that over the last few years her husband had been involved in a number of fleeting affairs with women he had met either in the course of his work or in his social life, and as time went by well-meaning friends were quick to tell her that he was still doing so. While all the older Priestley children had been aware of periods of severe tension in the household when they were growing up, now it was continual and there was no longer a houseful of young people to help break it. Angela, Barbara, Sylvia and, to a lesser extent, Mary were soon merely visitors. Rachel went to train as a nurse and then only Tom was still at school to come home for the holidays. The jolly family treks between London and the Isle of Wight were over, although the social weekends continued with as much hospitality as was possible, given the austerity of the times. Without the children the Priestley were thrown into each other's laps.

The atmosphere between them worsened. During the post-war period, Priestley considered buying a theatre in which he could put on his own and other productions. He also wanted to buy pictures, not only as an investment but because he enjoyed having them on his walls. Jane thought both ideas impractical and, as she had always handled their finances, she had her way. Her financial advisers told her that one of the best investments at that time was farmland and she decided that they would buy several farms. Priestley was unhappy about this from the outset: according to some members of his family, he had never remotely wanted to become a farmer. In the event, the advice Jane had been given proved wrong and, far from being a good investment, the farms became a permanent financial drain. She also felt they should leave Billingham and live nearer the farms, so they began to look for another property. But by that time, unknown to Jane, the event had taken place that would blow the marriage apart.

From 1946 onwards Priestley suffered from the depression that had always dogged him, and was increasingly frustrated with the new Labour Government. In a letter to Edward Davison he wrote,

> The chief trouble here is that the government is so unimaginative. They're letting it get dreary. They don't give the people any lift of the spirit and their public relations are shocking ... it's a revolution without bloodshed and cruelty but also, alas, without any fun and glory – a sort of London School of Economics job! I think their foreign policy is unrealistic, but there's nothing 'Imperialistic' about it: the trouble is, like most foreign policies,

it just goes on functioning mechanically without anybody giving the damned thing any fresh thought . . . I suspect the atom bomb is on the American conscience, and that many American minds are busy projecting their guilty feelings on to Russia, Britain, anything. The Russians are irritating – I should know having had plenty of dealings with them – but they want a war about as much as I want ten rounds with Joe Lewis. One wonders what the American press would say if the Russians sent a large fleet to prowl off Panama.[3]

A number of his friends and acquaintances had died recently, including, in August 1946, H. G. Wells. The two men had been friends since the late 1920s and admired each other's work. Wells had been particularly supportive when Priestley had been criticised by reviewers. He had found *Faraway* a pleasure to read, thought all the characters good except for the girl, but warned against what he saw as one of his own faults, the need to put in dissertations on deeply felt issues. After he had seen *Johnson Over Jordan* he wrote to tell Priestley that its design was magnificent, and that it was certainly one of the most impressive pieces to be seen on the London stage for a long time. Priestley was in the middle of rehearsals for a light comedy when Wells died and found himself yet again having to give a funeral address, this time 'for a man whose word was a light in a thousand dark places . . . Of all the English writers I have known, he was the most honest, the frankest, the one least afraid of telling the truth.'[4]

Also, in 1947 Mary, who was now playing the violin professionally both as a soloist and with other string players, went for further study to Geneva where she met a Danish music student, Sigvald Michelsen, with whom she fell in love. At the time she was having psychoanalysis for nightmares from Gerhard Adler but there had been no real warning of what was to come. In retrospect, she puts her years of frail mental health down to a variety of causes, starting with her childhood when she had not known which of the two men in her mother's life was her father. She also feels that her father was never happy about her choice of music as a career, although it played such an important part in his life. 'I think he wanted us to do something we were happy doing and able to be successful in. Well, I wasn't ever going to be *that* successful, you had to have tremendous talent to be a real success. He thought my real talent lay as a writer and that was what I really should have been doing.'[5]

She and Sigvald arrived in England in a romantic haze to be brought severely down to earth when neither of her parents would agree to their immediate marriage or even an engagement. Sigvald, who had been born into a working-class Danish family, was a penniless student and, however far they might have drifted apart, the Priestleys were united in feeling that the young couple, who had only known each other a matter of weeks, should separate for six months, then see how they felt and how they would live. Parental opposition merely fanned the flames and Mary and Sigvald became engaged regardless. Mary moved into Sylvia's house and tried to keep herself by her violin playing, supplemented by the allowance she still received from her father. But the estrangement from her family tipped her over the edge into a complete breakdown. This placed further strain on the Priestleys' marriage.

The immediate post-war period had seen the setting up of a number of major organisations under the auspices of the United Nations. One was UNESCO, the United Nations Educational, Scientific and Cultural Organisation, for which a six-week inaugural meeting was to be held in Mexico at the end of 1947. Among those involved with Britain's contribution was a woman who had been drafted into the civil service during the war and was currently a principal at the Ministry of Education. She was to be secretary to the British delegation, the members of which were to be chosen by her head of department, Sir John Maude. Looking through Maude's list of proposed delegates she saw that he had chosen J. B. Priestley to represent not only literature but the arts in general. She immediately went to him to protest that she considered Priestley too lightweight, too popular, and insufficiently intellectual to be considered, 'although I have to admit that I'd hardly even read anything he had written at that time', she recalled later.

Maude refused to budge. Priestley, he told her, had a wide knowledge of the arts and his own work encompassed novels, essays, plays. He was truly a man of letters. He was known internationally for his literary work and also as a wartime broadcaster. He was exactly right for the task. Maude's junior, realising there was nothing more to be done, returned to her desk, writing when necessary to Mr J. B. Priestley and signing off her letters 'J. J. Hawkes'.[6] For some considerable time Priestley assumed that she was a man.

He and Jacquetta met for the first time at a briefing session and reception given for the UNESCO delegation in Belgrave Square, London, when, they told Diana Collins, Jacquetta offered Priestley a rather horrible bright pink pudding. Over it, there had been a soundless communication between them.

Their second encounter was in July 1947 when a special meeting for senior delegates was held by UNESCO in Paris, which Priestley had to attend although Jane made it clear she did not want him to go. He was given two special assistants for the Paris trip, Jacquetta and another young woman, Helen de Mouliplied, who was the director of the film department of the Ministry of Information. Helen was in a highly emotional state as she had been involved for some time with one of her colleagues but was finding herself increasingly attracted to a new recruit to the film department, Denis Forman (who later became a distinguished television producer), and was unable to make up her mind what to do about it as both men were subjecting her to emotional pressure. In the course of the Paris visit Helen confided something of her distress to Priestley, who invited her out to dinner. Over the meal, as well as offering Helen what advice he could – she eventually married Denis Forman – he asked her to tell him what she knew about Jacquetta. 'What a woman!' he exclaimed to her. 'Ice without and fire within.'[7] The next night he took Jacquetta out to dinner and it seems they confessed their troubles to each other. Jacquetta had been having an extra-marital affair that had ended abruptly with her lover's death, and Priestley was now very unhappy with Jane and extremely worried about Mary's manifestly deteriorating condition. Although he was attracted to Jacquetta it does not seem at that stage that he had any real intention of taking the relationship any further.

He returned home to discover that Mary's condition was, if anything, worse, and was sufficiently alarmed to cancel a forthcoming trip to Mexico. By the autumn, Mary was critically ill and she was taken into St Andrew's Hospital, Northampton, for treatment. Her doctors thought it best that, for the time being, all family visits should cease. She received drugs, relaxation exercises and, finally, electro-convulsive therapy (ECT), which is now considered highly controversial. Various diagnoses of her illness were suggested, including schizophrenia, but it was decided that she was suffering from manic depression, from which she recovered and then turned her experiences to expert use as a music therapist.

As Priestley was no longer able to visit his daughter, he was finally persuaded that he should, after all, take his place with the UNESCO delegation and he withdrew his cancellation, insisting on paying his own expenses for the inconvenience he had caused. Although Jane felt uneasy, it was with her blessing that a few days later he joined the rest of the UNESCO delegation, including J. J. Hawkes, at Southampton and boarded the *Queen Mary* bound for New York, from where the delegates were to travel to Mexico City by train.

He arrived back in the first week in December and on the ninth Jane wrote to Natalie, thanking her for going shopping with Jack in New York and for all the things he had brought home with him. It was a nice chatty letter: 'Jack has come back looking so very much better. I never was so pleased to see him.' A postscript adds that Mary is 'not too good at the moment. She has just had a relapse and I am very anxious about her. Her heart has also given us cause to worry too and we shall have an anxious time for at least two months more. Twice while Jack was away I was warned she might die at any moment. I am VERY thankful to have him with me again but I feel it was worth making the effort to stick it out over here as he did such good work.' And she reiterated, 'He has come back so much better, so fresh . . .'

CHAPTER 23

Jacquetta

Jessie Jacquetta Hopkins was born in 1910. Her father was one of the most eminent scientists of his day: Sir Frederick Gowland Hopkins, OM, winner of a Nobel Prize for science, the discoverer of vitamins and generally considered the 'father' of biochemistry. His own father, a bookseller and amateur scientist, died young and his widow moved in with her brother, a figure later described by Jacquetta as a bullying, domineering man with fundamentalist religious beliefs who saw science as the devil's work. The young Frederick was, therefore, set to work in a local insurance office, and it was only as a result of his own persistence, hard work and, later, the support of a cousin of his father that in 1888, at the age of twenty-seven, he entered the medical school at Guy's Hospital where he qualified as a doctor, won the gold medal for chemistry, and simultaneously took an external degree in science at London University.

In 1898, aged thirty-seven, he met Jessie Anne Stevens, an orphan who also had an interest in medicine and was a probationer nurse at the Royal Free Hospital in London. They married within months of meeting each other and, according to their daughter, 'were to love each other for half a century or more'. Within a relatively short time Frederick was invited to become a fellow and tutor at Emmanuel College, Cambridge, and was given a house in the college grounds. Jacquetta was the youngest of three children, separated from her brother by eight years. Outside the confines of his own scientific discipline, in which he showed inflexible determination, her father was a gentle, imaginative and sympathetic person, yet Jacquetta told Diana Collins that as a child she saw this as weakness and found it difficult to relate to him.

Her mother was beautiful, lively, kind and practical, ran a

comfortable home, was immensely supportive of her husband, a good hostess and an excellent mother. From an early age her children were taken to places of interest, art galleries and museums.

In the year that Jacquetta was born, Frederick suffered a breakdown caused by overwork. On his recovery, Trinity College offered him a fellowship without any teaching responsibilities to enable him to pursue his own research. It also provided sufficient money to have a fine house built on the then outskirts of the city, to which the family moved when Jacquetta was nearly a year old. The improvement in the family finances also enabled them to employ a cook, a house-parlourmaid and a nanny for Jacquetta.

She was a precocious child, enjoyed being alone and liked to have her own way. She went first to a small private school, Miss Sharpley's, much patronised by Cambridge academics. Much of her spare time was spent outdoors and she had a passion for climbing, especially trees. She was also used to mixing with her parents' friends, many of whom were also distinguished scientists. At eleven she was sent to the Perse School where she firmly refused to wear uniform or to take part in organised games. She was, as she said, never 'a joiner'. In her first years at school she was not considered particularly bright and her main claim to fame was that she founded the Trespassers' Society, members of which were awarded marks for the relative daring of their illegal entry to other people's property.

Jacquetta later applied to Newnham College, Cambridge, and became the first woman to study the newly established full degree in archaeology and anthropology. She was an attractive young woman with striking, dark good looks and one of her earliest friends at Newnham, Peggy Lamert, said she 'stood out like a star'. By the end of her second year she was considered one of the most promising students in the college and was sent on her first serious 'dig', that of a pre-Roman Celtic capital just outside Colchester. The director was a brilliant young archaeologist, Christopher Hawkes, who promptly fell in love with her. He was already a leading expert on Celtic Britain and by the age of twenty-seven was a fellow of the Society of Antiquaries. When Jacquetta first met him, she found his appearance unprepossessing – he was rather small and wore glasses – but was, she wrote, lively, clever, immensely energetic, a master of my beloved subject – and the boss. I cannot remember just when or how he first declared his love for me but I think it must have been before the end of the season's excavation. Certainly he continued to court me, and meeting him on his own ground in London impressed me with his social confidence and knowledge of the world – largely illusory, but considerable when set against my own lack of them.[1]

She wrote about her marriage to Christopher in her strange book *A Quest for Love*, part-myth, part-fiction and part-biography. Later she regretted the biographical section: 'I really did treat him very badly,' she said, 'particularly when it came to Jack – but what could I do?'

Jacquetta took a first class honours degree and was awarded a travelling scholarship. She used it to go to Palestine, where caves were being excavated on the slopes of Mount Carmel; her special responsibility was to supervise the recovery of a Neanderthal skeleton. During her time in the Middle East she gave much thought to whether or not she should accept Christopher's proposal of marriage. She liked him a good deal, admired him, they had a mutual interest in the same compelling subject and she was flattered by his adoration. 'Did I "love" him? How could I tell?' His embraces had failed to move her, but she was prepared to consider that sex might well prove more exciting. She made up her mind and on her return they became engaged, their wedding planned for the following autumn. She was just twenty-two and in many ways young for her age. Almost immediately she ran into problems with Mrs Hawkes, who doted on her son and thought no girl could ever be good enough for him. She had been instrumental in the break-up of his two earlier serious involvements, even though on the last occasion he had also become engaged. It seems that at the last moment Jacquetta had doubts about the wisdom of going through with the marriage, but felt that it was impossible to back out. The wedding went ahead and was followed by a honeymoon in Majorca which she described later as 'neither a joy nor a disaster . . . While I came nowhere near to passion, it would not be just to say I was frigid. I wanted to please my husband and even gained some small pleasure in the attempt. As it was we enjoyed the sun, the bathing and visiting antiquities – and were not unhappy.

Similar words might be used to describe the following years of our marriage.'[2]

The couple returned to London where they had rented a flat in Paddington as Christopher was working at the British Museum. Life settled into a pattern of work in London, weekends in Cambridge and summers on excavations or visits to special sites. Diana Collins describes Christopher as a 'workaholic', at the museum all day and writing late into the night. As Jacquetta was working on a book of her own, *The Archaeology of Jersey*, the easy companionship that had sustained the marriage in its early days was showing signs of strain. However, by the end of 1936 she was pregnant, and gave birth to her only child, Nicolas, the following August.

While the arrival of another male Hawkes might be thought to have softened her mother-in-law's attitude to her, it had the reverse effect. Mrs Hawkes was so unpleasant that Christopher wrote to her, begging her to be more careful of her language

and – I mean this – your fatal passion for controlling others will lead to serious and irreparable harm if you do not check it where we are concerned. Your being 'horrified' and writing disagreeable things is extremely painful . . . More than that, coming as it does on the top of a great deal of previous exhibitions of the same kind, and accompanied with language to Jacquetta on the telephone and whenever you have come here by yourself to see things, has upset her more than I can say . . . I do not expect you ever to be fond of Jacquetta – that hope you killed a long while ago – but I do expect you to keep a proper hold on yourself . . . And as for Nicolas, it might well mean that he might never come to know his grandparents . . . But it is I who would have to decide, and a man's wife and family come inevitably first.[3]

In the summer of 1939, under the threat of war, Jacquetta undertook the first excavation for which she had sole charge, that of a Megalithic tomb in County Waterford where she met the head of Irish archaeology, Adolf Mahr, who was already packing up to leave. (He turned out later to have been head of German intelligence in Ireland.) Meanwhile Christopher was involved in packing British Museum treasures for storage in a safe place. After Jacquetta's return from Ireland they managed a short holiday with their son in Dorset, but it is clear that she was becoming increasingly dissatisfied with her marriage. Much later, and with hindsight, she wrote:

> In all things social and intellectual, it was admirably balanced and free. Yet it was also, I suppose, becoming every year more lifeless and stultifying. I will not say the lack was in our sexual life, that would be far too simple, but it was certainly in our union as a man and a woman. If we had known real passion together, everything else might have been well – but why had we not attained it? I now understand that all delight and intensity of love-making depend upon the mind and the imagination.

But if this was so, it explains to some extent what happened next. With the onset of air raids in 1940 Jacquetta left London, taking Nicolas with her, to stay with the Pinneys, a family with whom the Hawkeses had become friends while on their Dorset holiday. Jacquetta fell passionately in love with Betty Pinney. It was, she wrote, the sudden undamming of feelings of an intensity she did not know that she possessed. 'I shall never lose the beauties of spring in the Dorset countryside when my love was at its height.' Betty Pinney did not treat her obsessed devotee well, alternately encouraging then repulsing her, yet when it finally came to embarking on a full-blown physical relationship, Jacquetta drew back. Over the years she was

> to brood on these matters ... Much less of an artist than I would wish, but on the whole thankfully, no more a Lesbian ... I do not think it was timidity that confined it to emotion. My body was only mildly interested, if at all. From that time I have loved men, but still, on meeting other women, I can feel that instinctive message, the tremor of a nerve just penetrating consciousness, that triggers a true Sapphic presence.

From every point of view she felt it imperative to leave the Pinneys and took Nicolas and his nanny to her parents' home in Cambridge. As Christopher had been seconded to the Ministry of Aircraft Production, and with bombs now falling on London, Jacquetta felt her place was at his side and returned home, soon to find herself drafted into the civil service.

She spent weekends in Cambridge, her weekday evenings at home in the house they had bought in Hampstead where Christopher continued to write his new book, as *The Prehistoric*

Foundations of Europe had been published in 1940. In spite of the
war, Jacquetta began to look for a social life of her own and this
was provided by her old friend Peggy Lamert, who now worked
for the publishers Chatto and Windus. At a party in Peggy's
Kensington flat in 1943 she was introduced to the poet and
critic Walter Turner. Peggy Lamert described the effect the two
had on each other as 'electric'. He was sixty when they met, she
thirty-three. Rather like Priestley, he remained attached to his
wife in spite of having had a number of affairs and was happy
to stay married. At the time he and Jacquetta met he combined
the post of literary editor of the *Spectator* with that of music critic
for the *New Statesman*. He had also ventured into the field of
theatre criticism and, although he was not generally enthusiastic
about Priestley's work, he had admired *Johnson Over Jordan*, and
attacked its hostile reviews as 'typical of the sterile negative nature
of so-called intellectuals'. A short while later, however, Priestley
and Turner were involved in a literary row carried out in the letter
pages of the *New Statesman* of which Priestley was a director.

At first the relationship between Jacquetta and Turner was
on a literary level, encompassing, interestingly enough, Dunne's
theories on time, but it soon developed into something more.
Turner was a skilled and imaginative lover and Jacquetta became
infatuated with him, but it is clear that she never considered
leaving Christopher. The relationship with Turner continued, off
and on, throughout the rest of the war years until, in November
1946, he died suddenly from a brain haemorrhage. Beforehand
Jacquetta had experienced an inexplicable sense of foreboding,
and when she heard of his death she was prostrate with grief
'and an all-consuming sense of loss'. Eight months later she met
Jack Priestley.

If he had had shipboard romance in mind as the *Queen Mary*
left Southampton *en route* for New York in 1947, he was to
be disappointed. Jacquetta was a chronically bad sailor and
was confined to her 'cramped' cabin for most of the voyage,
which infuriated Priestley who could not understand what had
happened to her. Nor were matters much improved in the first
days in Mexico City. The hotel housing the British delegation
left much to be desired, not least that when the lavatory chains
were pulled the waste did not disappear down the drain but
overflowed on to the floor. The entire delegation went down

Tom Priestley's christening, 1932.

Jack with Rachel and Tom
in Arizona, late 1930s.

Jack and Jane with Buster Keaton in Hollywood, around 1938.

Owing to the sudden indisposition of Mr. Frank Pettingell, the Author of "WHEN WE ARE MARRIED" has consented to take his place until such time as Mr. Pettingell will be well enough to reappear or other arrangements for the performance of the part can be made.

Mr. J. B. Priestley will be appearing for the first time on any stage.

Priestley standing in as the drunken photographer in *When We Are Married* opposite Patricia Hayes at St Martin's Theatre, 1938.

Sir Ralph Richardson in the nightclub scene from *Johnson Over Jordan*, February 1938.

Jack and Jacquetta during the UNESCO trip to Japan, 1952.

Jack and Jacquetta with the cast of *Dragon's Mouth*, 1952. The actors are Michael Dennison, Dulcie Gray, Rosamund John and Norman Wooland.

With George Bernard Shaw, 1961.

With Soviet writers, 1962.

At a *New Statesman* dinner in the 1960s. Editor John Freeman sits at the head of the table; among those also present are Kingsley Amis and Richard Crossman MP.

In full flow, early 1970s.

Jack donating pictures to the City of Bradford,
having been given the Freedom of the City, 1973.

Jack and Jacquetta relaxing in the library at Kissing Tree House, late 1970s.

with gastroenteritis. Priestley, hearing that 'J. J. Hawkes' was ill again, went up to her room bearing brandy in a medicine bottle: 'That brandy, together with his irresistible voice, marked the beginning of a wonderful sense of being looked after – a thing I had never before known and have never lost.'

As soon as she recovered, he took her out to dinner where 'driven by compulsive honesty and a recklessness induced by the high altitude' (and her first martini cocktails), she told him that 'she didn't much like his writings'. He was, not unjustifiably, angry at first, but as they walked back to the hotel together along 'the noble and now quietening Pasa de la Reforma, there seemed to be just the two of us walking as one beneath the stars'.[4]

The conference lasted six weeks, and towards the end they told each other that it had just been a rather special 'conference affair', which had to end, although 'now, in my late thirties, I was to discover the pleasures and spiritual transformations of total love. I seemed to be created anew. I made rapid progress, for I remember one night in a country place when my whole being was filled with recognition of the sweet tragedy of mortal love, the union of love and death.' Priestley had to leave for New York before the end of the conference and they had agreed that, as there could be no future for them because they already had families, they would not communicate with each other again.

Yet almost as soon as his train left Mexico City, Priestley embarked on the first of an extraordinary series of love letters to Jacquetta, which continued intermittently throughout their clandestine relationship. 'I know I shouldn't be doing this', he wrote, 'it's against everything I meant or said, but I can't help it. I must write one letter to you – if only selfishly, to try and relieve myself of this terrible weight of sadness and loss . . . I feel older, emptier and sadder than I ever remember feeling before.' He thanked her for the enchantment she had brought into his life, telling her that her 'curious changing beauty' did not belong to this world and how he had recognised in her a priestess of 'the archaic cult'. 'Take this miserable letter, kiss it once, and then burn it,' he admonished her. 'I'll get hold of you somehow . . . I sit here in the damned train, holding your lovely image in my arms – I can hardly see for tears.'[5] Jacquetta received his letter, ignored his instructions and stowed it carefully away before wandering round the back streets of Mexico City in a happy daze, 'hunting for the post office which would put Jack out of his immediate misery'.

It must be said that he was also writing to Jane during those six weeks of 'enchantment'. His first letter, detailing how tired he was and that he was using ointment for the eczema on his hands, expressed his concern that he had had only one letter from her and was worrying about Mary. He was hoping to fly home earlier than planned, well before the conference finished, and he now ended, 'I think of you, my love, and of our dear Mary, constantly and with great love and tenderness. Bless you! Jack.' His next, in answer to two cables about Mary, reiterated that he expected to be home sooner than originally planned and that he now hoped to be able to return on 11 December on the *Queen Mary*.

> One day I hope we'll come here and explore this strange country together – outside the city, which I detest, it becomes fascinating though, a strange and arid landscape. I long for you, my dear love, for this sad business with Mary puts a great strain on me too, and I've found it impossible to join in most of the parties here, etc. though I try hard not to brood . . . But my heart's not in it. I'll be with you, my love, as soon as I possibly can.

Just what his archaic priestess would have made of this correspondence beggars the imagination.

This was the start of the complex double life he lived for the next six years. His return was not happy because although, in her letters to the Davisons, Jane said how pleased she was that he finally went to the conference, she berated him at home for leaving her to deal unaided with Mary's crises. There was still work to be done on *The Olympians*. *An Inspector Calls* and *The Linden Tree* were still running but needed his attention, while three other plays, *The Golden Fleece*, *Home is Tomorrow* and *The High Toby* were in progress, and he had a number of pressing commissions for newspapers and magazines.

Then there was still the necessity of finding a house on the Isle of Wight, although this, while disruptive, was largely left to Jane. The one they finally settled on was Brook Hill, which they rented, a large Edwardian stone house on top of a hill overlooking the sea. The view was an obvious attraction, but they chose it mainly because it was close to the farms.

Slowly Mary began to improve, and by early 1948 she was considered sufficiently recovered to be discharged from hospital. In spite of all her parents' efforts to dissuade her, she later returned to Sigvald Michelsen, married him and left England for Copenhagen. They had three children, including twins, but the marriage was dogged by problems, financial and personal, and also by Mary's fragile mental health: she had relapses in 1958 and 1964. 'I knew it would be a disaster,' Priestley told John and Diana Collins gloomily years later, 'and it was!' Over the years he wrote hundreds of letters to his daughter, aware of how much she needed the contact, but although they show care and concern and are friendly, they are strangely lacking in the warmth shown in those to Jane and his friends, especially the Davisons, let alone those to Jacquetta.

It seems that for some considerable time Jane did not know that he was again involved with another woman and that, even when she finally did, she still did not realise the seriousness of the relationship or the threat Jacquetta posed to her. By early 1948 Priestley was writing regularly to Jacquetta. He was enormously attracted by her air of coolness and reserve, which was often daunting to those who did not know her well, but he understood how deceptive that was: 'You have so much: a glorious honesty (which I deeply admire)', he wrote,

> passion, and a kind of frosty fire, like the Snow Queen on her birthday, a folded-in sort of handsomeness that turns into amazing beauty at the right moment . . . It is odd how everything is reversed for us. I, the easy sensualist regard you most unsensually, except when immediately excited by you; whereas you find love for me in your body, but little or none, alas, in your mind.[6]

They met whenever and wherever they could. Jacquetta wrote:

> So we embarked on several years of a relationship that could certainly be called disreputable and in our existing circumstances even deplorable. Yet I cannot deplore it knowing how it was to end and never forgetting how full of wonders it was even at the time – and how, too, it was always growing and deepening. In its younger days we seized every possible opportunity for meetings, delicious in themselves, but always with one end in view. We made love indoors and out, by day and by night, in borrowed offices and flats, in the box of a provincial theatre and the garden of the Institute of Archaeology.[7]

CHAPTER 24

The Tangled Web

Over the next six years Priestley's double life became tangled and fraught with problems. Meetings with Jacquetta were difficult and uncertain, and the lovers often had to fall back on correspondence, itself no easy matter as Priestley dared not risk receiving anything but the most innocuous letters from her, disguised under the cover of UNESCO business. While Jacquetta kept his letters to her, even though he continually asked her to get rid of them, he destroyed all but one of hers.

What comes across clearly from these years is his ability to keep separate the strands of his life. It is as if he saw himself as two different people: Jack, the passionate lover, and Jack Priestley, the husband and professional writer.

As well as keeping up with his writing commitments, in 1947 he was appointed a member of the Royal Commission on the Press and in 1948 chairman of the British Theatre Conference, of the London Philharmonic Advisory Council and of the National Theatre Institute Conference in Prague. For one who had previously shown no enthusiasm for committees he was now involved in a positive array of them and travelled continually. His son suggests that one reason for this might have been that the posts provided him with excuses to meet Jacquetta.

It was in his British Theatre Conference capacity that he again approached Shaw. He wanted him to join, but Shaw's response was almost exactly the same as it had been when Priestley invited him on to the Authors' National Committee in 1939. He had nothing, he said, to contribute, and from the information he had been sent the British Theatre Conference appeared to have no real agenda, much less a programme, 'and if there was I wouldn't agree with a single item'. He had done what he could for the Society of Authors, had been in at the birth of the

Authors' League of America, which boiled with high hopes but gave away right after right to managers and publishers, including film rights. 'You are too young to grasp their ignorance of the law, and incompetence in business, which makes them unemployable in any other occupation except that of sitting alone in a study and indulging their imaginations.' However, since Priestley had let himself in for this folly, he sent his blessing which, at the age of ninety-one and a half, was all he could spare.[1]

There is nothing in the letters written to friends and family between 1947 and 1950 that gives a hint of Priestley's personal situation. Letters to Mary, first from Billingham, then from Brook Hill, are full of domestic chit-chat interspersed with brief information on his work and, fairly regularly, admonishments in answer to her complaints over the lack of work for 'Sig' and their consequent financial hardship. In the spring of 1948, he wrote to her about the play he was working on: 'It takes place on an island in the Caribbean – it's really about the United Nations idea, though it is called HOME IS TOMORROW, which you probably feel applies to you just now. It is in two acts with two scenes in each act and I am working at the second scene of the second act.' Later he moved the action from the Caribbean to the South Pacific, feeling that he had to distance the play because of the frenetic 'yes and no' attitude towards international co-operation which shadowed the early years of the UN.

The play makes two points: that international co-operation is vital, and that it is difficult. It was not well received, considered too wordy by some, poorly plotted and inconclusive by others. Even Gareth Lloyd Evans, trying to be sympathetic, is in agreement with fellow reviewers that it was a lacklustre piece 'in which the dramatist makes a personal entrance at far too many points. He telegraphs his plot-line which bears little relation to the play's theme and this theme is pressed home without any real sense that characters and statements should be one flesh . . . in this [play] Priestley's time-complex, given such fruitful communication in his time-plays, stalks the action like a weary ghost.' The play is tired, he considers, 'as if Priestley is going through certain automatic responses which he sees about him, but has no energy left to make those responses mean anything beyond verbiage.'[2] The play opened in Bradford, in the autumn of 1948, and in another letter to Mary he writes of its apparent success, but it did not survive for long in London.

The move to Brook Hill proved as disruptive as any other house move, causing Priestley, that chronic grumbler, to grumble even more, his complaints spilling over in a letter to Jacquetta in which he describes all removal men as 'a race of morons', and accuses his furniture of acquiring a malignancy of its own. 'Yet in the muddle I think of you constantly and with delight. Friday was very special to me too – there is is no accounting for these queer ebbs and flows of feeling and pleasure and sense of rightness – the whole story seems to take place below the conscious level, which hasn't had much of a go with us, who rather tend to disapprove of one another on that level and have to be prodded from below – or is it above?' He ends: 'The sun is bright and I adore you, my sweet girl . . .'

During the late 1940s and early 1950s Priestley wrote a puppet play for children, *The High Toby*, and a number of conventional plays, which were simply not very good. The exception is *A Summer Day's Dream*, of 1949, which deserved more than the fifty performances at the St Martin's Theatre that it received. Meticulously plotted and well scripted, it was adopted successfully for television in 1994, with Sir John Gielgud in the leading role.

It is set at some unspecified time in the future in England in the aftermath of a nuclear war. A family of survivors in a large country house on the South Downs has managed to make a good, simple life by their own unaided efforts. Without warning they are visited by a delegation from the outside world and learn that Russia and America have now divided the world between them, using the countries of the third world as satellite states to provide them with raw materials, oil and new technologies. The house and grounds, the family is told, stand on useful chalk deposits and it has been decided that the land must be opened up for commercial development.

Gradually, though, the members of the party succumb to the spell of the place and the family. The young female Russian scientist falls in love with the son of the house while the young white American is enchanted by what he sees as a better way of living. Throughout there is a subtext of allusions to *A Midsummer Night's Dream* as a reminder of an older, rural England. At the end of the play the intruders have to leave the house with its magical garden, which they do reluctantly, but they have learned that it is wrong to exploit the land and its people purely for gain and that their respective governments have no right to destroy the lives of people who choose to live differently.

While *A Summer Day's Dream* is manifestly another Priestley play with a message, this time the message is timely and comes across unstrained while the characters are both sympathetic and rounded. The language moves from the complexity of devious argument to evocative and beautiful prose.

In July 1949 the Davisons' son, Peter, arrived at Brook Hill to spend the summer. Priestley, writing to his parents to say what a charming lad he was, informed them that *The Olympians* was to open the new Covent Garden season, that he would be bringing out a book of essays in September, a grumbler's apology called *Delight*, and also that he had been asked to write another film script, designed as a vehicle for Alec Guinness. When he remembered that holiday many years later Peter Davison painted a picture of a lifestyle reminiscent of that at Billingham before the war, with busy social weekends where distinguished guests were entertained with tennis matches, splendid dinners, talk and games, and the day started every morning with a positively Edwardian breakfast, an array of food on a sideboard groaning with kippers, kidneys, bacon and eggs.[3] There was nothing to show on the surface that the Priestleys were not living in perfect amity.

The Alec Guinness film was difficult to write but when he saw the final edited version, Priestley wrote to Mary, he thought 'it was looking pretty good, though it may be rather too ironical and grim for the big public'. It was to be called *Last Holiday* and

> It is about a man who is told he is going to die of some mysterious disease, so he chucks his job and draws all his money out of the Bank and goes to stay in an expensive hotel. Here he has more chances than he has ever had in his life before – and can't do anything about them because he is going to die. Then he discovers there was a mix-up in the X-ray plates and that he isn't going to die after all. But then he is killed in an accident. Although the main theme is rather tragic, most of the episodes are comic or comic/pathetic and there is some very good acting in the film, particularly that of Alec Guinness.

This letter was briskly friendly and informative. His previous one had commiserated with Mary on what seems to have been a miscarriage, and had pointed out that it might be sensible to wait 'until you are more settled down and Sig has found a steady job which I think he ought to do until he gets better known as a soloist'. He could understand her not liking Denmark very much, but he thought that this was largely due to their being hard up and unsettled: 'If Sig. were earning about £700 a year it would be very different. (And don't forget this is what he *promised* to do, in fact, he told me he could get a job any time with the Royal Chapel for £900 a year.)' It is clear that he felt impatient with them and their predicament: 'In my opinion it would be a mistake to come back to England yet because it is running away from Denmark just when something might turn up, and it is absolutely impossible for Sig. to get work at once here. And anyhow it's a mistake to make these sudden retreats just because everything is not wonderful.'

As he and Jane struggled to keep up the appearance of normality in front of family and friends, life in the Hawkes household was more placid. Denis Forman, who was now married to Jacquetta's old colleague, Helen, told Diana Collins later how normal everything seemed. He and Helen were regular visitors to the Hawkeses and were highly amused at the unsuccessful efforts of Sir Mortimer Wheeler, womaniser *extraordinaire*, to get Jacquetta into his bed. Christopher disapproved of Wheeler's personality and lifestyle and put up with him only on sufferance. Forman described Christopher at that time as 'the man in the kitchen', who did not appear to be master in his own house and could be overruled and corrected by Jacquetta.[4]

While Priestley was on tenterhooks in case their affair became public, Jacquetta describes in *A Quest for Love* how at that time she revelled in it.

> There was, I can now see, an element of display in my attitude, but a display directed not outwards but to myself. I think it can and should be forgiven. Having lived for so long without knowing what it was to love a man, and be loved, in a union of body, heart and mind and then to attain it so suddenly and mightily with a man who moved in so exciting a world – surely I can forgive myself if I gloried in it, indulged in a kind of foolish pride at this long-delayed fulfilment.

It was, presumably, this same 'element of display' which had driven her to write that intensely biographical chapter in *A Quest for Love*. It also surfaced again when, in her grief over Jack's death, she allowed publication of intimate and passionate love letters, a decision which, she told me, she wished she had never made, not least because she alleged that some of them had never been returned to her.

She wrote a great deal over the years about the strength of her relationship with Jack, and there is no doubt that it was a remarkable one. However, of one thing she was always adamant: that once she and Priestley met, there was never any rift between them, even during the period when they decided to marry. Each had discovered the perfect 'other'. Certainly their marriage was outstandingly successful, and Jacquetta was particularly delighted with what their friend John Braine wrote of their partnership in his book *J.B. Priestley*: 'They're absolutely complementary. You can't imagine one without the other.' 'This,' she wrote, 'is how it feels also from the inside and it expresses in the best, because the simplest, terms that we had to the full that mysterious polarity, that irresistible magnetism, that Christopher and I had been without.'

However, after her death in March 1996 a bundle of letters was discovered in her bedroom, carefully hidden away. Among these are some that show that on at least one occasion before they were married there was a serious rift and that either this, or their situation, had driven Priestley seriously to consider ending their relationship.

The rift grew from Jacquetta having told him of the 'Sapphic trigger' of which she had long been aware and also, perhaps, of her love affair with Betty Pinney. It was almost certainly 1948, as there are references to a visit to Prague and 1948 was the year in which he chaired a British Theatre Conference in the city. Jacquetta was there too, for at least part of the time.

The first letter, dated 13 July and written obviously in haste and distress, spells out what happened:

> Some of the things you said to me on the plane reminded me again that close as I often feel to you, there was, on this level of work, a desperate failure of communication and understanding which was worrying when I was feeling as I was. Then, what happened in that restaurant, innocent as it seems to you, hit me still harder.

The two had been dining when Jacquetta's attention was caught and held by an attractive young woman. It had seemed clear to Priestley that she had felt for the girl an immediate and unmistakable physical attraction:

> I felt you had moved clean away from me, unconsciously resented the surrender of the few days before, and so were swinging over to that attitude you had known some years before. If this seems to you a lunatic interpretation of something quite innocent, I must point out that you are in public an extremely reserved person and that I have never before seen you exchanging such glances with a stranger. And when you said – outside – that perhaps you were following her, you were speaking more truly than you imagined. But there was I, exhausted and depressed, left staring at this failure of communication and understanding, and at this quite unusual behaviour of yours which in another woman would have passed with me for what you say it was – merely an older woman's acknowledgement of a girl's charm and high spirits.

But, he continues, 'you had told me too much about yourself to enable me to take this queer little scene superficially, though I am not now arguing that my interpretation is right; I am only telling you what has been happening to me.' He knew that he had aroused jealousy in the women with whom he had been involved, but he found it almost impossible to handle such feelings himself. Whether or not he would have felt less strongly had the supposed threat come from a young man is not clear. So black was his mood that he told Jacquetta bluntly that he must be left alone to wrestle with it until he felt able to talk to her about his feelings 'which I am afraid (and this I can't help) may not be for some weeks yet . . .'

The second letter, undated and written some time later, is in answer to a message she had sent to him by his secretary at Waterloo Station, where he had been about to board the train for the Isle of Wight. In it he referred to attempts to contact her by telephone which had proved unsuccessful.

> But there are special reasons why I didn't want a showdown now. I must say I wouldn't blame you if you came to the conclusion that I was now a great deal more bother than I was worth; but I can't help it. I shan't be in London much in the near future and,

although it should be better later, there is a growing danger that I might not be up so much alone as I used to be, partly because the London flat, now that it is re-organised and decorated, makes a better family place for entertaining, etc. I don't like the way more and more people have to be brought into this . . . better write me off for a few weeks, though of course if I have a break, I'll get in touch. And no messages of any kind, please; and then as soon as the chance presents itself we'll have a really good long talk about ourselves.

The third letter, also undated and without an address, is later still, after the two had met. In it Priestley expressed serious doubts. She had, he conceded, written him 'a very nice letter' but it was no use talking of Jung's theories if

as soon as real life comes in, one abandons them – as one does, I think, when one gets back to vague talk about 'in love' and 'not in love'. Now I believe quite firmly that there is such a thing as anima projection, that when a man is doing this, a woman appears to have powers of magical compulsion over him, though he may resent them – and indeed resent her. This may not apply to young men being 'in love' but I am certain it applies to middle-aged men. That was the stage I was in at first and the stage I got out of, with the result that while the magical compulsion is no longer there (not due to familiarity but to some change in one's psyche), you, JJH, are there, yourself, your very loveable, intensely endearing self, clearly seen and deeply appreciated.

Throughout his life, whatever had happened, he had always been able to write. Now for the first time in his life the flow of ideas and inspiration had ceased.

He had, he wrote, always said he had little to give and now felt he had even less, due to 'some mysterious change inside', and he did not believe that either she or anyone else could help him much.

For the first time I am not full of ideas and zest for work – I feel I can do some little thing I am compelled to do, an article, a broadcast, and am even depressed about them when I'm doing them, but cannot create anything. This may mean I'm merely tired and rather disappointed, that I've worked the top soil and must now go deeper or pack up. I've heard it said men tend to go through a crisis at about my age and this may be it.

I would certainly be very unhappy if we no longer saw each other, but, at the risk of depressing or hurting you, I must say that there are times when I feel strongly that it would be far far better for you (who need more richness in a relationship than I can offer) if we did, and also better for me, just because then I can 'dree my weird' and come through or bust. Perhaps the truth is that I am by nature a clever technician, almost a subtle craftsman with a comparatively simple mind (I would have been happy in an easy time with a very elaborate art form) and that now everything is just too dam' complicated for me.

The strain was beginning to tell: their assignation had taken place in A. D. Peters' flat, where they had raided his larder ('he didn't mind at all'), but both were unhappy at having to make do with such rendezvous. Priestley wrote to her:

There is in fact great sweetness in you, and this, with your intellect and personality, makes you an astonishing wench. It is not difficult for a stupid woman to be amiable but an amiable (to put it at its lowest level) clever woman is a gem . . . Please destroy this letter – too many clues in it. Not possible for you to reply to this here, unfortunately.

CHAPTER 25

Endings

The strain of his double life told on Priestley: his output of books dropped and although he continued to write plays they were not good ones. He was also depressed by the failure of the Labour Government, which he had supported with such enthusiasm, to effect any real change.

During the war Priestley had become a household name but now new young writers were coming to the fore. In no other field was this more marked than in the theatre. In the 1950s, when Priestley was writing plays such as *Bright Shadow, Treasure on Pelican* and *Private Rooms* – let alone *Take the Fool Away* which almost nobody wanted to put on – he was up against formidable opposition. New types of drama were sweeping the board, such as Samuel Beckett's *Waiting for Godot,* which had its first production in 1953, and, of course, John Osborne's *Look Back in Anger,* which opened in 1956. Both offered a totally different view of the world from that presented by Priestley in his plays, the former bleak and enigmatic with overtones of dark humour, the latter the pioneer of what was to become known, somewhat vividly, as 'kitchen sink drama'.

After the publication of an amusing book of essays, *Delight,* in 1949 there was a two-year gap before Priestley published his next novel, *Festival at Farbridge.* Writing about it in *Margin Released,* he explains he wanted to write a large-scale comic novel about post-war England and 'stupidly as I see now' chose the Festival of Britain, 'which I welcomed and never sneered at, as a peg on which to hang the tale'. He had welcomed the attempts of the Labour Government to provide a focus for national celebration and saw the book as his own contribution to the festivities.

Its three protagonists set out to bring the Festival to Farbridge, with hilarious results and misunderstandings but at the end of which there is a truly splendid celebration. He never saw it as anything other than a lightweight work, but reading it now, forty years on, it has much to say about the nature of the English both then and now. Readers loved it and it was the Book Society Choice for May 1951, but many reviewers were unenthusiastic. 'Its reception,' he wrote later, 'disappointed me as that of no other novel of mine has ever done.' He had sent his latest play, *Golden Door*, to Ralph Richardson, who was not happy with it. In a letter to Edward Davison of 3 April 1951, Priestley wrote that he had had to spend a long session with the actor the previous Saturday 'and I agreed to reconsider some of it, to make the suicide more plausible and to heighten the tension there'. But it never went into production.

In the same year Jacquetta published to great acclaim what many regard as the best book she ever wrote, *A Land*, in which she told the story of Britain's land, its geology and archaeology and their relationship to the island's subsequent history. It is written in a style that manages to be scholarly, accessible yet evocative.

By 1950 Jane had known that there was another woman in Priestley's life, although she did not know who it was. She and Priestley were no longer close as they had been before the Peggy Ashcroft débâcle, and his preoccupation and frequent absences failed to alert her. She put down his incessant grumbling and outbursts of ill-humour to difficulties with his work; perhaps he had told her, too, that he was experiencing some kind of writer's block.

She began to write long, confiding letters to Charles Lack, the doctor they had met in Tintagel early in the war, about the turmoil she was in, that her marriage seemed to be falling apart and that she found herself swinging between a desire to force a confrontation that would end it for good or to say nothing in the hope that things might improve. Finally, a trivial disagreement about wine brought the Priestleys to the point of no return. Jane took to her bed with what she said was flu, and the two stopped speaking to each other, communicating only through messages carried between them by their unfortunate son.[1]

When Jack did finally decide to tell Teddy Davison the position, he laid the blame squarely on Jane. Even worse, he reiterated in every letter written during that period that he had agreed to a divorce only with reluctance because Jane was demanding it, as she was deeply involved with someone else and wanted to marry him. (Jane had indeed become friendly with the distinguished ornithologist Dr David Bannerman, who later became her third husband, but at this stage they were not involved in an affair and Priestley knew it. Tom Priestley notes that the whole family were aware of how scrupulously Jane had behaved throughout this period and, indeed, during the time when her friendship with Bannerman was leading to marriage.) Priestley wrote that he and Jane had recognised that they had insufficient in common now to make a satisfactory life together, and 'if we came together again one of us (and it has been me mostly in the immediate past) must sacrifice too much for a very doubtful gain. It was Jane who brought this out. I doubt if I would ever have had the courage, though I profoundly agree with it.' He added that he would like Teddy to tell no one but Natalie.

Two weeks later he wrote to Natalie, thanking her for her sympathetic letter and again reiterating, 'I would never have had the courage to tell Jane that we were really better apart, although I've known it for some time; but as she wants to marry someone else, who represents the kind of life she prefers now, I cannot but agree . . .' He would much have preferred a legal separation and had only with reluctance agreed to divorce, but would do the gentlemanly thing and allow her to divorce him 'in the usual faked style; but am hoping this will not be necessary while the present Government is in power because it may lead to savage attacks on me from the cheaper Tory Press'. Significantly he made a point to which he would return in subsequent letters: 'I do not particularly want divorce myself and in some ways would find it more convenient (and safer) to be officially married.'

Did 'safer' imply that if he was divorced he might have to decide whether or not to marry Jacquetta, and that he preferred to keep things as they were?

The Priestleys had gone to Paris in the late spring, Jane cherishing the hope that a holiday there might bring about some rapprochement. But Priestley had found fault with everything and, indeed, was writing to Jacquetta saying how much he wanted to get back to London. Jane had told Tom of how she had looked out of the hotel window at the wonderful view and asked herself, 'Why on earth should I continue to put up with this?'[2]

In an undated letter to the Davisons, she says,

> You've heard from Jack the miserable news. I am more deeply
> grieved than I can say. Why did it all go wrong? It is quite
> impossible I think for either of us to see the truth. We are each
> too involved and can only see it from our own viewpoint. I feel that
> our relationship has been gradually and increasingly undermined
> by Jack's continued infidelities. We have been together twenty-five
> years and ever since 'The Good Companions' there has been
> a procession of ladies. That was not the real trouble though
> because even during those years, 'til five years ago, there was
> something valuable. We could still be friends and talk.
>
>   Something went wrong about five years ago. I don't know what.
> It was nothing to do with me but since then our relationship has
> been empty.

She had become merely his business manager, housekeeper and
the recipient of his complaints. There was neither affection nor
friendship between them, only a mounting tension. 'I realised
I could not take it any more. I had done my part of the job,
the children were all grown up. I knew then [during the Paris
holiday] it was all ended for me.' Jack did not want a divorce,
she told them, and had told her solicitor 'that he wanted a wife
in name so that other people should not try to marry him'.

In a letter to Davison on 23 July Priestley mentioned Jacquetta
for the first time, but there is no suggestion of the true situation
between them.

> By the way I think you will notice a change in my work
> because from now on I propose to dig deeper and try to
> release stuff at a poetic unconscious level unless it is too
> late. This would chime with your own view, I fancy, and
> I have lately been encouraged to take this step by the
> observations of a brilliant woman friend, Jacquetta Hawkes
> (she is the wife of an Oxford professor, the daughter of a
> Nobel prize winner – her father Gowland Hopkins discovered
> vitamins and was the cousin of Gerard Manley Hopkins, and
> she is an associate Fellow of Newnham) whose book, a
> strange mixture of scientific scholarship and poetry called
> A LAND, has been the highbrow hit of the season here.
> Just as most contemporary writers are too introverted, I have
> been too extroverted – in my work if not in my thinking
> and feeling.

One person who had discovered the truth was Priestley's stepsister Winnie. At some time in the summer Priestley and Jacquetta had managed a short walking holiday in the Yorkshire Dales and had been seen by one of Winnie's friends. 'She wrote to Jack,' Jacquetta recalled, 'asking him who the very smart woman was he had been seen with out walking on the moors and later in a nearby hotel.' The woman was particularly striking as she was wearing a sombrero 'and smoking a cigar! Actually "it was a cheroot", said Jacquetta. I had something of a thing about them at that time.'[3]

In October 1951 Priestley went to America to discuss the possibility of productions of two plays on Broadway. Jacquetta had to undertake a lecture tour, after which the two would meet up in New York. On 9 October Priestley wrote to the Davisons saying that the legal separation had been sorted out, even though Jane 'is impatient for a divorce but has been made to realise, by her own solicitors, that that is out of the question this year so that she must wait. She is buying a farm in S.W. Scotland, which she likes very much, and it is I suppose where her new chap would like to retire to.'

When he arrived in New York he immediately wrote to Jacquetta to say he was rereading Jung and

> that analysis of me based on *Rain Upon Godshill*. It seemed to me rather better than it seemed first time, probably because I began last night by accepting its faults. You might probably agree with its conclusion that I am kind, generous, gifted, etc, etc. but over-extroverted, demanding from the outside world something it can't give and so on, and probably with Shadow and Anima trouble.

Yet even his shadow side Jung had considered to be honest and candid, 'and there are few people of whom so much could be said and my Shadow is neither repulsive nor evil but not unlike one of those genies or spirits in the fairy tales which accompany the wanderers in secret', and this was 'not too bad'. In 1946 Priestley had actually visited Jung, an event to which he attached great importance. He never wrote an account of their meeting at the time (though presumably this refers to it); but he interviewed Jung for a BBC radio talk, and eight years later wrote an article, 'Jung and the Writer', for the *Times Literary Supplement* (6 August 1954).

It was with Jung in mind that he went to see a production of Shaw's *Don Juan in Hell*, directed by Charles Laughton. It was presented as what we would now describe as a rehearsed reading, without a set, the cast in evening dress reading from scripts. It was then a novel notion that immediately fired Priestley with a brilliant idea. No sooner had Jacquetta joined him than he suggested they write a play together, which could be produced similarly with Laughton directing.

During this visit he introduced Jacquetta to the Davisons and was delighted to find that they all got on well. But this was not enough for him. On his return home, in a deeply unpleasant move that was most unfair to Jane, he wrote, to Edward, a lyrical letter about Jacquetta, adding 'It's a great pleasure to me that she's so fond of both you and Natalie . . . Jane liked you, because of old times, but never liked Natalie, who is, as I needn't tell you, a Treasure and Poppet and one of my three favourite women on earth. (She knows it and DOTES on me.)'

Even before leaving New York, he and Jacquetta began work on their joint venture. The play, *Dragon's Mouth*, would be for four actors, representing Jung's four functions of sensation, intellect, intuition and emotion. Jacquetta would write the roles for the first two, Priestley for the others, and the setting was to be a yacht cruising off the West Indies that belonged to Matthew, a tough businessman married to a professional singer. The second man would be an academic, and the second woman a personnel manager in Matthew's firm. The yacht is moored in an inlet surrounded by jagged rocks – the dragon's mouth of the title. A deadly plague has hit the crew, one has died and two more are sick. A doctor, summoned to attend to the sick, has taken blood samples from the four protagonists who, if they are found to be affected, face certain death. During the waiting time the four strip their souls to the bone. The play ends with the sound of the returning motor boat bringing the results of the blood tests, but the audience is never told if all or, indeed, any of them will die.

The collaboration was official and gave Priestley and Jacquetta valid opportunities to be seen in public together. The script, rushed out with impatience by Priestley, was sent to Laughton in New York, but he was told that because of Laughton's film commitments there was no hope of an early production in the USA. Undaunted, Priestley immediately started to put together one of his own and approached Michael Denison to play one of the men. According to Denison, Priestley handed him two scripts, informing him that it was the best thing he had ever done and how lucky he had been to find such a fine collaborator as 'Mrs Hawkes'.[4] He invited Denison and his wife, Dulcie Gray, down to Brook Hill to discuss it further and told them, 'I've just heard my wife has left me for a bird man and I told her she could take any furniture that she wanted, but she won't have done it yet,' although in reality he and Jane had been living apart for months. In fact, Jane had removed those pieces she claimed belonged to her, with the result that the Denisons arrived to find the house almost empty. 'Yet,' says Denison, 'never in our experience had his gift of hospitality been more hilariously displayed.' Priestley ended the evening accompanying the pianola in the role of a dancing cellist without a cello.[5]

The production of *Dragon's Mouth* was an exhausting experience for all concerned. It was finally decided that, although the actors would not be in costume, they would learn their parts and that a basic staging would suggest the deck of a yacht. Priestley had planned a terrifying tour worthy of the old barnstormers, with fifty-two different venues each for one night only. He hired a bus with the idea that he, the cast (the other two actors were Rosamund John and Norman Wooland) and the production team would undertake the tour together. This idea was vetoed by Dulcie Gray, who claimed that she got coach-sick and demanded that she and Michael travel in their own car. They were the lucky ones: the coach was slow, the driver kept losing his way and eventually Priestley stormed back to Brook Hill, only rejoining the company when the show reached Bournemouth. The tour was financially disastrous and he cut it short, ending in Cambridge on 13 May 1952, before putting it into the Winter Garden Theatre in London.

Its organisation had been a shambles, Priestley wrote to the Davisons,[6] as the concert booking agency had fouled things up by being late everywhere with tickets and advertisements, but he claimed that the play been an artistic success with enthusiastic press reviews. He was, however, worried about its prospects in London as the Winter Garden was an enormous theatre, and

he hoped that the play would still be running when they came
to London in June,

> but I have my doubts. There is a lot of prejudice against me
> in the theatre just now (some of it due to my supporting
> Labour) persuading playgoers very unfairly that I am always
> writing 'propaganda' plays, lecturing my audiences, etc. We
> found this out during our tour of *Treasure on Pelican*, now
> ended ... Ironically enough, I have now said in print that I
> no longer believe in socialism and that the socialist–capitalist
> duel is now out of date and the whole thing calls for fresh
> thinking instead of this wrangling about dead issues. But then
> I seem to have almost a flair for annoying people in power.

In fact, the reviews had been mixed, most of the enthusiasm
for Dulcie Gray's portrayal of Nina. To Priestley's bitter
disappointment Laughton never put it on in New York, and
his own attempt to revive it some years later failed. However,
he and Jacquetta were already working on another script, *The
White Countess.*

It had an even more dismal history. Nobody liked it. Priestley
offered the leading male role to Ralph Richardson, who read it
with what sympathy he could muster but said it wasn't for him,
then to Laurence Olivier who promptly turned it down. He tried
to persuade his old love Peggy Ashcroft to take on the female
lead but she told him tactfully that she felt she was too old for
the part. A. D. Peters disliked it from the first.

In the summer of 1952 the Priestleys were divorced. It is hard
to remember in these days of 'no fault' and relatively easy divorce
how archaic the system was in the 1950s. The three main grounds
were cruelty, desertion and, of course, adultery. Most men agreed
to take on the official role of adulterer, whether or not they
actually were, but the usual practice for those seriously involved
with another woman was to hire a 'professional co-respondent',
book a double room for the night, and ensure that a private
detective was on hand to see them leave in the morning. But
Jacquetta thought this dishonest and said that she should stay
with Priestley herself. It is not certain when Christopher Hawkes
became fully aware of Jacquetta's relationship with Priestley –
perhaps it was after Nicolas had been sent to Bryanston – nor
if she told him what she intended to do.

As Priestley wanted the minimum of publicity it was agreed that he and Jacquetta should spend the night together in Paris (along with a hired private detective) and that the divorce proceedings should take place in Exeter. There was a hiccup when the manager of the Paris hotel refused to give the private detective any evidence for use in court on the grounds that the 'English monsieur', or anyone else for that matter, should be allowed to take his pleasure when and where he wished without it being the business of other people. However a 'sort of retired police inspector' was found in Exeter, who took down a statement from Priestley about his night in Paris, and on 29 July 1952 the divorce went through without Jacquetta's name being mentioned, the decree absolute following in September.

Priestley had already been invited by a group of liberal newspapers in Japan to give a series of five lectures the same month. Somewhat rashly, Jacquetta decided to accompany him, and the two planned a holiday trip on the way home via New York as Priestley still hoped to find an American backer, not only for *Dragon's Mouth* but also for *The White Countess*.

The Priestley divorce had been achieved relatively easily but Jacquetta was still torn as to whether or not she should follow suit. Another aspect of the then divorce law was that, if a husband or wife was found to have 'colluded, connived or condoned' the behaviour of their partner to obtain a divorce, it would automatically be refused. Christopher's father was a divorce lawyer; Christopher informed him that Jacquetta was planning a trip to Japan with Priestley and asked what the position would be if it came to divorce. Hawkes advised him that, as a precaution against later being accused of collusion, he should ask Priestley to write him a letter, ostensibly about the purpose of the trip, giving innocuous reasons why it was necessary for Jacquetta to accompany him. Christopher duly wrote to Priestley, asking if he would do this so that he had something 'to show his family'.

Priestley found himself in what can best be described as a *Catch 22* situation. If he refused to write the letter he would look guilty and, as the Hawkeses still had no plans for divorce, he could hardly say that Jacquetta was his long-standing mistress. If he gave the valid reasons of their collaboration on two plays and their work with UNESCO, he felt this would be dishonest. In the end, though, persuaded by Jacquetta that it was all for the best (although she did not really understand the reasoning behind it), he did so.[7] The letter would return to haunt them.

So in September 1952 they went to Japan and, via the South Seas, on to New York, returning home just before Christmas. For Jacquetta it proved 'perhaps the most unpleasant period I have ever known'. The day after her return her housekeeper was taken to hospital, and she found herself in the unusual position of having to cook and shop for the festivities. Her father was now dead and her elderly, increasingly frail mother was one of the party. The tension was enormous and finally, as she disclosed in a letter to Edward Davison, on Boxing Day, 'without any advance intention of doing so', she told Christopher that she was going to leave him and wanted a divorce. He had been half expecting it since the Japanese trip but the news still provoked an emotional scene. Somewhat to her surprise she found she was deeply sad and 'kept weeping', although Christopher was 'very sweet about it'. She did not tell her son until the end of the holiday and he was, she said, 'horribly upset for a short time, for as Christopher and I always got on perfectly well superficially it came to him out of a blue sky . . . I think seeing that Christopher and I remain on excellent terms and will see each other freely when the period of legal enmity has finished has comforted him and reassured him.' It was, she concluded honestly, 'never against my personal principles to be unfaithful to my husband, but it was to let him down and break up his home.'[8]

Throughout, the love letters from Priestley continued to arrive. Jacquetta was, he told her, his 'last manifestation of the anima image, Sophia, the wise one, as well as my dear Jacquetta with her beautiful eyes and magnificent grin', even though he felt she was capable of 'strange and sudden passions which might wreck a man'. In the February following her confession to Christopher she wrote to Priestley that she had 'behaved in a way I don't like', which worried him. 'Did you mean the divorce?' he asked.[9] 'Or that keeping the relationship going during its worst passage demanded some sacrifice of pride?' Neither he nor Jacquetta, he continued, were 'pledge' people but must continue to share their major emotions and thoughts, 'never never never seeing the other as Conscience, an Accuser, a Prosecutor, an Enemy. This is what is fatal in marriage.' On a more mundane level he told her that he was about to embark on a strict health regime: cold baths (which were then supposed to reduce weight), *no lunch* and no drinks beyond a glass of beer or mild whisky at dinner. 'I will report progress on this front. I must get down to 13-and-a-half stone which is nearly a stone less than I am now.'

Two days later he wrote again in answer to another letter from her about her coming divorce.

> I feel myself that if I were simply a friend of yours and Christopher's I would advise the divorce, even if neither of you wanted to marry anyone else. On the ground that you were no longer good for one another. He is a good man but would be a better one married to someone else. You are so fairminded that you will not indulge in any of Jane's projections but don't go too far the other way, overplaying the role of guilty wife. Remember please if you had not had me to make you feel happy at times and make you feel rather guilty towards Christopher, it is doubtful if your marriage would have lasted through these last few years. Again, if you had saved your marriage but we had bust up (as we might easily have done) what do you think home life at 39 [her house] would have been like then? You were certainly anything but a happy or contented woman when we first met – and what was C doing about it and what could he do? I don't know what you have said to him but I do hope that you have suggested that all was far from well and probably[9] drifting to disaster before I came on the scene. I may be being a bit selfish here, but I certainly don't want people to get the impression that I was responsible for breaking up a happy home.[10]

He had prompted her to read Ouspensky and now sent her another time book, Maurice Nicolls' *Living in Time,*

> more confusing than Ouspensky, but more sympathetic. The chief clue to this Time thought is that we are our times, which I have long believed. Thus we are not living in order to die, to be the cross-section of ourself that lies on the death bed. Our real self is the long length of us along the fourth dimension. There is no time (in the ordinary sense) for us outside our own time. This is where conventional Christianity, Theosophy, Spiritualism, etc. go all wrong. [This view] is not at all easy. It is rather demanding and austere in its implications, but does suggest a larger and more just universe.[11]

Finally, in 1953, they decided to marry. In March Priestley told Tom the news 'and he seemed genuinely pleased. I also told him I wanted him to be specially nice to Nic and he understood that too.' Jacquetta and Nicolas had been invited down to Brook Hill and Tom had brought a friend to stay. It was quite like old times – good meals interspersed with walks and tennis.

Jacquetta's divorce, first set down for May, finally took place on 5 June. Needless to say, Christopher's mother, who had always disliked her daughter-in-law so much, had taken the whole thing very badly, which goes some way towards explaining what happened. The date might have been seen as an excellent one by those wanting to avoid publicity: newspapers in the early 1950s were thin and their few pages were crammed with features on the aftermath of Elizabeth II's Coronation, which had taken place a few days earlier. However the divorce judge, Judge Tudor Rees, ensured that in spite of this the Hawkes divorce was plastered across what remaining space there was. 'Mr. J. B. Priestley cited as "mean and contemptible," was the headline in *The Times*, 'Priestley "mean and cunning" says divorce judge', bellowed the *Evening Standard*.[12]

The grounds were not, as previously reported elsewhere, the same as those of the Priestley divorce but were based on 'misconduct by Mrs Jacquetta Hawkes while on a tour last autumn in Japan with Mr J. B. Priestley'. At the last moment, Christopher's father had advised him to make use of the letter Priestley had been asked to write him before the trip to Japan. Christopher, who was devoted to his father and under heavy pressure from his mother, agreed to do so, and it was that letter (not 'letters' as in the judge's remarks or in the press) that provoked Rees's ferocious attack on Priestley which made the headlines. The judge said,

Mr Priestley is a writer of fiction, a capacity which he has demonstrated in letters [sic] which were written to Professor Hawkes when the latter became suspicious about the relationship between his wife and Mr Priestley. In my view, he wrote those letters in a deliberate and cunning attempt to deceive Professor Hawkes as to his conduct. Mr Priestley and Mrs Hawkes collaborated in writing and producing plays in Japan and elsewhere and it is quite clear that it was not only a literary collaboration but an adulterous one. Mr Priestley's conduct was mean and contemptible

Priestley was devastated.

Christopher's solicitors advised him also to sue Priestley for heavy damages, pointing out he was an extremely wealthy man, but, to his credit, Christopher refused to entertain the idea.

Christopher's biographer, Diana Webster, wrote that he destroyed the letter shortly afterwards in a fit of anger and remorse. 'His way of dealing with emotional problems was to dig the biggest hole he could, shovel in as much heavy material as he could lay his hands on and build an impregnable fortress on top of it . . . I know that he was deeply ashamed of the hurt his action caused but what was left of his pride refused to let him admit it.'[13] Priestley was not alone in being hurt by the letter. Jacquetta, aware of what the press would do, immediately wrote to Nicolas at school warning him of what had happened and hoping he would be able to see the matter in perspective, but it was too late. Another pupil had acquired a copy of one of the papers carrying the story and circulated it around the school, along with a number of choice comments.[14]

On 23 July 1953, Priestley and Jacquetta were married at that fashionable venue for civil weddings, Caxton Hall. Jane Priestley married David Bannerman and the two spent many happy years travelling all over the world on ornithological expeditions. Jane's sister told Priestley when they met by chance that she looked happier than she had seemed since she was eighteen, and appeared to have shed years. Six years later Christopher Hawkes also married again. Writing to his fiancée, fellow archaeologist Sonia Chadwick, just before the wedding, he told her he no longer felt any emotion for the Priestleys, 'who seem to me people in another world'. He could now look back and see that the break-up of his marriage to Jacquetta had been just one of those things, but she had remained 'a charming and affectionate mother to Nick all through . . .' He had no grudges, no grievances, no burden of inner woe.

CHAPTER 26

Journey Down a Rainbow

On the surface, at least, Priestley's way of life continued much as it had before the traumatic events of the last years, but underneath there were big differences. Jacquetta was not Jane. She had her own many-faceted career to pursue, as an archaeologist, as a continuing representative of UNESCO and, increasingly, as a writer. That the domestic side continued so seamlessly in its usual routine was in no small part due to Jane having generously suggested that Miss Pudduck, along with Gertrude, remained with Priestley to oversee the housekeeping.

The early years of the marriage were marked by many trips abroad, in part for holidays but mainly for professional reasons. Priestley was greatly in demand as a lecturer and presence at major literary events in both Europe and North America, and Jacquetta's UNESCO commitments also took them abroad fairly frequently.

There was another major change. From the time of their marriage, for Jacquetta, and to some extent for Priestley, it was as though their previous lives had never been and everything began anew. Friendships are often lost in the aftermath of divorce and this happened to the Priestleys. However, they also formed new, lasting and intense friendships. Some older relationships survived, such as that with the Davisons, but on the whole it was truly a case of 'tomorrow to fresh fields and pastures new'.

Interestingly, this is reflected in the views of two of the couples with whom they became increasingly intimate over the following years, Diana and John Collins, and Barbara and Gareth Lloyd Evans. Both Diana Collins and Barbara Lloyd Evans recall how life before their marriage was rarely discussed, apart from references to past work.[1]

Where the immediate families were concerned, the new

marriage took place when most of the children had their own lives. Barbara, Sylvia and Rachel all had families of their own and both Barbara and Sylvia were taking up the threads of their own careers again. Mary's health continued fragile and her marriage collapsed. That Priestley continued to worry about her is shown in the continuing volume of their correspondence. When Tom Priestley and Nicolas Hawkes left school they went to university, did their National Service and embarked on very different careers, both of which were highly distinguished, Tom as a film editor and Nicolas as an academic. All were regular visitors to Brook Hill, then to Kissing Tree House outside Stratford-on-Avon, bought in 1959, but there is little doubt that Jacquetta felt she now came first in her husband's life.

There is also little doubt that many members of the family were to feel that right up until Priestley's death – his youngest daughter, Rachel, particularly. During the upheaval of the deteriorating marriage and the long-drawn-out divorce, Jack had become particularly confiding. They had gone for long walks together and spent hours in conversation on a variety of subjects, not least the work he had in hand. On his marriage that stopped at once, and the close relationship with it. It was obviously nothing like as drastic as his sending away Granny Tempest on his marriage to Jane, but, once again, he found himself in thrall to a strong woman and put behind him what had gone before.

It is something of a truism to say that children of famous parents have many problems with which to contend, some of which they are never able to overcome. Obvious examples come to mind such as the offspring of Sir Winston Churchill and Bertrand Russell, not to mention such show business stars as Judy Garland. It was something Jack himself became aware of in later life. In a letter to Tom Priestley written in 1971[2] concerning payments to the different members of the family from the Good Companions Trust, he writes:

> May I end with a point I ought to have made long ago? If I have seemed, for many years now, to be too detached from the family, it is not because my interest is concentrated only on my writing, etc. for I have always been deeply concerned. The point is, I have always had to steer a course between leaning too heavily on my family, trying to influence them too much,

reducing freedom of opinion and action, and risking appearing
to be too detached, too unconcerned. It is not easy to be the
children of a well-known father – I have always realised that –
but equally it is not easy to be the well-known father either. But
in these, my final years, I must get closer.

It is one of the rare occasions in which he appears to express
regret for what might have been and to apologise to his children
for not being closer to them.

Now that he was relieved of emotional and domestic trauma,
Priestley was soon as busy as ever; the writer's block had vanished.
He was still trying to put on *The White Countess*, a film was being
made of *An Inspector Calls* and he was thinking of writing a
book with the provisional title *The Wrong Planet: And How to
Make the Best of It*, 'all about life in general'. Jacquetta wrote
on 10 September to Edward Davison about the little festival
Priestley had organised privately at Brook Hill for a number
of years: they were presently accommodating Leon Goossens
('a powerful, healthy-looking man dressed in whipcord and
corduroy, a kind of John Bull with oboe') and his quartet.
Their concert had proved so popular that even baby chairs
and pillows had to be used as seating. After it was over and
Priestley had finished his next novel, *The Magicians*, they went
off on holiday to southern Germany.

By February 1954 *The White Countess* was in rehearsal, dogged
by every kind of problem. It finally opened in Dublin 'hopelessly
under-rehearsed'. According to Priestley, the Dubliners hated it
anyway 'partly for easily remedied faults in production but mostly
because they hate sex taken seriously and there was enormous
Catholic prejudice against our theme and ideas'. This was picked
up by the Beaverbrook press ('which hates me anyway') and,
although reviewing previews (which were then called 'try-outs')
is not useful, 'they dished the dirt out fast and increased our
troubles'. However, he had great hopes for London where the
play was to open on 25 March. These were soon dashed. As
Jacquetta wrote to Natalie on the twenty-sixth, the play was 'the
world's most complete and noisy flop! The press this morning
was so bad that we haven't looked at much of it. We weren't
booed but it came near . . . the First Night audience came in
a hostile mood and the poor piece fell to pieces.'

For a while it seemed that, whatever the setback, Priestley

would remain undaunted, and by the beginning of May he had finished the script for what he described as a cheerful, disreputable, anarchical comedy, *Mr Kettle and Mrs Moon*. He was also consumed by enthusiasm for a new joint project with Jacquetta: they would both go to the USA, he on a lecture tour to Texas, she to the native reservations of the Navaho and Zuni in the south west. They would write a book based on their joint experiences, contrasting the lifestyle of the citizens of Texan cities with that of the remaining indigenous population of the region. It worked brilliantly.

Read at the time of publication in 1955, the Priestley contributions to *Journey Down a Rainbow* seemed sharp, amusing and possibly somewhat over the top – even if what he wrote of 1950s' American culture was true, he was surely overdoing it when he suggested that all too soon it could happen here. After all, the British were much too sensible. But what he wrote was indeed prophetic. He pictured a society devoted, in a word he coined himself, to the 'Admass' commercial philosophy, the uninhibited release of market forces and the putting of profit before anything else, the irresistible rise of those who know the cost of everything and the value of nothing. This, he wrote, had spread into almost every aspect of life in the American cities, not least the rhetoric of politicians.

At a lunch in Houston he met a Republican politician from the Deep South who believed anyone to the left of him was a Communist. 'He was the first man I had met who really talked as those newspaper correspondents I had read seemed to think . . . he was a bit dotty.' The man spoiled his day

> . . . not because he was quarrelsome, too loud, too violent, his manners were civil enough, but because there was something frightening in his political dottiness, his monstrous unreason, his refusal to question any evidence that supported his case, his bloodshot anger. A thousand like him, all fiery with bourbon, would be ready to lynch anybody merely on suspicion. And among a lot of ADMASS people, no longer really interested in politics, merely anxious for complete security without reference to ideas, a man so passionately single-minded, so forceful and fluent, so ready to appeal to prejudice and to the violence that lurks behind the ADMASS sense of frustration, could soon stampede crowds into lunatic action

... I don't believe in ADMASS as a bulwark of political democracy.

Jacquetta fell in love with the deserts and their people, both the Navaho and the Zuni. She visited the caves at Sandias, watched the women at work on their weaving and fine pottery, sought out information on the culture of the Navaho people. But for her the high point of the journey was to be allowed to see most of the complex ceremony of the Zuni Shalako from its beginning with the tying of forty-nine knots in a special piece of rope and the appearance of the Katchinas, the masked gods, with their prayer sticks and dancing.

Each downward drive of the feet is marked by a clank of bones. Now again, as they reach the hole, that weird cry I heard before: *ha tu tu* I know it is written but to my ear it sounds like a ghost coyote in the hollow of a moonlit night. The dancers wheel away, then renew the approach; something is being softly driven home, softly but powerfully reiterated to the earth by the moccasined feet.

She emerged from the long day and night of the Shalako feeling that she had truly visited another and better world.

Between the light of the crescent moon and the light of the Morning Star I have known the Shalako night, have gone out to it, and been – as by all living experience – a little changed. I shall not stay to see the sacred races by the river, nor even to see Long Horn climb on a roof at dawn to untie the last of the forty-nine knots in the ritual tally cord which have marked the days leading to this one. He will be climbing his ladder any minute now, for already the peacock blue is bleaching above the eastern mesas. But I want to leave Zuni while moon and star still chime in my mind, holding taut between them the bright pattern of this night.

Before the publication of *Journey Down a Rainbow*, Priestley had outraged half the American media by writing of his experiences in Texas that November, although at least one appreciated his comments: 'J. B. ("Jack the Ripper") Priestley spent a fortnight in Texas last November, a memorable fortnight,' wrote Lon

Tinkle, of the *Dallas News*, on 2 January 1955. 'If we can gauge by the press, Houston particularly found the distinguished British novelist memorable. A mere writer has not occasioned so much sputtering since Edna Ferber was invited by Houston critics of "Giant" to attend her own lynching. (She declined.) Houston seemed to agree with a line attributed to Ogden Nash: "Mr. J. B. Priestley is simply beastly." '

Dallas had found him infuriating too. He was outspoken and had the British touch of malice. But the *Dallas News* admitted that some truth was on his side. It lists his criticisms of society at length and his own apparent superiority to it. But at the end of the day 'it seems to us healthy to have a literary lion say, in effect, what he thinks . . . the real artist has little concern with pleasing. What he has is something to give, not to sell. He is not collecting success . . . ultimately the artist is a serious man. And only the serious can discern the difference between gaiety and frivolity, between the real and the counterfeit.' It ended: 'Come back, Jack!'

Back in England, in March he began a weekly series of television programmes partly to familiarise himself with the medium and partly to promote his books and plays, before leaving for a short trip to Vienna where he had been invited to lecture. As well as trying to get *Mr Kettle and Mrs Moon* into production he was also trying to find some enthusiasts for *Take the Fool Away*. Nineteen fifty-five was an election year and the Conservatives were returned to power. Labour, Priestley felt, had deserved their defeat because the party had become barren of ideas, and he felt the situation was probably for the best: the Tories had got in with only a small majority, thus precluding a 'nasty swing to the far right'.[3]

Mr Kettle and Mrs Moon opened in London in September and, according to Priestley, was a smash hit with the public and a matter of indifference or worse to the critics. However, his disappointment was mitigated by the reviews for *Journey Down a Rainbow* in the previous Sunday's papers, which had been very good indeed.

In *The Art of the Dramatist*, published in 1957, Priestley outlines three types of comedy: high comedy (intellectually challenging) had never been popular with English audiences although he had attempted it several times; light comedy was the kind of play designed mainly as a vehicle for popular and highly skilled performers 'without whom these flimsy pieces look very thin indeed'; broad comedy was strong on both character and situation, as in *When We Are Married*. On examination, though, few of Priestley's own comedies fall so neatly into such categories; styles tend to overlap or change direction. Yet whatever the mode and label and whatever the technical experimentation, a number of commentators have pointed out factors common to all, one of which is that Priestley comedies are purposeful, which was generally assumed only to apply to a serious work: 'The assumption is frequently made that if a playwright has anything of moment to communicate, then it can only, and ought only to be done through the medium of a "serious" play.' Catastrophe, gloom or deep speculativeness are, for many people, the only correlative to serious intention. The English are the most difficult people in the world to rouse to action or speculation through the medium of creative art. Priestley had known from *Dangerous Corner* days that the average audience required dramatic entertainment which did not tax them too much but which had to hold their attention. Most of his own comedies were written with several aims in mind: to entertain, to show people as they are, what motivates them and how they behave in a given set of circumstances and, where possible, to put over his own ideas, social and political.

Jacquetta was heartily grateful that *Mr Kettle and Mrs Moon* was successful as she felt that, if it had flopped, Priestley 'could hardly have got on to the London stage again'. However, he was still unable to find backing for a London production of *Take the Fool Away* and by mid-autumn he had agreed that it should have its first production in Vienna. Rehearsals were continually postponed throughout the autumn of 1955 and its opening was finally set for 29 December. He and Jacquetta decided therefore to spend Christmas in Vienna, as Jacquetta wrote to Natalie, 'thus escaping much that one no longer enjoys and bringing the greatest delight to Gertrude and Miss Pudduck, who haven't been home for Christmas Day for a decade or two . . .'

Take the Fool Away was a success in Vienna, *Mr Kettle and Mrs Moon* was going into production in Sweden, Denmark and Germany, and Jacquetta was embarking on a history of UNESCO, having had a modest success with her book *Man on Earth*.

In the spring of 1956, Priestley left for a gruelling lecture tour of Canada. Whether it was because he found living so tiring now or because he went down with a gastric upset, he viewed Canada and the Canadians with a jaundiced eye. His criticisms of the American way of life were repeated by columnists in the local papers wherever he went, and the tour ended with a row at a lunch given by W. H. Smith in Toronto when the chairman announced, without consulting Priestley first, that he would be available for a book signing. He refused. He was missing Jacquetta desperately, and wrote to her, on 23 April 1956, in a tone reminiscent of the early days of their relationship: 'God knows I miss you and look at your photograph fifty times a day, longing and longing to be back.'

That year was marked by a book of essays, *All About Ourselves and Other Essays,* and a longer single essay, 'The Writer in a Changing Society'. The next saw published *The Art of the Dramatist* and *Thoughts in the Wilderness,* the essay collection taken from his contributions to the *New Statesman.* From then on, his attention was devoted to working on *Literature and Western Man.*

Another pressing issue was causing him increasing concern. In *Journey Down a Rainbow* Jacquetta had written a chapter on a visit she had made to Los Alamos, birthplace of the atomic age. It is unlike her style in the rest of the book, far more like Priestley's – perhaps he had a hand in it. 'Unfortunately', she writes, 'it wasn't nearly so horrible as I'd expected.' Los Alamos was presented as just another neat company town, full of ordinary folk. Passing the towering Black Mesa mountain on her way there, she felt it would have been more suitable if Los Alamos had been built on its summit, 'a devil's stronghold without disguise', rather than as a place of 'sweetness and light, all pastel shades and golfing greens'. Entrance was via a guard post and the area was enclosed in barbed wire which, apparently, some of the inhabitants liked as it made them feel secure. The 15,000 people who lived there were assigned houses according to their status, although this was denied in the 'propaganda talk' to which Jacquetta was subjected by the chief administrative officer. He spoke of a community with its own town council, just like everywhere else, although unfortunately there was a handful of 'chronically non-cooperative neurotics who didn't always appreciate what was done for them'.

One of these, a scientist's wife, told her that the chief

administrative officer was a petty tyrant, that she couldn't even change the colour of her front door without his permission and that there was no choice of house, neighbours or street. Homes were allocated on the basis of how many people there were in a family, which resulted in a kind of black market in grannies who moved in for just long enough to force the authorities into providing a family with a larger home. Jacquetta was driven round the town and shown its amenities, the library, schools, hospitals, shopping centre, the dramatic tree-filled canyons with their picnic areas. Everything was designed to give an air of normality. Yet how, she asked, could that be? 'As the brochure says, their "primary responsibility is the development of new and better military applications of atomic energy". I respond to the word *better*.'

Both she and Priestley were haunted by Los Alamos and the implications of what it stood for as the international political situation worsened: relations between East and West were tense, and the USA, the USSR and Britain undertook continuing series of nuclear tests. The coming of the nuclear age has been variously described: as the loss of man's innocence, as the participation by mankind in a Faustian bargain. Possibly the most apposite comment, however, was made by J. Robert Oppenheimer, the so-called father of the atomic bomb, as he watched the first successful explosion of his device at Los Alamos. Quoting from the Hindu religious text, the *Bhagavad-Gita*, he said: 'I am become Death, shatterer of worlds.'

CHAPTER 27

Banning the Bomb

The years between 1956 and 1960 were busy ones for Priestley, professionally, politically and domestically. He became involved in the founding of the Campaign for Nuclear Disarmament, moved from the Isle of Wight to Warwickshire and undertook the enormous amount of work required to research and write *Literature and Western Man.*

Throughout this period he was a regular and popular contributor to the *New Statesman*, then edited by Kingsley Martin with assistance from John Freeman. It was in the *New Statesman* that Priestley published the famous piece that is said to have launched CND, but before that he had upset the literary establishment with two pieces of polemic, greeted with glee by those who felt that the subjects of both had had it coming to them. He first tackled that academic ikon, Dr F.R. Leavis. His essay 'Thoughts on Dr Leavis', published on 10 November 1956, attacked a recent Leavis lecture, 'Literature in My Time', given at Nottingham University, and other published gems of Leavis's criticism. He had, wrote Priestley, 'knocked hell out of everybody'. Hardly any contemporary writer had escaped his lash: Stephen Spender was talentless, Auden remained fixed in time as an undergraduate, Lytton Strachey was irresponsible and unscrupulous, Virginia Woolf a minor luminary and as for J. B. Priestley: 'Fielding,' Leavis had written, 'is important not because he leads to J. B. Priestley but because he leads to J. Austen, to appreciate whose distinction is to feel that life isn't long enough to permit of one's giving much time to Fielding or any to Mr Priestley.' Indeed even the eighteenth-century writers fared little better. Dr Leavis would have liked to drop Smollett, Sterne, Goldsmith and, of course, Fielding into the dustbin. Who, then, should be admitted to the Leavis pantheon? enquired Priestley.

Well, D. H. Lawrence, possibly a couple of Leavis acolytes and, of course, Dr Leavis himself, 'after that nothing'.

'This is where the arrogantly dogmatic, absolutist critic, behaving more like the Grand Inquisitor or Calvin than a sensible man of letters, walks into a trap,' he continued. He freely admitted to being as 'vain, touchy and aggressive as the next man', indeed the odds were ten to one that he was actually *more* vain, touchy and aggressive than the next man, but when *he* was confronted with original talent – the most precious thing in the world – at least it made him feel humble. He painted a pen portrait of Leavis, pale-faced and glittering of eye, marching out to close down whole libraries and wrench books of which he disapproved out of the hands of readers, or working away in some dim study to bring about the ruin of literary reputations. 'Truth compels me to add that I think he and his kind in universities both here and in America have done much mischief to the art they are boarded and lodged to serve . . . Literature is not well served when its giants are mutilated and slaughtered to fit a critical theory here today and gone tomorrow.'

Rumour has it that Leavis, when shown the offending article, commanded that it be returned to its author or to the gutter where it properly belonged. Not so all those who had longed for someone to say publicly what so many people said in private. Edith Sitwell wrote on 12 November,

> Dear Mr Priestley, Your 'thoughts' on Dr Leavis have so delighted my brother Osbert and me – indeed they have been our sole delight at this terrible time – that in sheer gratitude I am writing on behalf of both of us to thank you. I think the article may kill him! There has been *nothing* like it yet, nor will there be – although he has had a pretty bad time of it this year! Incidentally, did you see his interminable whine about the way in which he has been treated, in a letter in 'The Listener' a fortnight or three weeks ago? He is certainly in a very bad state of mind. You are certainly right when you say his goings-on are the result of 'some strange neurosis as if he had been frightened by an Alsatian in early childhood'. I also hear, on the best authority, that some time ago, returning from giving a lecture at Downing College and finding Mrs Queenie Leavis darning socks in the drawing-room, he, shutting the door behind him, spread his arms across it as one being crucified,

and cried, '*they* nearly got me that time!' We don't know who 'they' were!

Next in line for the Priestley treatment was Evelyn Waugh in a review of his latest book, *The Ordeal of Gilbert Pinfold*, published on 31 August 1957. At the outset, Priestley suggested that it was obvious that the drunken protagonist of Waugh's novel, Gilbert Pinfold, half out of his mind on sleeping pills and bromides, was no other than Waugh himself. Like Waugh, Pinfold lived in a charming old country mansion, was in his middle years, was a Roman Catholic and an arrant snob. For Waugh, Priestley wrote, was not a Catholic landed gentleman pretending to be an author, but an author pretending to be a Catholic landed gentleman.

Like Leavis, Waugh had come to believe everything his admirers said of him. A letter from no less a person than John Betjeman, written to Waugh in 1946, fulsome, even sycophantic, was all too typical in its praise: 'You are,' he had written, 'the greatest living English novelist. Everything perfect from ear for dialogue and learning to observation, the gift of storytelling and your carefully written, economical, unslushy English.' Compare this, he continued, 'with the average slushy core or the polished surfaces of such good technicians as Priestley and Coward'. It is unlikely that either 'technician' knew of the letter but it is quite possible that Betjeman had made his views known elsewhere.

His pride hurt by Priestley's diatribe, Waugh refused to reply in the columns of such 'a dubious rag' as the *New Statesman*, preferring a full page in its right-wing rival, the *Spectator*. What got Priestley's goat, he raged, was that he, Waugh, at least tried to behave like 'a gentleman'. Twenty years earlier Priestley had been one of those involved in a literary treason that had embraced the social revolution and had gone to great lengths to 'suck up' to the lower classes and 'identify themselves with the workers'. He dragged out *Blackout in Gretley* to prove his thesis: in it, he said, the workers were the patriots while the 'gentleman', Tarlington, a smart Conservative awarded medals for gallantry in the First World War, had been 'of course' a German spy. Yet, he continued, for all that Priestley had written about the need for major social change and the empowering of the workers and the taking of decision-making away from the political and social establishment, it had come to nothing. The workers themselves remained uninterested as long as they could pile into charabancs and tramp round the nearest stately home.

While both essays caused a flutter in literary circles it was as nothing to the effect of 'Britain and the Nuclear Bombs', which appeared on 2 November 1957. Like the 1940 BBC *Postscripts*, it caught a popular mood even if only a section of it. Priestley had had no idea of the impact it would make. What he wrote was not new; it had been said often enough before and with increasing vehemence as the long shadow of Los Alamos and the nuclear deterrent reached out across Europe.

The idea for the piece had come originally from John Freeman, although he was not a supporter of the anti-nuclear movement, and before he sat down to write it Priestley had asked the *New Statesman*'s library to provide him with all the material they had containing arguments in favour of the Bomb. Then, having read them carefully, he set about demolishing them. He dealt roundly with the supposedly 'realistic' arguments for Britain keeping its own deterrent and for an American–Soviet defence policy based on the promise of mutual destruction. The public were regularly told that no military men or politicians in their right minds would set off a train of events leading to mutual destruction, and therefore any criticism of the policy was mere 'woolly idealism'. But Priestley had seen his contemporaries slaughtered as a result of a policy that lacked all coherence and common sense, and he had no such faith in world leaders: 'Surely it is the wildest idealism, at the furthest remove from sober realism, to assume that men will always behave reasonably and in line with their best interests.'

He also attacked the hero of the left, Aneurin Bevan, who had shocked the Labour Party conference by telling it that, unless Britain retained the Bomb, he would be sent, as Foreign Secretary, 'naked into the conference chamber'. He had begged his outraged listeners to embrace reality: they must not confuse 'emotional spasms with statesmanship'. Yet 'so-called statesmanship', Priestley wrote, had produced little else recently but 'emotional spasms'.

The Bomb, he said, was not even the ultimate deterrent: each new nuclear weapon was immediately countered with another, even more destructive. After the atomic bomb, the hydrogen bomb; after the bomber, the rocket and the nuclear submarine, carrying warheads that could be loosed against any country in the world. Even if Britain held on to the Bomb, Priestley said, she would be in no position to mediate between the two great blocs: she could not afford to compete in a race to make weapons,

> an insane regress of ultimate weapons that are not ultimate', and 'we cannot at one and the same time be both an independent power bargaining on equal terms and a minor ally or satellite . . . Our "hard-headed realism" is neither hard-headed nor realistic just because it insists on our behaving in a new world as if we were still living in an old world, the one that has been replaced.

He was not, he assured readers, a pacifist. He did not suggest the abandonment of a strong defence for Britain – indeed, he argued, by giving up the nuclear race and putting the cost of it into conventional forces our defence capability might be considerably strengthened.

The people of Britain had never been asked what they thought, he said. As the preparations for nuclear war and the build-up of weaponry continued, they had never been asked their opinion. The whole mad conspiracy had been 'conducted in the stifling secrecy of an expensive lunatic asylum'. Nor was the danger of a zealot unleashing nuclear war the only one. What about war by accident? 'Three glasses too many of vodka or bourbon-on-the-rocks and the wrong button may be pushed.'

If realism was the name of the game, then how realistic was it to suggest that we could survive a nuclear war? Russia had survived vast losses in the last war because of its huge population and its vast territory, whereas Britain, so small and overcrowded, could be totally destroyed by a mere handful of bombs. If there was one country that should never have gambled in the game it was Britain: 'We may have been fooling ourselves, we have not been fooling anyone else.' Were we therefore to accept that civilisation was bent on self-destruction, 'hurriedly planning its own doomsday?'. Foreign affairs were conducted in an atmosphere of the wearisome recital of plot and counter-plot, in that 'curious and sinister air of somnambulism there is about our major international affairs'.

He concluded that Britain had ended the Second World War high in the world's regard:

We could have taken over its moral leadership, spoken and acted for what remained of its conscience; but we chose to act otherwise – with obvious and melancholy consequences . . . Alone we defied Hitler: and alone we can defy this nuclear madness . . . there may be other chain reactions besides those leading to destruction: and we might start one. The British of these times, so frequently hiding their decent kind faces behind masks of sullen apathy or cheap cynicism, often seem to be waiting for something better than party squabbles and appeals to their narrowest self-interest, something great and noble in its intention that would make them feel good again. And this might well be a declaration to the world that after a certain date one power able to engage in nuclear warfare will reject the evil thing forever.

'Britain and the Nuclear Bombs' had an immediate and dramatic effect. Letters poured into the *New Statesman* office by the thousand. There was already an infant anti-nuclear campaign, the National Campaign Against Nuclear Weapons, based in Hampstead, with Bertrand Russell as its president, the Quaker Arthur Goss as chairman and Peggy Duff as secretary. Kingsley Martin and his small staff, quite unable to deal with the deluge of correspondence, passed it on to the Campaign asking for help.

Martin, hitherto ambivalent about the nuclear issue, decided that he must now reflect the views of his readership and called a meeting at his flat to which he invited Commander Sir Stephen King-Hall, Professor P.M.S. Blackett, George Kennan (who had just given the 1957 Reith Lectures on 'Russia, the Atom and the West', questioning the entire nuclear strategy) and the Priestleys. Priestley himself had already contacted Blackett asking 'if we would join some kind of non-political arts/science etc. Group to denounce nuclear warfare'. The meeting decided that the time had come to launch a major national campaign, and it was decided that the small Hampstead group would sink its identity into a larger movement and hand over its bank balance of £450, its new office in Fleet Street and its February booking of the Central Hall, Westminster, to a newer and larger organisation – along with Peggy Duff. It was she who suggested that a more central meeting place would be needed and that Canon John Collins of St Paul's might be approached to see if he would agree to the use of his home within the cathedral precinct, 2 Amen Court.

John and Diana Collins were seasoned campaigners against the apartheid regime in South Africa and he was already involved in anti-nuclear activities. It seems that Priestley had doubts about the involvement of a high-profile priest in the new campaign, so Peggy Duff arranged a meeting between them in the Albany flat. According to Diana Collins, John returned in high spirits, impressed by Priestley whom he had found immensely sympathetic.[1] A dinner invitation followed to which Diana went alone as the Canon was unable to attend. She arrived apprehensively at the Albany, whose entrance she described as 'awesome', where she was met by a uniformed doorman. She was directed to the Priestleys' flat along a corridor set with rows of blue plaques in memory of all the famous people who had lived there. She finally climbed a huge stone staircase to a door with a brass plate bearing the legend 'J. B. Priestley'.

She had assumed that, although the invitation was for dinner, it would be an informal affair made up of others interested in launching the new movement, so she arrived in an ordinary short dress only to find the Priestleys resplendent in immaculate evening wear. The only other guest was Laurens van der Post's wife, Ingaret, whom she already knew and liked. Both Priestleys, however, put her at her ease. Priestley, she thought, could not be described as 'handsome':

He was not particularly tall, was thick-set and a bit fat, with a high-domed forehead and head that was losing hair on top. His mouth was rather heavily sensual, and there was a knowing twinkle in his eye. He immediately put me at ease by explaining how happy he was to be dining with three women, preferring their company to that of men – they were usually more interesting. It was a happy, easy evening and I felt greatly drawn to both of them. There was no call for party manners, nor social small talk. In so far as anyone can, I had only to be myself. I quickly discerned that no kind of personal falsity could long flourish here. How mischievous, malicious and false are those sedulously propagated public images.[2]

It was the start of an intense friendship between the Priestleys and the Collinses that lasted for the rest of their lives, ending

only with Jacquetta's death in the spring of 1996, which left
Diana the sole survivor of the quartet. They visited each other
regularly and took holidays together.

After the deaths of Priestley and her own husband Diana
wrote,

> These instant friendships are some of the delights and mysteries
> of life. They are often unexpected as was John's and mine with
> Jack and Jacquetta. I wonder what it is that so immediately draws
> people together, before you have had any chance of getting to
> know one another, and when you may only have exchanged
> a few words? Sometimes, not always, there may be a hidden
> sexual element – people talk in a reductionist manner about
> 'the chemistry' – but I think it is very much more: psychological
> in the deepest sense, almost as if there are people whom your
> true inner self instantly recognises. When that happens you soon
> discover that you have not been mistaken.[3]

The Campaign for Nuclear Disarmament was launched at the
Central Hall, Westminster, on 17 February 1958. The main hall
was packed and so were five other overflow halls. Speakers
included Michael Foot, A. J. P. Taylor and, of course, J. B.
Priestley. Although the speeches were splendid, the response
rapturous and a gathering on such a scale had not been seen
since before the Second World War, the event was ignored
by the press. The lesson learned from this was that packed
meetings expressing public outrage were not enough. Other
methods also had to be tried. CND became a household name
only with the marches from the nuclear facility at Aldermaston
in Berkshire.

At the beginning, both Priestley and Jacquetta threw themselves wholeheartedly into the Campaign. He stomped the
country as a speaker and in September 1959 organised a
fund-raising event at the Festival Hall, *Stars In Our Eyes*, calling
on his many theatrical friends to participate. He also persuaded
the BBC to put on a play he had written especially for television,
Doomsday for Dyson, along with another by Marghanita Laski, *The
Offshore Island*.

Priestley had strong reservations about the proposed marches
and never himself took to the streets, even for the first Good Friday march, from London to Aldermaston. Afterwards Jacquetta

suggested that the marches should end at the seat of power in Westminster, which was what happened. Over the years, she was regularly seen at the head of the march beside Canon Collins in his cassock.

She also set up a women's group within CND around a committee of distinguished female writers and scientists, and organised an all-women public meeting. Led by Jacquetta and Diana, the group lobbied Parliament and the Geneva Disarmament Conference and in 1962 took their campaign to the United Nations in New York and the White House in Washington.[4]

This is not the place to follow the history of the Campaign for Nuclear Disarmament. For those who want to find out more there are a number of histories of the movement, some written by those closely involved, other by outside observers. Nor is there any point in rehearsing yet again the splits and politicking which occurred over the years. Suffice it to say that the first and most major of these was the formation of the Committee of One Hundred in 1962 under the aegis of Bertrand Russell, committed to taking direct action against government policy on the grounds that ordinary protest was having no apparent effect. Also, those involved in CND had to contend with the flood of black propaganda purveyed in the media and elsewhere to the effect that all the leading protagonists in CND were either Communists or fellow-travellers and that the movement was financed by sacks of Moscow gold. Certainly there were Communists within CND, easily recognisable by their views and rhetoric, but there were also people from every political persuasion and none, those who believed in a variety of religions and those who were agnostic or atheist. It was, truly, a broad church.

For those born after the event it needs to be said that many of us who were young at the time really did think that we would not see middle age, let alone old age, and that we were bringing into the world children who would never grow up. It was a letter sent by me to the *Guardian* in November 1961 when pregnant with my youngest son (which also triggered off an enormous response) which brought about my own involvement with the Priestleys. Among the hundreds of letters I received from all over the country and all walks of life were some from extremely distinguished correspondents, among whom were Ritchie Calder, Bertrand Russell – and J. B. Priestley. 'You are obviously articulate and can communicate,' he wrote. 'Fight for the right to live.'

Finally, however, Jack was to resign from CND. He was, as Jacquetta said, 'a great resigner'. He had indeed, as has already been shown, a long track record of such resignations dating back to before the war. He was also to resign from UNESCO and, later, from the committee formed to launch the National Theatre. Basically he was simply not a 'joiner'. He was a fine innovator, thoroughly enjoyed helping to get a project off the ground and up and running, but he intensely disliked the long haul and all that went with it. While preaching democracy, he did not enjoy it in practice. Executive and committee meetings bored him. Endless talk and the passing of resolutions sent him running for cover. Where CND was concerned, according to Diana Collins he found her husband too gentle and reasonable a chairman, preferring a brusquer no-nonsense approach and always wanting to race through the business under discussion.

Priestley found his opportunity to resign from CND when Bertrand Russell left to lead the civil disobedience campaign, saying that, as there was now no longer a president, there was hardly a place any longer for the 'vice'.

In April 1958 Mary, who was by this time living in London in a flat in Earl's Court, had another breakdown, which alarmed Priestley. Jacquetta was covering a 'dig' in Mosul, Iraq, for the *Observer*, for whom she had become the archaeology correspondent, and he wrote to her that Sylvia had found Mary in a dire state, 'things smashed, no food for at least a day, rambling talk', and that she had been admitted to a sanatorium in Surrey. She had become involved with another man, and while Priestley did not consider him a suitable partner for Mary, he did not blame him for her relapse. He felt, though, that however indirectly, he must have had something to do with it. He hoped that, as the illness had been caught early, with treatment she would come through it faster than she had in 1947.

Several more letters followed: Mary's doctor was pessimistic about her chances of a quick recovery, but Barbara and Tom had been to see her and found her calmer. Later Priestley visited her twice and was relieved to discover that she did not seem to mind being in hospital again:

Both times she was obviously unbalanced but the second time not deranged, more like a child of about eight in a rather excitable mood. I find it terribly distressing myself, but luckily her sisters seem to mind less and visit regularly – at least Ba and Angela are. Tom goes at the weekend and is very sweet with her. She's certainly not as bad as she was eleven years ago – not violent and badly schizophrenic . . . but I can get no proper information about her.

In 1959 he and Jacquetta started house-hunting. Brook Hill was difficult to keep up and the journey to and from the Isle of Wight by ferry was increasingly inconvenient. Priestley had put up for sale the remainder of the lease on Brook Hill, and sold it quite quickly in June to a relative of the family who had originally built it. Their search led them to various parts of the country until Jacquetta found a house in the village of Alveston, just outside Stratford-on-Avon. On her recommendation Priestley made an offer for it, although he had not seen it. 'If it's good enough for her, it's good enough for me.'[5] They considered it highly suitable as it was close to the Cotswolds, which Priestley loved, yet also convenient for London, Oxford and, of course, the theatre. They moved there late in 1959, and called it Kissing Tree House after the lane running beside it. It was a fine Georgian house, and although it did not have the magnificent views of their Isle of Wight home, it had pretty gardens with a lawn large enough for Priestley to allow the local cricket team to use it on special occasions.

A long marble-floored passage ran from the front door to the south side of the house and in the alcoves along it they displayed many of the rare objects they had collected. Priestley had a huge study on the ground floor with long windows facing out over the garden and lined from floor to ceiling with books. It had something else too, something that no one who visited the Priestleys at Kissing Tree ever forgot and which they looked forward to seeing each time they came. Before lunch or dinner, guests would be taken into the study where Priestley, with a flourish, would press what appeared to be shelves of books (they were in fact imitations) and a section of the wall would swing out to reveal a splendid bar.

Although they were happy with their new home, and Priestley's anxiety about Mary had abated as she had now left the sanatorium, he and Jacquetta were becoming increasingly worried about Natalie Davison. Edward had first written to them about her illness the previous September. Although the Davisons had remained together and were always treated by Priestley as a couple, they had grown steadily apart. During the war Natalie had taken a high-powered political post in Washington in the Office of War Information. She had found it deeply satisfying: for the first time she had a professional identity which was not dependent on that of her husband. As the years passed she spent more and more of her time involved in Democratic Party politics. Although Edward had made a reasonably successful career as an academic, he had not fulfilled his early promise. According to their son, Natalie felt that he had allowed his literary talents to atrophy and his artistic energy to flag. He also suffered from a deep-seated drink problem. It is hard to say whether his deterioration drove her to become more independent or whether his problems came about through her continual absences.[6]

However, Natalie was now with Edward in New York and had cancer – which she was determined to beat. Priestley wrote to him, 'I certainly agree with you that if constitution and courage can win the day, Natalie will win it – bless her! She is to me almost a symbolic figure of brave optimisim, and though our respective patriotisms and prejudices sometimes clash, I am particularly devoted to her as one of the most truly lovable women I know.'

In the summer of 1959 Priestley wrote again to say that he hoped to be in New York at the end of September and that Jacquetta would join him a few days later:

Tell Natalie she is never far from our thoughts. I cannot believe the rich deep feeling I have for her is without meaning and significance. Of one thing I have always been sure, all my adult life, and that is that in our intellectual interpretation of this vast infinitely complicated universe, we don't begin to grasp its reality, what it is *really* like, or what our lives consist of, where they begin or end, and that in sincerely felt personal relationships and the arts alone do we have any glimmering of the truth of things. I don't speculate about Time any more; it is too difficult, at least for my intellect; but I *know* it hides a mystery, and that within this mystery we may discover our lives are richer and bigger and more far-reaching than we think, except at certain heightened moments.[7]

He arrived in New York just before Natalie died on 22 September 1959. Edward, his son Peter wrote, went to pieces. 'Luckily Jack Priestley was in New York . . . he sat with my father and they drank whisky while I dealt with the undertakers as neither of them could face it.' At her funeral, 'Jack Priestley paid her tribute in a heartfelt and eloquent eulogy.'

Back in England again, Priestley wrote to his old friend just before Christmas. He hoped Edward would have a good Christmas 'with some help . . . you are often in our thoughts, as indeed is Natalie herself, who insists – bless her – in being very much alive in my mind as if nothing had really happened. I have never felt this so strongly about anyone before, perhaps because now I am myself much closer to where she has gone than I ever was before.' He had just turned sixty-five.

CHAPTER 28

Into the Sixties

By far the biggest event for Priestley of 1960 was the publication of *Literature and Western Man*. He had considered the project through 'hours and hours with pipe tobacco and desultory reading', but the atmosphere of the late 1950s had prompted him to do it: 'What really tempted me, so that I fell,' he said, 'was my conviction that ours is an age of supreme crisis, when the most desperate decisions have to be made, and that some account of Western man, in terms of the literature he has created and enjoyed, might help us to understand ourselves (and doing the work certainly helped *me*), and to realise where we are and how we have arrived here.'[1] It was not an academic work in the strict sense of the term, rather his own personal survey of Western literature from the fifteenth century and the Renaissance to the present, in which 'Western' also included Russia and America as well as Europe. It covers seven hundred authors, admittedly personally selected because he, Priestley, was the Western man 'I knew best'. For John Braine it was 'the result of a lifetime's voracious and intensive reading, an almost inhumanly retentive memory, a capacity for organisation of the highest order and, above all, the strength to carry a workload that would break many a younger man'.[2] But it was not, as Priestley himself stressed, 'a literary history. The emphasis in the title should be not Literature, but Western Man. It might be considered as a possible volume on Literature in, say, a twenty-volume series on the history of Western Man.'

It took him eighteen months to write and, he said later, it nearly killed him. He begins with the religious basis and accepted framework of life in the Middle Ages and ends with the loss of both by the late 1950s. He divided the book into five sections, 'The Golden Globe', broadly the

Renaissance; 'The Order'd Garden', the eighteenth century and the Enlightenment; 'The Shadows on the Moon', the Romantics, nineteenth-century writers and philosophers; 'The Broken Web', European and American literature; and, finally, 'The Moderns', twentieth-century writers, with Freud, Adler and, most of all, Jung. There was a slight break between the completion of Part Four and the start of Part Five because at that stage he was still unsure who would publish it and in exactly what form, 'because this last part of the book can be more elastic than others, shorter or longer according to the agreed length and size of the book. Certain leading ideas emerge – it is those which keep me going – and it is in my treatment of these that the value of the book will lie, though I think my inside knowledge of fiction and drama is useful to the criticism,' he wrote to Davison.

He took 'literature' in its broadest sense and included political writing, beginning with Machiavelli and ending with Marx and Engels. Above all the book allowed him to indulge his own passions for his favourite writers, not least Rabelais, Cervantes and, of course, Shakespeare.

He is, perhaps, particularly entertaining when dealing with those who will not believe that Shakespeare wrote Shakespeare:

Whole libraries have been written about Shakespeare. There are shelves and shelves of books all attempting to prove that the plays attributed to him were really the work of other people – Bacon, the Earls of Oxford, Rutland and Derby, the Countess of Pembroke (probably a member of a syndicate), his fellow-poets Marlowe and Raleigh, even Queen Elizabeth herself. The authors of all these strange claims make the same mistake as many Shakespearean scholars who tell us that he must have been at one time a soldier, a sailor, lawyer, traveller in Italy, and so forth: they cannot grasp the simple fact that a highly imaginative and sharp-witted young man like Shakespeare, familiar with theatres and their various patrons, dodging in and out of London taverns, could soon pick up all the scraps of expert knowledge and professional jargon he needed for his plays. The astonishingly wide acquaintance and sympathy with all manner of folk, including yokels, tapsters, pedlars, harlots, bawds, broken-down solders that we find in the plays do not suggest they were written by a great aristocrat or a committee of earls and countesses. We happen to know that *Pickwick Papers* and *Nicholas Nickleby* were the work of the young Charles Dickens, but if we were uncertain about their authorship we would hardly consider the contemporary Lord Chancellor or the Duke of Norfolk to be likely claimants ... What the objectors do not make any allowance for, because they do not understand it, is dramatic genius.

He finished the final section musing on the state of Western man at that time, noting that the 'patterns of living that have existed for thousands of years have been destroyed within a generation' and that man, now without a religious framework, is driven this way and that at the mercy of his own unconscious drives and by the power of the huge, political and social, 'dehumanising collectives'. There now seems to be nothing left but sex, and 'we are now piling on to sex the whole gigantic load of our increasing dissatisfactions, our despair, a burden far greater than it can safely take'. And the man who had no belief in organised religion wrote of the need to establish order, justice, real community, and expressed the hope that

> we can at least believe that Man lives, under God, in a great mystery, which is what we found the original masters of our literature, Shakespeare and Rabelais, Cervantes and Montaigne, proclaiming at the very start of this journey of Western Man. And if we openly declare what is wrong with us, what is our deepest need, then perhaps the despair and death will by degrees disappear from our modern arts ...

He aimed the book, he said, neither at critics and literary scholars nor at the section of the public that asks only for digests, bottled and packaged culture. It was for the considerable numbers of people in many different countries who 'are sufficiently sensitive and intelligent to enjoy most good literature but are, for various good reasons, rather wary of it, especially the literature of our own age'. He dedicated it simply 'For Jacquetta'.

In this book, writes John Braine,

> Priestley makes his declaration of faith in literature and in the traditional values of the West. His purpose is serious, for nothing

can be more serious than survival. He doesn't write down, he doesn't trivialize, again and again he emphasizes the fact that the purpose of great literature is to enable us not to pass our time but to use our time, to be explorers of eternity . . . In the section on Tolstoy it is all summed up: 'Art should be religious in origin and feeling and ought to be widely understood and appreciated, not the possession of a few, but by the mass of people.'

While *Literature and Western Man* had its detractors, it also found enthusiastic support in Britain with a glowing review from Michael Foot, then a Labour MP. He was not so fortunate, however, in the USA where it did not do well, due, Priestley said, to the 'Eng. Lit' establishment who 'killed it stone dead'. Also, in spite of all the efforts of A. D. Peters, publisher after publisher turned it down for publication in paperback. But if any one work can be said to have earned J. B. Priestley the title 'Last of the Sages', then surely this must be it.

John Braine describes the twenty-four years between the publication of *Literature and Western Man* and his death as Priestley's 'Long Indian Summer', but he was as busy as he had ever been.

He was content at Kissing Tree, with its even tenor of country life and carefully regulated day, and it appears that at least until nearly the end of his life he kept at bay the depression that had always haunted him – even if he remained an insomniac. As for his health, he was overweight, suffered from twinges of gout, and had a bout of trouble with his colon when it was thought for a time that he might be suffering from a growth, but for a man of almost seventy he remained full of vitality.

He had also developed a new hobby: painting. Barbara and Sylvia were established artists in their own right, while Priestley was surprisingly good, and improved with practice. He preferred to work in gouache, often on sugar paper, and enjoyed painting landscapes. Holidays were taken up with it and Jacquetta's correspondence continually refers to 'Jack painting away' or 'Jack painting like mad'. The easel, the paint box and the beret accompanied them to locations as exotic as Ceylon and the wilder parts of Sicily and, nearer home, to Ireland, Scotland, the Welsh Marches and, of course, the Yorkshire Dales.

Not all the holidays were a success and he grumbled almost continually throughout the Ceylon trip, but even this paled beside the working 'holiday' at Daytona Beach. He had gone to write up the participation of the London Symphony Orchestra in the First Florida International Music Festival in 1967, an event for which the LSO had cancelled a host of other engagements.

Against Jacquetta's advice, Priestley decided extravagantly to fly out the staff of Kissing Tree House too. He soon decided that the whole idea had been madness and that it could only have been 'a rising tide of male grandeur and folly' that had driven him to ignore his wife's pleas for common sense. He had rented an expensive house but the air-conditioning failed in the intense heat, when he turned on the shower the water cascaded through the downstairs ceiling, and the house had not been properly cleared of the possessions of its previous occupants. 'I even found myself hammering on a bathroom door as I couldn't get out.' To cap it all an American official slammed a car door on his hand. It was, he wrote in *Trumpets Over the Sea*, a collection of writings he made at the time, and published by Heinemann in 1968, the world of slapstick and custard pies, 'at any moment it seemed Buster Keaton might materialise out of the floor'.[3]

In 1961 he and Jacquetta visited Russia in different circumstances from those he experienced on his former trip with Jane in 1945. This time he was able to travel more widely, funded by the royalties accrued by the Russian translations of his books and plays. They visited the house where Chekhov had written *The Cherry Orchard* and travelled to Armenia where they saw a thousand-year-old monastery. They went to Georgia, Tashkent and, finally, to Samarkand, which proved disappointing. No golden road to it, no merchants selling rich silks and all the spices of the East, just a rather dreary modern town choked with lorries. The great conqueror Tamburlaine had built Samarkand and under his despotic rule it had housed 150,000 people. The finest artists and craftsmen had been employed to make it one of the wonders of the East, yet now nothing of that legendary city or its founder remained. Once Priestley knew of the persecution Soviet writers were undergoing, he never went back.

It was during the Stratford years that the Priestleys became close friends of Gareth and Barbara Lloyd Evans. They had come to the town at about the same time as the Priestleys, as Lloyd

Evans was to take up a post at the Shakespeare Institute. On the surface, he and Priestley were unalike, certainly in appearance, for he was a small, thin, mercurial Welshman. As well as his academic work – he was an international Shakespeare scholar – he also contributed to a number of newspapers, including the *Guardian* and the *Birmingham Post*, was a drama critic and also an occasional interviewer for the BBC. He and Priestley met for the first time when Lloyd Evans was asked by the *Guardian* to interview him.

According to Barbara Lloyd Evans, they did not initially take to each other but 'then they suddenly clicked and we got to know Jack and Jacquetta better and better from then. We stayed close friends of Jack's right up until his death. I think Gareth was one person who, at the end, could still make Jack really laugh. They would talk theatre for hours. Gareth could – I won't say *manage* Jack, but if Jack was in a grumpy or switched-off mood he could always bring him back and make him laugh about something, or he'd do one of his mimic things – he loved mimicking the local doctor (his father was an actor) and Jack used to roar with laughter even when he was getting steadily more ill. They were both good for each other.'[4]

Priestley had taken to Lloyd Evans in part because he was not a conventional reporter or feature writer. 'He was in the true sense a freelance, he wasn't tied to any theatre or paper or attitude and Jack respected his knowledge of the theatre as well – not that he agreed with everything Gareth wrote in his book, but then you wouldn't expect him to!'

Like many visitors to Kissing Tree, Barbara at first found the lifestyle somewhat daunting: 'What struck me was the extreme formality of the way everything was run, the house, the garden, everything, and the total informality of Jack. There was such a contrast.' Both he and Jacquetta could be somewhat daunting, 'when he was in a huff or just sounding gruff about something', and Jacquetta possibly even more so 'in a haughty kind of way. She could appear very cold. But she was warm inside and we had lots of good talks in the small hours of the morning when she was relaxed and funny. I think she'd been brought up in a regimen of great formality and I think Jack actually loved all that. It was something he'd never had in his own childhood. She brought a most remarkable atmosphere to Kissing Tree. She was always, I think, a man's woman. There are some people who are men's women and she was one that responded in that way. She and Gareth got on very well together, he used to tease her a lot.'

One of the happiest memories Barbara has of those early days was the Easter Sunday soon after they had got to know the Priestleys when she was taken in to the local maternity hospital to give birth to one of her sons. 'The next day the matron came bustling through saying, "There's someone out here who says he's Mr Priestley and he's got some things for you." Now I knew Jack hated hospitals, loathed women being pregnant, and simply couldn't cope with small babies, so I said would she go back and say it was very kind of him, thank him very much indeed, bring whatever it was in and tell him I'll be writing to him. She returned with a pile of books under one arm and a whole armful of daffodils from Kissing Tree House under the other. Jack had brought them all himself for me. I said to him afterwards that I was sorry I didn't say I'd see him but that I'd thought he wouldn't really like it and he said, in that deep voice, "Thank God you didn't!" He hadn't actually wanted to come into the hospital but he'd made himself do it, which was lovely, and his daffodils filled the ward.'

Both Barbara Lloyd Evans and Diana Collins were captivated by him. He told Barbara, as he did other women friends, that he believed men and women had elements of both sexes, and that some women had more of the male in them and some men more of the female. He felt he had something of the woman in him, just as Jacquetta had male elements in her. Barbara and her husband found this interesting because, although it was clear that he had a great empathy with women and how they felt, his stage women somehow never came off.

There has never been any suggestion that Priestley strayed once he was married to Jacquetta, but he remained profoundly attractive to women and loved their company. As time went by he spoke to both Diana Collins and Barbara Lloyd Evans about how easily he had been attracted into physical affairs. 'I think Jack was just a very sexy, sensuous, yet in some ways, a very naive person,' says Barbara Lloyd Evans. 'When his imagination became engaged with a woman, his body was engaged as well. He would talk to women about it but not to men, certainly not to Gareth. He was never interested in that kind of "boys-together" conversation. With men it was literature or politics or theatre, with women he was different. He was a person who was totally committed to people, and if he was interested in you he would be imaginatively taken up and involved with you, and he certainly did attract women. He was very sensitive towards the female sex – and, of course, he had such a sexy voice and wicked eyes when he wanted them to be, and a lovely smile.

'Jack would flirt with anyone if he got the chance but there was no longer any seriousness in it. Jacquetta was everything to him. I truly believe that in his eyes she could do no wrong. It was always such a heady relationship and he was lost when she wasn't there, like a bear in a cage. The real love, the real commitment, was totally and utterly to her, as it was from her to him. I never even heard them bicker like most couples.'

In 1963 Priestley had his last West End success with a new play, and during the nine years that followed *Literature and Western Man* he published a further sixteen books, either original work or collections of existing essays.

The play was the well-received adaptation of Iris Murdoch's novel *A Severed Head,* which ran at the Criterion Theatre for almost two years. A collaboration between such different writers appears unlikely, but Iris Murdoch had met Priestley on a television programme in the 1950s and 'adored him at once! And I adored Jacquetta too,' she told John Braine, 'I'd never met anyone so beautiful and regal. Yet Jack is also Falstaff – I always think of him as expressed by his own essay on Sir John.' She had already attempted to adapt her own book, but realised the result was no good and set it aside. She told him about it one night in the Albany over a bottle of whisky and, after 'laughing a greal deal', she agreed to let him see the script. After which 'we wrote the thing in no time at all, and of course Jack's great theatre wisdom solved all the problems and the process taught me a lot about plays and playwriting. Jack was the *essential* partner, and could not have been a nicer one. He is a rational and a good man and exceedingly generous, and all deep benevolence. Not just a humane man but a powerfully benevolent one, while being a "bonny fighter" too.' She also admired him as 'a wonderfully shrewd *political* critic'. He was, she concluded, not only a vastly talented and exceptionally versatile and wise writer, he was also a remarkable human being. 'And such an *Englishman!*[5] I love him very much.'

As for Jack, he had been disappointed so often over the past ten years by the failure of his plays to make the impression he had hoped or, indeed, even to get some of them on at all, that this unexpected triumph was highly satisfying. Whether or not he realised this would be his last straight play he does not say, but at least he finally bowed out with a critical and financial success.

He wrote two thrillers, *Saturn Over the Water* and *The Shapes of Sleep*, in 1961, and another in 1966, *Salt is Leaving*, which seems to have been missed off all the bibliographies. In 1962 he published one of his finest collections of essays, *Margin Released*, and in 1964 a comic novel, *Sir Michael and Sir George*, followed in 1965 by one of his best, *Lost Empires*. In 1964 there was also *Man and Time*, in 1966 *The Moments*, and a novella, the fantasy *The Thirty-first of June*. In 1968 the two volumes that make up the massive novel *The Image Men* appeared, as did his account of the Florida Festival, *Trumpets Over the Sea*, and in 1969 *The Prince of Pleasure* and *The World of Charles Dickens*. Collections of existing work included *The World of J. B. Priestley*, edited by Donald McCrae in 1967, *All England Listened*, the wartime *Postscripts*, in 1968 and *Essays of Five Decades*, published to celebrate his seventy-fifth birthday in 1969, selected and introduced by Susan Cooper, a writer who had been born and educated in England but who had married an American and now lived in the USA.

Saturn Over the Water was dedicated 'To Diana and John Collins, Best of Campaigners, This Tale with Affection'. It is told in the first person, as Priestley thrillers often are, and the author is in message-giving mode, beginning with a death from leukaemia and warnings about nuclear testing, taking in a sinister Institute in South America and ending with a warning against the 'Saturn' people who would destroy most of the world for their own ends. *The Shapes of Sleep* follows the lively adventures of an investigative journalist in his quest for the truth. But the best of the three, and the one closest to the classic tradition of the genre, is *Salt is Leaving*, a straightforward story of murder and local corruption in which the protagonist is a middle-aged, pipe-smoking, irascible Yorkshireman . . . In many respects Salt predated today's popular sleuth Morse, for he too enjoys good beer and malt whisky, grumbles, lives alone and listens to classical music. However, unlike Morse, at the end of the book he gets the girl.

Priestley thrillers are rather reminiscent of the old days of radio crime drama, of Basil Radford and Naunton Wayne and the long-running series of *Paul Temple* mysteries. As John Braine put it, while they are splendidly ingenious and their pace never slackens, they carry the reader irresistibly to a satisfyingly neat and wholesomely happy ending: 'What is present even in a run-of-the-mill American thriller – sudden death, violence, pain – simply isn't there.' He points to the difference between the feeling of evil generated at the beginning of *Treasure Island* and the general atmosphere of a Priestley thriller, and goes on: 'Yet Stevenson's experience had included nothing even remotely to compare with Priestley's four years as a front-line soldier . . . About this side of life he is as prudish as the Victorians were about sex.'

It might also be added that another missing factor – except in *Salt is Leaving* – is the sense of place that permeates Dorothy L. Sayers's Cambridge and East Anglia, Raymond Chandler's Los Angeles, Simenon's Paris and Colin Dexter's Oxford. But, although Priestley always said he wrote his thrillers for fun, he took umbrage at the suggestion they were potboilers: 'In the first place, I really enjoy telling a story. In the second place I believe the novel of action can sometimes give readers a more vivid and impressive picture of the kind of world we live in – this is particularly true of *Shapes of Sleep* – than the so-called "serious novel".' He felt the same about *The Thirty-first of June*.

There is no doubt that the work is uneven: he still wrote as he always had, believing that you did not wait for inspiration to come but sat down at your desk every morning with cotton wool in your ears and *worked*.

In *Lost Empires* he returned once again to the world of Swan Arcadia, the pre-1914 era that haunted him more as it receded from him. Its Yorkshire hero, Richard Herncastle, is a talented young artist who is out of work and without family. He is taken up by his uncle, a magician and illusionist, who tours the music halls. The 'Lost Empires' of the title are not Britain's rapidly diminishing colonies but the old Empire halls.

In between *Lost Empires* and *Image Men*, Jack returned to an old preoccupation with his book *Man and Time*, in spite of what he had written to Teddy Davison when Natalie was dying. The book was prompted in part by the results of an appeal he made in the written media and on television, in which he asked people to write to him about any experiences they might have had of precognitive dreams. This produced, as one might imagine, an almost overwhelming response. However, the difference between this later book and his earlier writings on the subject is that by this time he was also giving consideration to the suppositions of twentieth-century science, in particular Einstein's Theory of Relativity. This latter, he considered, gave weight to his existing belief that time is not fixed; more than that, while Ouspensky had suggested it might be possible to look down on the past from a spiral above it, if you accepted Einstein's Theory then it might well be possible to travel forward in time as well. But the book is a strange and indigestible mixture including, as it does, a chapter devoted to the controversial views of the then popular guru Gurdjieff. Priestley ends, however, by returning once again to his mentor Jung and his belief in life as a preparation for an existence outside time.

The Image Men was published in two volumes, Out of Town, in 1968, and London End, later the same year. Priestley thought of it as his best work of fiction. The saga follows the fortunes of two men, Cosmo Saltana and Dr Owen Tuby, both gifted and persuasive, but who are first discovered down on their luck in a shabby back-street London hotel. They encounter a rich widow, Elfreda Drake, who is persuaded to help them set up their money-making scam in the Institute of Social Imagistics, which soon acquires academic status as part of a university. Priestley lards the dialogue with the kind of meaningless jargon with which we are all too familiar and he shows the triumphant progress of the advertising and public relations 'industry'. He anticipated much that has taken place since he wrote the book, from the fashioning of a nonentity into a media personality to the team of spin doctors without whom few politicians dare move, act or even open their mouths, and the novel ends with Saltana and Tuby providing the Conservative and Labour parties with virtually identical image-crafted leaders complete with interchangeable, sanitised, public-relations-friendly policies.

There is a lot that is good in The Image Men and much that is very funny, but for many readers the joke simply goes on too long. Priestley had found it almost impossible to let go: 'Image Men just flowed out,' he said. 'I loved those two characters, Tuby and Saltana. I'd gone on for three hundred thousand words and yet it was a wrench to leave them. I could have written a novel of two million words about those two. But I had to say goodbye to them and I've been a little sadder since . . .'[6]

The thrillers pleased the crime reviewers and *Lost Empires* was highly praised. He was all the more disappointed, therefore, with the critical reaction to *The Image Men.* The *Times Literary Supplement* summed up the general opinion that it fell below the standard expected of its author and 'it would be patronising to pretend otherwise'. It found the storyline weak, the plot unbelievable, and that 'cut to a third of its length these two novels would have made a lively little comic novel'.[7] Worst of all, as far as Priestley was concerned, it didn't sell.

As ever he refused to be daunted. In 1969 he produced *The Prince of Pleasure,* a portrait of the Prince Regent, and *Charles Dickens and His World.* He had already contributed the text for a pictorial biography of Dickens, which had inspired him to return to his subject for he had never lost his love of Dickens' work. Talking to Gareth Lloyd Evans on its publication, he said, 'We can't understand the popularity of Dickens unless we realise that to get a similar popularity today you'd not only have to be a novelist but a TV and radio celebrity, a film star and a lot of other things. We've divided it all up now, but Dickens had the lot.'

He had, he said, seen all the films adapted from Dickens, 'but to me it's like turning over illustrations in a book. What a film can't give you is the way in which he could animate the whole scene. He brought everything alive, not just people, but the furniture, the doorknobs, the windows, everything. He could make the world seem as it does for an imaginative child.'[8]

On 13 September 1969, Heinemann, Priestley's publishers, gave a party at the Savoy Hotel to honour his seventy-fifth birthday. It celebrated, too, his loyalty to his publishers, to whom he had remained faithful for over fifty years. In 1961 the firm had been taken over by the Tilling Group and it was proposed that Heinemann be merged with the Bodley Head, which Tilling had also acquired. It was suggested to Priestley that he and several other prestigious Heinemann authors should move to the Bodley Head but he resolutely and robustly refused to do any such thing, although a number of other writers did. In the event the merger did not take place, and Priestley remained with Heinemann until his death.

The guest list at the party included family, friends and colleagues from every area of Priestley's life. The broadcaster Robert Robinson made a television programme to mark the event which ended with Ralph Richardson performing the closing scene from *Johnson Over Jordan*. Priestley had agreed that Susan Cooper might write a brief biography of him to mark the occasion, and she was present when he and a few friends were given a preview of the programme. For the last time Priestley saw his old friend in the role he had made his own in the play that had meant so much to both of them. Susan Cooper writes: 'I don't know what I expected him [Priestley] to offer us: a non-committal snort, perhaps; a rumble of technical criticism; at the most, a bit of knowledgeable praise for Richardson. But Priestley sat silent for a moment, gazing into space, looking unusually small in a very large armchair; and then he rubbed his eyes. "I shed tears," he said, rather gruff and low, "not for what I have seen, but for what I have been remembering."[9]

CHAPTER 29

Order of Merit

The 1970s was a period in which many of the threads in Jack Priestley's life were drawn together, and in which he was honoured both locally and nationally.

He was a regular visitor to Bradford and continued for many years to walk the Dales. When such exercise was no longer possible, he returned there to paint. He never ceased to take an interest in the city's affairs, to give his name to worthy causes and to speak at special events. But there is no doubt that he and the city fathers consistently rubbed each other up the wrong way.

The difficulties had begun in 1952 when he asked if he could present a performance of *Dragon's Mouth* on a Sunday night, hopeful that Bradford's embargo on Sunday entertainment had been lifted. It had not, and his forcibly expressed views did not go down well. The mutual antipathy was compounded by his divorce, and especially Jacquetta's, which had resulted in such notoriety. The general reaction of Bradford to it, writes Peter Holdsworth, was 'cruel and deplorable. I can vividly remember comments in my own street which were savage in their censure. Nor will I forget overhearing, while walking along a Town Hall corridor, one city father saying to another, "No longer want to know t' chap; no longer want him here." It was all shameful.'[1]

Next came the matter of *The White Countess*. Bradford had been offered its second showing after the disastrous Dublin première. After heavy pressure from Priestley, it went on in his home town where it was panned. From the *Telegraph and Argus* ('there is something very saddening in the sight of a great author and playwright floundering as Mr J. B. Priestley does in *The White Countess*') to the *Yorkshire Observer* ('this play lumbers along like a gun carriage'), the local reviewers sang from the same hymn sheet. It is very stilted: no one seems to have found

the courage to say of *The White Countess*, at least in public, that
Jacquetta could not write plays, even with her husband.

The reviews attracted a further diatribe from Priestley, which
was printed in the *Argus* and was followed by his complaint that
the paper's headline two weeks before – 'Priestley Play a Flop
in Dublin' – had ensured its failure in Bradford.

This was compounded by the television programme *Lost City*
in 1958, in which Priestley revisited and talked about Bradford.
Before it was even screened the title alone produced uproar,
causing him yet again to go into print to defend himself. 'The
suggestion that my TV film about Bradford may have offended
some people because it was called *Lost City* is absurd,' he told
Peter Holdsworth later for local publication. 'It was essentially
a nostalgic piece – as the music from Brahms' third symphony
must have suggested – and the *Lost* in the title referred to the
passing of time and my youth, and I think this ought to have
been clear to anybody who saw the programme.' Before it was
shown, the *Argus* had run a satirical piece based around the title
and its TV critic launched a sustained attack, taking particular
exception to Priestley's last words as he sat in the train and it
pulled out of Bradford, that 'it [the city] is simply not good
enough for the real Bradfordian'. 'One wonders,' wrote the
critic, 'how Mr Priestley can know what is good or bad for
the "real Bradfordian". Surely the "real Bradfordian" must be
one who was not only born here but who has continued to live
here? Pontificating from his Isle of Wight fastness, Mr Priestley
hardly fills the latter role.' According to Priestley, part of the
problem was that the film had been badly edited and much of
it had been left on the cutting-room floor.

The feud with the local papers continued. In 1959 they
criticised him for the anti-nuclear TV play *Doomsday*: an editorial
in the *Argus* read, 'We are sorry for Mr. J. B. Priestley . . . He
is allowing himself to grow old more quickly than he should;
and in the old-man tradition he talks about the wonders of the
past and the faults of the present . . .' After that, according to
Peter Holdsworth, he stayed away for five years. In 1964, when
the *Argus* tried to interview him on his seventieth birthday, he
would not even come to the telephone and sent a message saying
that they could use some of the material he had already given
to the *Sheffield Telegraph*. Then, however, he relented, gave the
interview and resumed his regular visits to Bradford.

In 1969 to celebrate his seventy-fifth birthday Bradford University conferred on him the honorary degree of Doctor of Letters, which he received from its vice chancellor, the then Prime Minister Harold Wilson. He marked the occasion with a speech that came right to the point: 'It is no good teaching children to read Shelley and Wordsworth,' he said, 'if there isn't a good book shop in the city; it is no use learning to enjoy Shakespeare if there is nowhere to see the plays. The university can help to change all that.' But he was deeply upset when he learned that the city council had decided against offering him the Freedom of Bradford: 'Only one among the eight responsible for making Freedom decisions voted in his favour,' said Peter Holdsworth. 'It was a cruel snub and it hurt him hard.'

In 1972 the Yorkshire actor Leslie Sands, a friend of Priestley, suggested they put together an entertainment based on excerpts from Priestley works, a project to which Priestley readily agreed. The result, *The World of J. B. Priestley*, opened in August at the little Phoenix Theatre in Leicester. It was a good choice. Although small, it had an excellent reputation, was able to attract actors of the calibre of the young Ian McKellen and was regularly reviewed in the national press. The show was directed by the theatre's artistic director Stephen Macdonald (himself an actor) and the rest of the cast was made up of Sands's wife Pauline Williams, Derrick Gilbert and Judy Loe. It was a great success, particularly the excerpts from the essays (Barbara Lloyd Evans has described these as 'almost little poems'), and the audience at the first night gave Priestley a standing ovation.

Then it went off on tour, and Priestley was eager that it should go to Bradford, which it did, opening in September at the old Alhambra on his seventy-eighth birthday. He was not feeling well and was also tired. He had squeezed in television and radio interviews and a civic lunch at which, according to Peter Holdsworth, he couldn't resist several digs at the council who had continued to argue among themselves as to whether or not they should offer him the Freedom of the City. The evening proved a severe disappointment: the theatre was less than half full and remained so for the rest of the week. Holdsworth gives two possible reasons for this: the theatre was shabby and run down, and to young audiences Priestley was an old man, a far-off writer whose works were unfamiliar to them: 'Many of them had not only never seen any of his plays at the Bradford

Civic Theatre or the Prince's Theatre, they would have had', he says, using a Yorkshire phrase, 'all on to tell you where the Prince's had stood.'

In 1973 Bradford finally gave Priestley the Freedom of the City. The decision was in large part due to the intervention and public outburst of another outspoken Yorkshireman, the popular entertainer Wilfred Pickles. In an interview with Peter Holdsworth, during which Pickles asked if he knew whether or not the honour was in the wind or whether it had been decided yet again that Priestley was not to have it, he said: 'If the reason is political – and I've a feeling that has something to do with it – it is even more shameful. I love Bradford. I love its character and I love its forthrightness. That's not smooth talk, I mean it. And because I love it, I'll give it you straight. It is showing itself up because of Jack Priestley. He's an old man now – seventy-eight. Surely they won't deny him this honour . . .' On the whole the readership went along with this, the one dissenting voice that of a Shipley man who felt the only proper recipient of such an honour was someone who had stayed and worked in Bradford all his life. The interview was followed up by Bradford Trades Council, which carried a motion criticising the previous attitude of the city council: 'J. B. Priestley is as much associated with Bradford as Joyce with Dublin and Lawrence with Nottingham.'

On 8 September 1973 J. B. Priestley formally accepted the Freedom of the City. The *Telegraph and Argus* went so far as actually to invite him to use the paper to speak to its readers as bluntly as he wished: 'J. B. Priestley's bluntness has obviously delayed, for many years, the decision to bestow on him the Freedom of Bradford. However, Bradford has now decided, if somewhat belatedly, to embrace its most famous son, warts and all. He is delighted by this one honour which he obviously desired above all others.' If at the ceremony Priestley should feel impelled to speak, then the writer of the article hoped that he would say exactly what he wanted to: 'If he has critical things to say about "Bruddersford", let him say them. We want him to be blunt.' The occasion was marked with a production of *I Have Been Here Before* at the Bradford Playhouse and this time the theatre was full. It was after the Freedom ceremony, said Peter Holdsworth, that Priestley made his famous and oft-quoted remark: 'I am *not* a genius – although I do have a hell of a lot of talent.' He continued to visit Bradford, on one occasion taking with him John and Diana Collins; Diana described his stroll around what remained of his old haunts as 'almost like a Royal Progress'. Nowadays the city's pride in him is evident: close to his much-loved Alhambra Theatre, a statue of Priestley stands four square to the winds, his overcoat flowing out behind him.

The 1970s were full of the deaths of Priestley's friends, including Edward Davison. Six months after Natalie's death in 1959 he had married his second wife, Rose, a singer. It is clear that Priestley never came to terms with this, although the correspondence between the two men continued, as did visits both ways. When the Davisons visited Kissing Tree House Priestley would boast that he could always get tickets for the Royal Shakespeare Theatre even though the house was 'sold out' or 'booked solid'. He was a familiar figure in the theatre and at Royal Shakespeare Company and Birthplace Trust functions, and while he did not join the parade through the town on the poet's birthday celebrations on 23 April he was generally to be seen at the festivities afterwards, and on at least one occasion was the guest speaker at the lunch. His views on what happened on stage were as forthright as ever. In 1970, shortly after the opening of Peter Brook's famous production of *A Midsummer Night's Dream*, with its white 'empty space' and fairies on trapezes, Priestley said 'Do you know, I've seen the most extraordinary production of Shakespeare's most magical play. It appears to take place in a clean, well-lighted garage . . .'[2]

Edward Davison died in the early spring of 1970, of cirrhosis of the liver – too much whisky compounded by heavy pipe-smoking, according to his son.[3] His last academic post had been that of Dean of General Studies at Hunter College, and he no longer wrote. 'He kept few of his literary friends,' said his son, 'although his devotion to Jack Priestley and Jack's loyalty to him remained unchanged. When he was dying he babbled poems upon poems, Shakespeare verses, fragments of poetry on which his young manhood had nourished itself and which had served him in the solitudes of his life.'[4]

Priestley did not say how his friend's death affected him, and in his letters to Peter Davison in 1970 he seemed almost distanced from it. Looking back on their long relationship, he

wrote that Teddy's great time had been 'his whole three years
at Cambridge. With his all round success there, he must have
felt himself to be in a strange, wonderful dream. But these years
in Wonderland were bad rather than good luck.' He recalled
Davison's unhappy love affairs, his getting into debt and how
Natalie had rescued him from both. 'Apart from a very genuine
love for her (though not altogether satisfactory in a sexual way),
he always felt under a deep obligation to her, knowing that she
had rescued him from the London mess – though perhaps in
the long run the decision to go to America was a mistake.'[5]

Although at the time of Natalie's death Davison had sat up
with Priestley drinking whisky night after night, he had never
confided his true feelings. 'He had a queer attitude towards
me because while a deep affection was there he had a trick,
especially just after I'd arrive, of making "snide" remarks as
if he were envious of what I had done and was doing and of
my capture of such a brilliant creature as Jacquetta. I'm not
blaming him and I always allowed for it, always tried to start him
writing again, as you know, though I must confess his marriage
with Rose left me feeling rather hopeless and sad.' He ended by
telling Peter that he was a far better poet than his father had
ever been.

Priestley continued to correspond with Peter Davison almost
up until his own death, but the letters, of course, were of a different order from those written to his old friend over so many years.
In Peter Davison's to Priestley himself, that correspondence was
'an extraordinary record of your life and more especially your
career . . . when the time comes for your biography to be written,
these letters should be indispensable'.[6]

Priestley continued to publish books well into the 1970s, of
which only two, the volumes of social history *The Edwardians*
(1970) and *Victoria's Heyday* (1972), are substantial works. He
employed researchers to assist him in gathering information
and, if his letters to Peter Davison are anything to go on, he
must have been a trying and testy employer. Both *The English*
(1973) and *English Humour* (1976) make pleasant reading, but
to some extent recycle material that had been used before.

Until the mid-1970s he also continued to travel, and in 1973
he and Jacquetta visited New Zealand at the invitation of the
New Zealand Government, against all the advice of Priestley's

doctors. His account of his last major journey was published in 1974 under the title *A Visit to New Zealand*. Shortly before they left, Priestley had been in hospital for a relatively minor operation after which he had insisted on discharging himself. The long flight to New Zealand, followed by his explorations of the countryside by car, tired him and he was flagging well before the trip was over. Yet he found much to enjoy and, indeed, to marvel at, from the 'wonder' of Lake Taupo to the view from half-way up Mount Possession, where he discussed his philosophy of life with a sympathetic sheep farmer.

His one new piece of fiction was a children's story, *Snoggle* (1971). In this story a spacecraft arrives on earth from a far galaxy and lands two small, friendly, if strange-looking aliens, who are found by three children who call them Snoggle and Snaggle. The children look after them to protect them and conceal them from the authorities, finally rescuing them from the police and army who are determined to catch the creatures and shoot them since they are convinced they have been sent to take over the world. As in the smash-hit film *E.T.* which came much later, the children succeed in outwitting everyone and returning the two lovable creatures to their parent spaceship and back home to a more advanced, tolerant and compassionate planet. In 1975 Heinemann brought out a book of three short stories under the title of the first, *The Carfitt Crisis*, all of which had appeared elsewhere. The title story and the last were both written in romantic vein (Priestley had originally intended the theme of the latter for a play) but the most interesting is the middle story, 'Underground', a true horror tale full of a sense of evil he never achieved in his thrillers. In it his villain travels, in spite of an anonymous warning, on the Northern Line of the London Underground where it delves deepest below Hampstead, only to find that after the train has pulled out of Belsize Park he is the only passenger, that the ticket collector has no face and that he is plunging ever downwards.

From his letters to Peter Davison, it is clear that until the mid-1970s Priestley was also still trying to write for the theatre, but nothing substantial emerged. However, in June 1974, two months before his eightieth birthday, he was to be found sitting in a London rehearsal room, 'keeping a parental eye', as he put it, on a musical version of *The Good Companions*, which boasted an enormous array of talent: André Previn wrote the music, Johnny

Mercer the lyrics, and it starred John Mills as Jess Oakroyd, Judi Dench as Miss Trant and Christopher Gable as Inigo Jollifant. The idea had originated with Previn who, he said, had always loved the book not least because there were so few picaresque novels. Some years earlier, Previn had asked unsuccessfully for permission to turn it into a musical. Then he was contacted out of the blue by Johnny Mercer, who had had the same idea, and together they approached Priestley again. This time he agreed.

Interviewed during rehearsals, Priestley was lively and enthusiastic.[7] He said with glee that even if he *was* nearly eighty, he had been involved in the process of seeing the show put together, and that he was particularly pleased with the music. It all had to be in period, and not a send-up of the period. The music for the concert party, he said, 'can't be very good because they weren't', while that for the rest of the show had to be different, and better, but still in the idiom of the late 1920s or early 1930s. He thought the songs hit it just right, 'very whistleable – I hope people will take to them because they're catchy'. Watching the cast going over and over one particular scene he commented, 'Have you ever seen the last rehearsal of a big commercial musical? It lasts about twenty hours. The chorus are exhausted and unable to do anything more, while the man who wrote the lyrics is in the bar getting drunk and saying he washes his hands of the whole thing.'

André Previn, at the same rehearsal, said at the time that Jack's hands-on approach, his 'parental eye', had meant exactly that. 'He told me the other day,' he said, looking at the rotund figure which had been sitting there all morning, 'what he was working on and his future plans and it would be remarkable for a lad of twenty at Oxford let alone a man of eighty!' As the rehearsal drew to a close, Priestley reminisced about those far-off days when *The Good Companions* had rocketed him to fame and fortune and how 'the elephant suddenly turned into a balloon'. Unfortunately the musical ran for barely six months in the West End.

There were also several collections of essays, *Over the Long High Wall* (1972), *Outcries and Asides* (1974), *Particular Pleasures* (1975) and *Instead of the Trees* (1977). The last subtitled 'A Final Chapter of Autobiography', is in some ways rather sad. Priestley writes again of his Bradford childhood, his own philosophy of literature and life, of remembered trips at home and abroad. He stoutly defends *The Image Men,* which 'remains – and must remain, for I can no longer write fiction on that scale – my own first favourite. Alas that its sheer size will not enable it to follow *Angel Pavement* and *Bright Day* into the Everyman Library list of what it takes to be modern classics: Still, *The Image Men* shines the brightest in my memory and my heart.'

In a last section, called 'Afterthoughts', he dwells on the unpleasantness of flying, remembers his first essay into journalism, looks back to his Cambridge days, dreams of the Isle of Wight and considers what might constitute Heaven. He had originally intended to write a volume of autobiographical essays following on in sequence from *Rain Upon Godshill,* which would have been written in California 'among or near to the ancient trees, the giant redwoods', but because of the war and other work he had never had time. Now he felt too old to make the journey and it was too late, hence the title. His epigraph for the book is taken from *King Lear,*

> . . . Men must endure
> Their going hence, even as their coming hither:
> Ripeness is all.

Physically he was no longer well. By the beginning of 1982, his hearing, although he hated to admit it, was deteriorating and he was suffering from an accumulation of the problems of old age, none incapacitating in themselves but tiring and annoying when added together.

Over the years he had been regularly approached on the subject of honours, but he had always refused to accept one, including a knighthood, on the grounds that he did not believe in patronage and that he did not want an honour of the kind awarded to politicians. Indeed Jacquetta told Diana Collins that one of their rare near-quarrels had come about when he had met her at Heathrow on her return from an archaeological excavation and told her that he had just refused the award of Companion of Honour. She felt that at the very least he might have consulted her before doing so. He had also turned down a life peerage offered to him by Harold Wilson because he disapproved of the Labour Government's support for the American bombing of Vietnam. Wilson explained that the Government had had no choice because it needed an International Monetary Fund loan to shore up its balance of payments deficit, but Priestley did not change his mind.[8]

However, in 1977 he was offered the Order of Merit, which he simply could not refuse. It is the most prestigious award of all, in the sole gift of the Queen. It is also the rarest, as only twenty-four people can be members at any one time. It is given for meritorious services in the armed forces or for the advancement of the arts, literature or science.

John and Diana Collins, with John Bayley and Iris Murdoch, were invited to spend the weekend at Kissing Tree House. Just before dinner, as they all waited in Priestley's study, Miss Pudduck arrived with champagne. 'Our glasses were filled and Jacquetta stood up in front of the fireplace to announce: "I want to share with you, our dearest friends, and with Miss Pudduck the news that beloved Jack has been given the OM."'

On 17 November 1977 he took his place with twenty-one other members of the Order in the Chapel Royal of St James's Palace where, in front of the Royal Family, he listened to music composed by other members on whom the honour had been bestowed, Sir Edward Elgar, Vaughan Williams and Benjamin Britten. Vaughan Williams, like Priestley, had steadfastly refused any honour until he had been awarded the OM. After the choir of the Chapel Royal had finished singing, the Duke of Edinburgh stood up and read from the Apocrypha the rousing sentiments of Ecclesiasticus 44.i which begin: 'Let us now praise famous men and our fathers that begat us.'

CHAPTER 30

A Dream of Birds

After *Instead of the Trees* in 1977, there was no new published work from J. B. Priestley although he did not stop writing until the early 1980s. In that book he had written movingly of the difficulties he was experiencing in his efforts to keep going. It would be easier, he noted, if he accepted the role of the elderly 'properly', living a fireside-dressing-gown-dotage existence, behind a huge beard garnished with crumbs and egg. 'But I don't live that kind of life at all.'

At that time he was keeping up the daily pattern he had followed for half a century and continued to keep an eye on business connected with his books and plays, 'even using the long-distance telephone when I feel I can afford to use it'. He still worried endlessly and unnecessarily about money, for although the settlement he had made to Jane was generous (half his capital and a percentage of his earnings), royalties flowed in from all over the world. Indeed, his eightieth birthday had brought about a revival of interest in his plays, with productions of *Dangerous Corner, Eden End, I Have Been Here Before, Time and the Conways* and *An Inspector Calls.*

In the late 1970s he described how he spent his day: down to breakfast, if in his dressing gown, at nine, followed by the dictating of letters, and, after shaving and dressing, writing at his desk until about 12.50. Unless it rained he took a short walk around the lanes in the afternoon, 'rarely seeing walkers, only cars', read a little, took tea and worked again between five thirty and six thirty, 'only an hour now but an hour of actual writing, not thinking about writing'. Bed followed at about eleven thirty even if sleep did not.

However, while this might sound an easy schedule, old age meant that it demanded of him both effort and patience. Even getting dressed or going to bed seemed the equivalent of a workout. He had to wrestle himself into his trousers.

> Just coping with the mere arrangements of ordinary living, requires that there must be an exercise to will. To get by from nine in the morning until midnight I use enough willpower to command an army corps. Is there no fun along the way? Yes, of course; but I wish there was more – and much less effort. Any serene old age is well out of sight. I am in a fair way to become one of the really grumpy old meanies, cackling at the deaths of acquaintances. But, of course, not of friends.[1]

He retained his sharp wit: according to Peter Holdsworth, a television script writer had written a novel whose potential publishers said they would take it on if 'J.B.', who was on their board, liked it. The young man met 'J.B.' on one of his increasingly rare visits to the Albany and found him still in his dressing gown and carpet slippers, standing under a Renoir puffing his pipe. 'It's all right for a first novel, lad,' he boomed. 'Construction excellent, characterisation fine, but your punctuation's terrible.' The would-be novelist explained that this was because he modelled himself on successful American writers like Norman Mailer. 'They don't worry much about punctuation. I do a first draft, then I do a second one and take all the commas and semi-colons out.' Priestley drew thoughtfully on his pipe, then said, 'Aye, well, lad, when you get to my age, you'll start putting 'em all back in.'

His insomnia returned during the last ten years of his life with even greater intensity, and during the nights he mused again on time and death. He could no longer ignore the latter, as death followed death among those he knew, 'for here the loss is hideous, really hard to bear'. At his age he was outliving his friends on a desolating scale. Only two of those young literary lions who used to meet every week in a Fleet Street pub in the late 1920s and early 1930s to drink and air their wit now survived: himself and J. B. Morton, 'Beachcomber' of the *Daily Express*. When they wrote to each other it was, he said, like 'two small ships flashing signals across a huge darkness'. Friends vanished, leaving enormous blanks. Looking back over his long career, he felt he had spent too much time in writing and wished that he had devoted more to painting, playing the piano, planting things in his garden, and study: 'Astronomical discoveries and speculations fascinate me – think of those *black holes*!'

He wrote many times during that period that he had no fear of death. Still resolutely a non-Christian, he remained unable to accept that nothing of the human spirit survived death, whether in a different dimension or time or along Ouspensky's spiral. 'We don't understand our lives and what happens in them,' he had written to Peter Davison after the death of his father, 'we don't understand who we are or what we are – and make little attempt to solve the age-old riddles, just pretend they aren't there. And we live in a society that now hates itself. I am hoping, God willing, to write a shortish book, longish essay on LIFE, DEATH and TIME . . .' But he never did.[2]

In *Instead of the Trees* he devotes an essay to death and the question of an after-life. He did not accept conventional teaching – simply could not believe as do some 'earnest and sturdy souls' in the Last Trump, 'or some other alarm device, which will bring them out of their graves with newly resurrected bodies, to await a final judgement . . .' But while some ideas of an after-life 'are so silly that I propose to ignore them', he did not accept the case for extinction. 'The Dr Knowall who defies you to prove that life survives death is asking the question the wrong way around. It is up to him to prove it doesn't.' And if the mediums could communicate with the dead, surely the great minds of the past such as Plato, Aristotle and Shakespeare would have sent reliable messages as to what was in store across the great divide. But, he continued, if we believe that there is nothing, that they were all snuffed out like guttering candles, then the victory of death cannot be challenged for it would mean that 'when our time runs out, we are extinguished forever. Our fate then is worse than that of the most cruelly hunted animal', and he could not accept that either.

Shortly after Edward Davison's death, his old friend had appeared to Priestley in a dream, acting in a gentle, tentative fashion quite unlike himself in life. Priestley had welcomed him and put his hand on his shoulder, could still feel the rough tweed of his coat under his hand, but at that point he had woken up. What the dream meant he did not know. Finally he returns again to Jung, who believes that preparation for death entails making a gradual detachment from the ego and the Self in all its aspects. Jung also believed that if there is life after death then it might well not be superior to ordinary life, the survivors no stronger or wiser than we are, and that indeed they might well be anxious to learn from those who came after them rather than trying to teach them. Jack then posits his own belief that he thought there would be no marked change in the mind and personality that survived but that the corporeal 'body' would be less substantial. What remained would be 'our old etheric friend', and the after-life, possibly four-dimensional, would seem to us now like a dream life. He hoped that beyond the grave we would encounter those we had loved, recapture former peak experiences, great moments in art as well as love: all he felt able to contribute to the debate on man's immortality was a few guesses. 'But let us not go, taking the sap and juice out of our lives, in fear of Death.'

In his last years he no longer went far afield from Kissing Tree, content with the lanes of Warwickshire and his beautiful garden. Eventually he had to stop writing, which he found deeply distressing because, he told Diana Collins, 'I seem to have said it all and I am a creative man or I am nothing.'

Jacquetta, on the other hand, was to publish in 1980 a book quite unlike those on which her reputation as a writer and academic had previously been based. A Quest for Love was inspired in part by a mystical experience she had undergone years earlier, on Mount Carmel, of ' "oneness" with the past . . . but a common past, not my own'. The book consists of a series of accounts of brief lives or reincarnations, written in the present tense, from when man was barely sentient to the present day.

What gave the book its notoriety at the time of publication was, as has already been noted, its final chapter which is quite definitely not fiction and therefore seems wildly out of place. A Quest for Love provoked real controversy because of her apparent need to describe her love affairs, including her lesbian attachment, although she did not name her lovers – not to mention her full and explicit description of her long relationship with Jack prior to her marriage. For it must be remembered that both Christopher Hawkes and Jane Bannerman (ex-Priestley) were still alive and that the Priestley children and grandchildren and those of Nicholas Hawkes were regular visitors to Kissing Tree.

Without the stimulus of writing that had kept Jack going all his life, his depression returned, although, according to Diana

Collins, this did finally settle into a gentle melancholy. His secretary's image of him staring into space as he re-lived the Somme remains a haunting one. It is impossible to speculate how he might have developed as a writer had he written at length about that war in its immediate aftermath. A previous Priestley biographer considers Robert Graves's *Goodbye to All That* so excellent and definitive an account that a Priestley book would have been unnecessary, but Graves's whole attitude to the 1914–18 War was quite different from that of Priestley. Graves was fresh from public school and its cadet corps, and was its boxing champion. The war was all something of an adventure to him and nowhere in the book, good as it undoubtedly is, does he give any thought or time to considering why it happened, the way the British Establishment conducted it or what its appalling slaughter did to the human psyche, all of which would surely have been part of a Priestley brief for such a book, as he touches on all these things – and the class distinction with which the Western Front was riddled – if only briefly in *Margin Released.* John Braine's suggestion that the millions of words over half a century were needed to blot it out of his mind now seems all the more plausible.

Priestley was always pleased to see his children and grandchildren but recognised, in a final television interview he gave to his son immediately before his death, that he had always had some difficulty communicating with his family on a personal level. Referring to *Margin Released*, he said: 'Speak now and I will answer, but too often we don't speak, in a sense. We are affectionate and have plenty to say on general topics but we have never spoken from heart to heart, not I to my father, not my children to me. With us, the Lord our God is an inhibited God, visiting the awkward silences and unspoken endearment of the fathers upon the children.'

In the early 1980s there were several incidents which made his friends concerned about the state of his health. On one occasion Jacquetta had to go to London and suggested that Barbara and Gareth Lloyd Evans spent the evening at Kissing Tree to give Jack some company and keep an eye on him. 'He'd gone back into that lovely little room where he kept all his books and records and where Jacquetta occasionally rustled up a supper if we came back late from somewhere, eggs and bacon or that sort of thing, on a stove at the back of it, to refresh the drinks. Suddenly and quite neatly he slid to the floor. He didn't fall, just slid, and would you believe it, by the time he got on the floor he'd still got the two drinks and he hadn't either dropped them or spilled them. But we got the doctor and rang Jacquetta. He was all right the next day but he'd obviously had some kind of attack. When the doctor saw him in the morning he said, "What happened, Jack, what was the matter?" "I was bored," was all he said. I suppose it was an early warning, I don't know. They took him into hospital to check him out, by which time he seemed fine and wouldn't go to bed but stayed up and about.'[3]

His deafness increased, which annoyed him greatly, and he began to suffer from short-term memory-loss, which Jacquetta lovingly and cleverly covered up when visitors were present. At first he had recognised it, writing much earlier in *Outcries and Asides* how he would go upstairs for something and on the way forget what he had wanted: 'Remembering in detail the face, voice, habits of a man met in 1909 but no clues to the man who called last week and who is coming again this afternoon.' Later he did not realise it was happening.

The Collinses were still regular visitors and the pleasant weekends and picnics in the countryside continued. But it was all about to change. At the end of November 1981 John Collins retired as Canon of St Paul's Cathedral, an event celebrated beforehand with a special dinner party on 5 August in Amen Court on Jacquetta's birthday. The Collinses had invited a number of old friends, John and Marghanita Howard, Peggy Lamert, Denis and Helen Forman and her editor from Chatto. Once away from St Paul's and now in their pretty converted millhouse on the Essex–Suffolk border, Diana felt that she and John could look forward to a happy retirement after all the years of campaigning. But on New Year's Eve 1982 John Collins died suddenly from a heart attack.

At about the same time Gareth Lloyd Evans was diagnosed as having leukaemia. Barbara, convinced he would retreat into Welsh darkness and give up and die if he knew, persuaded his doctors not to tell him, and he was given another name for it. and as a result he fought it hard until a doctor, unbriefed by his colleagues, casually told him the truth. The disease and its treatment were weakening and debilitating but he remained a regular visitor to Jack in those last months of Priestley's life. Both retained the ability to amuse, entertain and cheer each other up, despite being aware that time, at least for one of them, was fast running out.

The end, when it came, was somewhat unexpected. As all Priestley's later birthdays had been celebrated in style, plans were afoot for something special but not too tiring for his ninetieth. There was no question of his going to London, so a booking was made for a special birthday lunch on 13 September 1984 at a nearby hotel. In February he had suffered a series of gastric attacks, which had resulted in an operation to remove a blockage. According to his family he did not have cancer, as has been suggested elsewhere, although he had needed intensive care afterwards. He rallied well and was enjoying his convalescence at home when in mid-August Barbara and Sylvia visited Kissing Tree to finalise the arrangements for his birthday.

Shortly before they arrived Priestley collapsed with pneumonia, and although he was given penicillin, it was clear that he was not responding to it and was having difficulty with his breathing. Jacquetta arranged first for a day nurse, then a night nurse, to look after him. Barbara and Sylvia stayed on and they, Jacquetta and Miss Puddŭck took it in turns to sit with him so that he was never alone. According to Diana Collins he knew that he was dying, was calm and unafraid, and said goodbye to his family 'very sweetly'. Finally, unable to talk, he squeezed their hands.

He slipped away, surrounded by his family and the faithful Miss Pudduck, on 13 August 1984, exactly a month before his birthday, so peacefully that no one is quite sure when he actually died, only that his hands became cold. The nurse checked his pulse, then nodded. Jacquetta leant over, kissed him, and said, 'Goodbye, my love.' Outside in the dark garden, owls were hooting in the trees, something Barbara and Sylvia have not forgotten because of the ancient belief which links owls with death.

Shortly before Priestley died, Barbara Lloyd Evans, concerned that Gareth's condition was deteriorating, had taken him on holiday to Mallorca. On the afternoon of 14 August they were sitting on a headland. Beneath them the sea, rushing into a long inlet, made a continual roaring noise. 'I said to Gareth that it sounded like the Minotaur and wondered what Jacquetta would have made of it, and then added that I also wondered how Jack was. "Oh, Jack's gone," Gareth replied. "Gone where?" I asked, for I hadn't thought him well enough to go far afield. Gareth looked at me. "He's gone. Dead." I could only think he'd read it in an English newspaper in the town and hadn't liked to tell me, but he assured me it wasn't so. He was simply convinced that Jack was dead. In order to reassure us both I rang Stratford when we got back to the hotel, only to find that it was absolutely true.' Priestley would have been intrigued.

Although a number of Priestley's love letters to Jacquetta survive, there is just one from her to him. It was found only after her death. Some time before 14 February it looks as if he asked her to write him a letter for Valentine's Day, for her reply of that date, from her old home at 39 Fitzroy Road, begins, '*Give me your letter on Tuesday.*'

> You know, of course, that I enjoy this sort of thing, that a large part of the female in me loves the feeling of toughness and masterfulness hidden in you; likes even to be ordered to write a love letter. You wouldn't have got one without it. But as I think you know, this isn't the main thing – it represents a delectable country, but too well known. I've explored it extensively. No, what is to me so wonderful in you is a power of humanity, a tenderness that is strong enough to wake my own. My own, it seems, has been pent up for years. Your greatness in this quality gives me an indescribably sweet sense of being cared for, and, when coupled with toughness, possessed.
>
> This is, as it were, on the more homely, comprehensible side of our relationship. In the world of pure magic I love you wholly and instinctively. My body asks nothing better than to be at your disposal and I wear your ring, not as a token of gratitude for an evening, but, while the magic lasts, very humbly as I think a woman should. But with all this we have both, I believe, ancient bits, wild bits, mockeries which the other one will never come near; we are a little afraid of them and so are saved again. I believe that our love can add to the communion of saints and the world without end. That is why I am, have become, perfectly simple and serious about our relationship and shall not try any devices to prolong it.
>
> You have given me the most intense happiness this last week. Often I have hardly been able to endure the rightness, the significance of the world – or the sparrows in the trees, the ducks and swans on the lake, people moving about and smelling of bonfires. It has been like a prolongation and refinement of

the best moments of drunkenness. You pulled me to this from such a dismal pit where I had thought, work apart, to die.

Dear heart, above all, I want to be beautiful in your eyes, and to give you, too, more than a passing satisfaction.

Jacquetta.

Priestley's cremation was a private affair but there followed a memorial service in Westminster Abbey. Jacquetta turned to Diana Collins, who, of course, had wide experience of church services, for advice as to what would be most appropriate and to give the main address. The chosen hymns were the paraphrase of Francis of Assisi's 'Hymn to the Sun', Addison's 'Eternal Ruler of the Ceaseless Round' and Blake's 'Jerusalem'. Denis Forman read from Ecclesiastes, the passage about the golden bowl that cannot be broken, and his publisher, Charles Pick, from *Margin Released*; Dame Peggy Ashcroft read the essay 'Whatever Happened to Falstaff?' and then the fine actor Richard Pasco moved the congregation to tears with the last great speech from *Johnson Over Jordan*.

His ashes are buried in the graveyard of the tiny church at Hubberholme at the farthest end of Wharfedale. A simple plaque inside records: 'Remember J. B. priestley O.M. 1894–1984 Author and Dramatist, whose ashes are buried nearby. He loved the Dales and found 'Hubberholme one of the smallest and pleasantest places in the world.'

The views of those who knew him vary as to what Jack Priestley believed when he died, whether or not in the end he accepted that death was the end or that something of the human spirit or soul survived. But it seems appropriate to end with his famous passage about the dream that haunted him all his life:

I dreamt I was standing at the top of a very high tower, alone, looking down on millions of birds all flying in one direction; every kind of bird was there, all the birds in the world. It was a noble sight, this vast aerial river of birds. But now in some mysterious fashion the gear was changed and time speeded up, so that I saw generations of birds, and watched them break their shells, flutter into life, mate, weaken, falter and die. Wings grew only to crumble; bodies were sleek and then, in a flash, bled and shrivelled. And death struck everywhere at every second. What was the use of all this blind struggle towards life, this eager trying of wings, this hurried mating, this flight and surge, all this gigantic meaningless biological effort? As I started down, seeming to see every creature's ignoble little history almost at a glance, I felt sick at heart. It would be better if not one of them, if not one of us all, had been born, if the struggle ceased forever. I stood on my tower, still alone, desperately unhappy. But now the gear was changed again and time went faster still, and it was rushing by at such a rate, that the birds could not show any movement, but were like an enormous plain sown with feathers. But along this plain, flickering through the bodies themselves, there now passed a sort of white flame, trembling, dancing, then hurrying on and as soon as I saw it I knew that this white flame was life itself, the very quintessence of being; and then it came to me, in a rocket-burst of ecstasy, that nothing mattered, nothing could ever matter, because nothing else was real, but this quivering, hurrying lambency of being. Birds, men or creatures not yet shaped and coloured, all were of no account except so far as this flame of life travelled through them. It left nothing to mourn over behind it; what I had thought was tragedy was mere emptiness or a shadow show; for now all real feeling was caught and purified and danced on ecstatically with the white flame of life.

Bibliography and Chronology

Select Bibliography

Agate, J. *The Ego Books*, London, 1935–1948
Atkins, J. *The Last of the Sages*, London, 1981
Braine, J. *J. B. Priestley*, Weidenfeld & Nicolson, London, 1978
Billington, J. *Peggy Ashcroft*, John Murray, London, 1988
Brome, V. *J. B.Priestley*, Hamish Hamilton, London, 1988
Collins, D. *Time and the Priestleys*, Alan Sutton, Stroud, 1994
Cooper, S. *Portrait of an Author*, Heinemann, London, 1970
Evans, G. Lloyd, *J. B. Priestley, Dramatist*, Heinemann, London, 1974
Hawkes, J. *A Quest for Love*, Chatto & Windus, London, 1980
Hobson, H. *Ralph Richardson*, Rockliffe, London, 1958
Holdsworth, P. *The Rebel Tyke*, City of Bradford Libraries Department, Bradford, 1994
Jung, C. G. *Memories, Dramas and Reflections*, Fontana, London, 1967
Ouspensky, P. D., *New Model Universe*, London, 1931

UNPUBLISHED SOURCES

The Davison Correspondence: six volumes of letters, Beinecke Rare Book and Manuscript Library, Yale University USA

Miscellaneous correspondence from the Priestley Collection of Letters, Harry Ransom Humanities Research Center, University of Texas, USA

Letters in the possession of Nicholas Hawkes, Lady Barbara Wykeham and Tom Priestley

J. B. Priestley – Own Works

Unless otherwise specified, all works were published by William Heinemann Ltd.

FICTION

Adam in Moonshine, 1927
Benighted, 1928
Farthing Hall (with Hugh Walpole), Macmillan & Co. Ltd, 1929
The Good Companions, 1929

The Town Mayor of Miraucourt, 1930
Angel Pavement, 1930
Faraway, 1932
Wonder Hero, 1933
They Walk in the City, 1936
The Doomsday Men, 1937
Let the People Sing, 1939
Blackout in Gretley, 1942
Daylight on Saturday, 1943
Three Men in New Suits, 1945
Bright Day, 1946
The Magicians, 1954
Saturn Over the Water, 1961
Salt is Leaving, Pan Books in association with Wm. Heinemann, 1961,
Lost Empires, 1965
The Image Men: vol. 1. *Out of Town*, vol. 2 *London End*, 1968 (later published
   in one volume)
Snoggle, 1971
The Carfitt Crisis, 1975

NON-FICTION

The Chapman of Rhymes, Alexander Morris, 1918
Brief Diversions, Bowes and Bowes Ltd, 1922
Papers from Lilliput, Bowes and Bowes Ltd, 1922
I for One, The Bodley Head, 1923
Figures in Modern Literature, The Bodley Head, 1924
George Meredith, Macmillan & Co. Ltd, 1926
Essays of Today and Yesterday – J. B. Priestley, Harrap & Co. Ltd, 1926
Open House (Essays), Heinemann, 1927
Thomas Love Peacock, Macmillan & Co. Ltd, 1927
The English Novel, Ernest Benn Ltd, 1927
Apes and Angels (Essays), Methuen & Co. Ltd, 1928
English Humour, Longman & Co. Ltd, 1929
The Balconinny and Other Essays, Methuen and Co. Ltd, 1929
Self-Selected Essays, 1932
I'll Tell You Everything – J. B. Priestley and Gerald Bullett, Macmillan & Co.
   Ltd, 1932
English Journey, 1933
Charles Dickens, Thomas Nelson, 1936
Midnight on the Desert, A Chapter of Autobiography, 1927
Rain Upon Godshill, A Further Chapter of Autobiography, 1939
Postscripts, 1940
Out of the People, Wm. Collins, in association with Heinemann, 1941
Britain at War, Harper Brothers Inc., 1942
British Women Go to War, Wm. Collins, 1943
Manpower, HMSO, 1944
Russian Journey, Writers Group, 1946
The Secret Dream, Turnstile Press, 1946
Arts Under Socialism, Turnstile Press, 1947
Delight (Essays), 1949
The Priestley Companion, Penguin Books, 1951
Journey Down a Rainbow (J. B. Priestley and Jacquetta Hawkes), 1955
The Writer in a Changing Society, Hand and Flower Press, 1956

All About Ourselves and Other Essays, 1956
The Art of the Dramatist, 1957
Thoughts in the Wilderness (Essays), 1957
Literature and Western Man, 1960
Charles Dickens – A Pictorial Biography, Thames and Hudson, 1961
Margin Released (Essays), 1962
Man and Time, Aldus Books, 1964
The Moments, 1966
The World of J. B. Priestley, 1967
Essays of Five Decades, Little Brown Inc., 1968; Heinemann, 1969
The Prince of Pleasure, 1969
Charles Dickens and His World, Thames and Hudson, 1969
The Edwardians, 1970
Victoria's Heyday, 1972
Over the Long High Wall (Essays), 1972
The English, 1973
A Visit to New Zealand, 1974
Outcries and Asides (Essays), 1974
Particular Pleasures (Essays), 1975
English Humour, 1976
Instead of the Trees (Essays), 1977

PUBLISHED PLAYSCRIPTS

Dangerous Corner, 1932
The Roundabout, 1933
Laburnum Grove, 1934
Eden End, 1934
Cornelius, 1935
The Good Companions (adaptation with Edward Knoblock), Samuel French Ltd, 1935
Three Plays and a Preface, 1935
Bees on the Boat Deck, 1936
Time and the Conways, 1937
Mystery at Greenfingers, 1947
I Have Been Here Before, 1937
People at Sea, 1937
When We Are Married, 1938
Johnson Over Jordan, 1939
Desert Highway, 1944
Ever Since Paradise, 1946
An Inspector Calls, 1947
Music at Night, Samuel French Ltd, 1947
The Long Mirror, Samuel French Ltd, 1947
The Rose & Crown, Samuel French Ltd, 1947
The Linden Tree, 1948
The Golden Fleece, Samuel French Ltd, 1948
The Olympians (Opera Libretto), Novello & Co. Ltd, 1949
Home is Tomorrow, 1949
Bright Shadow, Samuel French Ltd, 1950
Summer Day's Dream, Samuel French Ltd, 1950
Dragon's Mouth (with Jacquetta Hawkes), 1952
Mr Kettle and Mrs Moon, Samuel French Ltd, 1956
The Glass Cage, Samuel French Ltd, 1958

A Severed Head (with Iris Murdoch), Chatto & Windus Ltd, 1964.

Dates of First Performances of Priestley Plays

The Good Companions (adaptation), 1931
Dangerous Corner, 1932
Laburnum Grove, 1933
The Roundabout, 1933
Eden End, 1934
Duet in Floodlight, 1935
Bees on the Boat Deck, 1936
Spring Tide, 1936
I Have Been Here Before, 1937
Time and the Conways, 1937
People at Sea, 1937
Mystery at Greenfingers, 1938
Music at Night, 1938
When We Are Married, 1938
Johnson Over Jordan, 1939
The Long Mirror, 1940
Good Night Children, 1942
They Came to a City, 1943
Desert Highway, 1943
How Are They At Home?, 1944
An Inspector Calls, 1946
Ever Since Paradise, 197
The Linden Tree, 1947
The Rose & Crown, 1947
The Golden Fleece, 1948
Home is Tomorrow, 1948
The High Toby, 1948
Summer Day's Dream, 1949
Bright Shadow, 1950
Dragon's Mouth (with Jacquetta Hawkes), 1952
Treasure on Pelican, 1952
Private Rooms, 1953
Mother's Day, 1953
A Glass of Bitter, 1954
Mr Kettle and Mrs Moon, 1955
Take the Fool Away, 1956
The Glass Cage, 1958
A Severed Head (with Iris Murdoch), 1963
The Pavilion of Masks, 1963

Notes

CHAPTER 1 Beginnings and Childhood

1. *New Statesman,* 29 July 1966.
2. *The Rebel Tyke.*
3. *Margin Released.*

CHAPTER 2 Growing Up

1. *Instead of the Trees.*
2. *The Listener,* 23 July 1959.
3. *The Edwardians.*
4. *Margin Released* and in conversations noted by John Braine in *J. B. Priestley.*
5. Winnie Scott, née Priestley, in conversation with Peter Holdsworth.
6. *Margin Released.*

CHAPTER 3 The Swan Arcadian

1. The general material in this chapter is drawn from the collections of essays referred to in the text, interviews with JBP by Peter Holdsworth and information given directly to the author by residents of Bradford.

CHAPTER 4 Into Print

1. *Bradford Telegraph and Argus,* 19 September 1994.
2. *Margin Released.*
3. Ibid.
4. Interview with Tom Priestley.
5. Interview with Lady Barbara Wykeham, née Priestley.
6. *Margin Released.*

CHAPTER 5 Into the Inferno

1. *Margin Released,* Part 2, 'Carry On, Carry On!'
2. Vincent Brome, *J. B. Priestley,* Chapter 3.

3. *Time and the Priestleys,* also in conversations with the author.
4. All JBP's letters from the Front are quoted by permission of Mr Tom Priestley.
5. Ibid.
6. Papers of George Oswald Mitchell, Document Dept., Imperial War Museum Archive.

CHAPTER 6 Flowers From Dead Men

1. Mitchell papers, as above.
2. Ibid.
3. Papers of Private Gilbert Isles, also in IWM Document Dept. as above.
4. Ibid.
5. Papers of Stanhope and Elizabeth Forbes, The Tate Gallery Document Archive.
6. This and following from *Margin Released.*
7. Ibid.
8. *J. B. Priestley – A Workmanlike Man.* Tape in Sound Archive, Imperial War Museum.
9. Ibid.
10. Susan Cooper, *J. B. Priestley.*
11. *Midnight on the Desert.*
12. Ibid.

CHAPTER 7 Brief Diversions

1. Peter Holdsworth, *The Rebel Tyke.*
2. Ibid.
3. Ibid.
4. Conversation with author.
5. *Instead of the Trees.*
6. Ibid.
7. Vincent Brome, *J. B. Priestley,* noted as 'interview' but no source given.
8. Interviews with Barbara Wykeham (née Priestley) and Sylvia Goaman (née Priestley).
9. This and following information on Davison from Peter Davison, *Half Remembered.*
10. A servant returns from the market to his master, a wealthy merchant, in great fear and asks if he can borrow a horse to return to his family in Samara. The merchant asks why, and the servant tells him that he saw Death sitting in the market place in the guise of a beautiful woman and that she made a threatening gesture to him. After he has galloped away the merchant, intrigued, goes down to the market to confront Death, asking her why she had made a threatening sign to his servant. 'Oh, but I did not,' replied Death. 'It was a sign of surprise because I was amazed to see him here in Baghdad. For I have an appointment with him tonight – in Samara . . .'
11. Judith Cook, *Daphne – A Portrait of Daphne du Maurier.*

CHAPTER 8 Dark Hours

1. *Margin Released.*
2. Interview with author.

3. Ibid.
4. Peter Davison, *Half Remembered.*
5. Peter Holdsworth, *The Rebel Tyke.*

CHAPTER 9 Jane

1. Interview with author.
2. Letter in possession of Mr Tom Priestley.
3. Davison correspondence, Beinecke Rare Book and Mss Library, Yale University, USA.
4. *Margin Released.*
5. Ibid.
6. Letters in possession of Lady Barbara Wykeham.
7. Interview with author.
8. Ibid.

CHAPTER 10 Picking Up the Pieces

1. Interviews with Lady Barbara Wykeham and Mrs Sylvia Goaman.
2. Letter, 2 February 1922.
3. Letter, 29 January 1926.
4. Interviews with author as note 1 above.
5. Ibid.
6. Judith Cook, *Daphne – A Portrait of Daphne du Maurier.*
7. This and subsequent quotes, interviews with Angela Wyndham Lewis and Mary Priestley.

CHAPTER 11 Mr Walpole and Dear old Jack

1. Barbara Wykeham to author.
2. Letter, 28 May 1926.
3. Letter, 31 May 1926.
4. Rupert Hart-Davis, *Hugh Walpole.*
5. Letter, 22 May 1926.
6. Letter, 12 April 1928.

CHAPTER 12 Fame

1. *Margin Released.*
2. Letter, 29 March 1928.
3. Letter, 25 July 1928.
4. Letter, 15 August 1928.
5. Peter Holdsworth, *The Rebel Tyke.*

CHAPTER 13 'Oh she doth teach the torches to burn bright. . .'

1. Michael Billington, *Peggy Ashcroft.*
2. Ibid.

CHAPTER 14 Time and the Dramatist

1. *Margin Released.*

CHAPTER 15 An English Journey

1. Barbara Wykeham to author.
2. Ibid.
3. Sylvia Goaman to author.
4. Mary Priestley to author.
5. Sylvia Goaman.
6. Diana Collins, *Time and the Priestleys.*

CHAPTER 16 Theatre, Hollywood and Arizona

1. 29 November 1933.
2. Basil Dean, *Mind's Eye.*
3. Judith Cook, *Daphne – A Portrait of Daphne du Maurier.*
4. 29 April 1934.
5. *Margin Released.*
6. Ibid.
7. Ralph Richardson.
8. Ibid.
9. Susan Cooper, *J. B. Priestley.*
10. *Midnight on the Desert.*
11. Ibid.

CHAPTER 17 Aspects of Time

1. 1 April 1936.
2. Letter to Walpole, 12 July 1936.
3. And following *Rain Upon Godshill.*
4. Ibid.
5. Ibid.
6. 12 August 1937.

CHAPTER 18 America Again

1. *Rain Upon Godshill.*
2. Gareth Lloyd Evans, *J. B. Priestley – Dramatist.*
3. 23 October 1937.
4. *Rain Upon Godshill.*
5. Ibid.

CHAPTER 19 The Dogs of War

1. *A Note From the Workshop,* Malvern 1937.
2. *Rain Upon Godshill.*

3. *J. B. Priestley – Dramatist.*
4. *The Times*, 23 February 1939.
5. *Ralph Richardson.*
6. Ibid.
7. 20 April 1939.
8. 2 March 1939.
9. *Postscripts.*

CHAPTER 20 Postscripts

1. *Postscript*, 1 September 1940.
2. Letters, 2 October 1939 and 11 October 1939.
3. Letter, 29 April 1940.
4. Jane Priestley, unpublished manuscript.
5. *Postscript*, 14 July 1940.
6. *Margin Released.*

CHAPTER 21 Through the War

1. Taped discussion with Gareth Lloyd Evans.
2. Letter, 1 August 1940.
3. For this and much more information on Priestley's relationship with the 1941 Committee and Common Wealth, I am indebted to Diana Collins.
4. This and the following from Jane Priestley's unpublished mss.
5. Letter to Tom Priestley, 4 September 1984.
6. Unpublished mss. as note 4 above.
7. Vincent Brome, *J. B. Priestley.*
8. Letter to Tom Priestley, 3 September 1984.

CHAPTER 22 Post-War

1. *J. B. Priestley – The Dramatist.*
2. Jane Priestley, unpublished letters, September 1945.
3. 16 September 1946.
4. Letters from H.G. Wells to Priestley, 23 February 1939. and 27 February 1939. Also Michael Foot, *H. G. – The History of Mr Wells*, Doubleday 1995.
5. Interview with author.
6. Interview with author.
7. Diana Collins, *Time and the Priestleys.*

CHAPTER 23 Jacquetta

1. Jacquetta Hawkes, *A Quest for Love*, Chatto & Windus 1980.
2. Ibid.
3. Diana Collins, *Time and the Priestleys.*
4. *A Quest for Love.*
5. Letter, Tuesday (date unknown), November 1947.
6. Undated letter, January 1948.
7. *Quest for Love.*

CHAPTER 24 The Tangled Web

1. Letter from GBS, 16 January 1948.
2. Gareth Lloyd Evans, *J. B. Priestley – Dramatist.*
3. Peter Davison, *Half Remembered.*
4. Conversation with Diana Collins.

CHAPTER 25 Endings

1. Information from Tom Priestley.
2. Ibid.
3. Jacquetta Hawkes in conversation with author.
4. Michael Denison, *Double Act.*
5. Ibid.
6. 18 April 1952.
7. Information from Diana Collins.
8. 1 February 1953.
9. 2 February 1953.
10. 4 February 1953.
11. 6 June 1953.
12. 5 June 1953.
13. Diana Webster, *Hawkeseye: A Biography of Christopher Hawkes.*
14. Ibid.

CHAPTER 26 Journey Down a Rainbow

1. Conversations with author.
2. 20 March 1971.
3. Letter to Teddy Davison, 27 May 1955.

CHAPTER 27 Banning the Bomb

1. *Time and the Priestleys* and also conversations with the author.
2. Ibid.
3. Ibid.
4. The *Guardian* followed up my letter with an interview immediately after my
son was born – which produced even more post. With no qualifications to
do so, no political or campaigning experience and great naivety, I formed a
British group of Voice of Women. Both this, and Women Against the Bomb
founded by the late Eve Latimer, sought to bring together ordinary women,
many of whom like us had been daunted by the array of wealthy, academic
and expert women who formed the membership of CND's women's section.
Even with hindsight, I have no idea whether this was the right or wrong
thing to do – it just seemed an imperative at the time. Again, the history
of these women's protests can be left to others, but suffice it to say that
clutching my new son I also went to the UN and the White House (with
Labour MP Anne Kerr) and to Moscow to a conference held there in the
summer. I met Jacquetta for the first time in New York (very briefly),
told her how delighted I'd been to receive a letter from her husband and
thought we were unlikely to meet again. However, on my return home
I was invited for the first time to Kissing Tree House and returned as a

guest, and I hope a friend, on a number of occasions up until the year before Jack Priestley's death.

5. Letter to Davison, 13 June 1959.
6. Peter Davison, *Half Remembered.*
7. Letter to Davison, 19 December 1959.

CHAPTER 28 Into the Sixties

1. From the Introduction to *Literature and Western Man.*
2. John Braine, *J. B. Priestley.*
3. *Trumpets Over the Sea.*
4. This and following from interviews with the author.
5. John Braine, *J. B. Priestley.*
6. Susan Cooper, *J. B. Priestley – Portrait of an Author.*
7. *Times Literary Supplement,* 22 February 1969.
8. From a tape recording by kind permission of Barbara Lloyd Evans.
9. Susan Cooper, *J. B. Priestley – Portrait of an Author.*

CHAPTER 29 Order of Merit

1. And following information, *The Rebel Tyke.*
2. Conversation with author.
3. Peter Davison, *Half Remembered.*
4. Ibid.
5. Letter to Peter Davison, 1 August 1970.
6. Letter from Peter Davison, 9 August 1970.
7. The following is taken from an account of the rehearsal written by the author for the *Guardian,* 5 June 1974.
8. Information given to author by Tom Priestley.

CHAPTER 30 A Dream of Birds

1. *The Rebel Tyke.*
2. Letter to Peter Davison, 1 August 1970.
3. Conversation with author.

INDEX

Acknowledgements

First and foremost I would like to thank Mr Tom Priestley for his extremely valuable and kind assistance during the progress of the book, the unrestricted access he gave me to papers, and for permission to quote from both his father's letters and those of his mother, Jane Priestley. I am also grateful for his permission to quote from Priestley books especially *Margin Released.* He has been an exemplary literary executor for a biographer.

I also had much sympathetic assistance from Priestley's daughters Lady Barbara Wykeham and Mrs Sylvia Goaman, and must thank them for the information they gave me and for their permission to quote from the letters of their mother, Pat Priestley. My thanks also to Mary Priestley for access to correspondence between herself and her father and Mrs Rachel Littlewood. Until her final illness early in 1996 I also had assistance and encouragement from the late Jacquetta Priestley, who gave me access to papers; and I am extremely grateful to her son, Nicolas Hawkes, for permission to quote from letters to his mother which were not discovered until after her death.

Many other people contributed to this book and require acknowledgement, including Angela Wyndham Lewis, Jane Priestley's daughter, and Mrs Epsi Hutchings, Jane's cousin. Two close friends of Jack and Jacquetta Priestley have proved invaluable in providing information: Mrs Diana Collins and Mrs Barbara Lloyd Evans. Diana Collins also gave me access to notes and writings on Jack Priestley and permission to quote from her own book, *Time and the Priestleys;* Mrs Barbara Lloyd Evans allowed me to use taped interviews by her husband, the late Gareth Lloyd Evans, which he recorded with Jack Priestley, and also permitted me to quote from *J. B. Priestley – Dramatist.* I would also like to thank Mrs Rosalie Batten, who was J. B. Priestley's last secretary and also acted in that capacity for his widow until Jacquetta Priestley's death.

A number of institutions and literary executors have also been involved in this project. I would like therefore to acknowledge with thanks the assistance of the Yale Collection of American Literature, Beinecke Rare Book and Mss Library of Yale University for access to the Davison Correspondence, and the special assistance of Ms Ngadi W. Kponou over two years across the divide of the Atlantic – she became by fax and telephone something of a personal friend. Also Cathy Henderson, research librarian at the Harry Ransom Humanities Research Center of the University of Texas at Austin for access to the vast archive of letters, many from celebrities, which they hold.

The assistance of the Document Department of the Imperial War Museum was invaluable in providing access to war letters and diaries of J. B. Priestley's Yorkshire contemporaries on the Western Front in the 1914–1918 war. Unfortunately, despite every effort having been made both by myself and by the Museum, it has not been possible to trace and therefore obtain permission from all copyright holders of papers held by the Museum which are used in this book. By allowing me access to their letter columns, the *Bradford Telegraph and Argus* enabled me to gather hitherto unpublished information on the family of J. B. Priestley's mother, Emma, née Holt or Hoult (it is spelt both ways). I was also given assistance by Bradford Library who published *The Rebel Tyke*, by Peter Holdsworth.

Permission for quoting from correspondence was given by The Society of Authors on behalf of the Bernard Shaw Estate; Sir Rupert Hart Davis on behalf of the estate of Hugh Walpole; Michael Sissons of Peter, Fraser and Dunlop on behalf of the estates of A. D. Peters, C. S. Forester and Clifford Bax; and David Higham Associates on behalf of the estate of Edith Sitwell.